Vattimo and Theology

Thomas G. Guarino

t & t clark

Published by T&T Clark International
A Continuum Imprint
The Tower Building   80 Maiden Lane
11 York Road   Suite 704
London SE1 7NX   New York, NY 10038

www.continuumbooks.com

Thomas G. Guarino has asserted his right under the Copyright, Designs and Patents Act, 1988, to be identified as the Author of this work.

British Library Cataloguing-in-Publication Data
A catalogue record for this book is available from the British Library

ISBN: HB: 978-0-567-03232-4
        PB: 978-0-567-03233-1

Typeset by Newgen Imaging Systems Pvt Ltd, Chennai, India
Printed and bound in Great Britain by MPG Books Ltd, Bodmin, Cornwall

Contents

Acknowledgments

The generosity of many people and institutions has made this monograph possible. Pride of place belongs to The Center of Theological Inquiry (CTI) in Princeton, N. J. The book was largely written at this unique establishment dedicated to fostering advanced theological research. I would like to thank William Storrar, director of CTI, for kindly inviting me as a resident member of the Center and for his gracious and warm welcome. My colleagues at CTI, with their acute insights and generous friendship, were also a source of great pleasure.

A special word of thanks should be tendered to the Rev. Dr. Robert Coleman, dean of the school of theology of Seton Hall University, for encouraging this work and for kindly approving an essential research leave. My Seton Hall colleagues, Anthony Sciglitano of the department of religious studies and Anthony Ziccardi of the department of biblical studies, unselfishly read and insightfully commented on the entire work.

Howard McGinn, dean of Seton Hall University libraries was extraordinarily helpful in providing the necessary research materials. The librarians at the Speer and Luce libraries of Princeton Theological Seminary were also an unfailingly helpful resource as were the librarians of my home institution.

I would like to acknowledge as well the important assistance with this project (as well as the continuing friendship) kindly offered by Edward Oakes of Mundelein Seminary, David Lotz formerly of Union Theological Seminary; Avery Cardinal Dulles (†) of Fordham University and Robert Jenson, formerly senior scholar at The Center of Theological Inquiry. A special word of thanks goes to Petra Daschbach, S. P. for her friendship and support.

I am grateful to The Association of Theological Schools (ATS) for offering a Lilly Research Expense Grant thereby helping to defray costs associated with this undertaking.

Acknowledgments

Finally, I thank those students who have been introduced to Vattimo in various seminars, not always willingly, but, one hopes, not without rewards.

Abbreviations of Vattimo's Works

Italian works

ADD: *Le avventure della differenza* (Milano: Garzanti, 1988).

AEC: *Analitici e continentali: Guida alla filosofia degli ultimi trent'anni,* by Franca D'Agostini, Preface by Gianni Vattimo (Milano: Raffaello Cortina, 1997).

AOC: *Atei o Credenti?: filosofia, politica, etica, scienza,* by Paolo Flores d'Arcais, Michel Onfray, Gianni Vattimo (Roma: Fazi, 2007).

CC: *Credere di credere* (Milano: Garzanti, 1996).

CRO: *Cos'è la religione oggi?* With Giovanni Filoramo and Emilio Gentile (Pisa: ETS, 2005).

DC: *Dopo la cristianità. Per un cristianesimo non religioso* (Milano: Garzanti, 2002).

DCN: *Dialogo con Nietzsche. Saggi 1961–2000* (Milano: Garzanti, 2000).

FDR: *Il futuro della religione. Solidarietà, carità, ironia* (Milano: Garzanti, 2004).

FM: *La fine della modernità* (Milano: Garzanti, 1985).

NEE: *Nichilismo ed emancipazione: Etica, politica, diritto* (Milano: Garzanti, 2003).

OA: *"Ontologia dell'Attualità"* in *Filosofia '87,* ed. Gianni Vattimo (Roma–Bari: Laterza, 1988), 201–223.

OC: *Opere complete* (Roma: Meltemi, 2007–).

OI: *Oltre l'interpretazione* (Roma–Bari: Laterza, 1994).

PD: *Il pensiero debole,* ed. Pier Aldo Rovatti and Gianni Vattimo (Milano: Feltrinelli), 1983.

RSC: *La Religion: Seminaire de Capri* (Paris: Éditions du Seuil, 1996).

ST: *La società trasparente* (Milano: Garzanti, 1989).

VFD: *Verità o fede debole?: Dialogo su cristianesimo e relativismo,* by Gianni Vattimo and René Girard (Massa: Transeuropa, 2006).

Abbreviations

VM: *Verità e metodo*, tr. Gianni Vattimo (Milano: Bompiani, 1983). Vattimo originally translated Hans-Georg Gadamer's *Wahrheit und Methode* in 1972. At that time, he published a long introductory essay, "*L'ontologia ermeneutica nella filosofia contemporanea*," 1–29. In the 1983 edition of the work, Vattimo also includes a short note, reflecting on the eleven years since the translation appeared.

English works: Translations and articles

AC: *After Christianity*, tr. Luca D'Isanto (New York: Columbia University Press, 2002).

ACT: *Art's Claim to Truth*, ed. Santiago Zabala, tr. Luca D'Isanto (New York: Columbia University Press, 2008).

AD: *The Adventure of Difference: Philosophy after Nietzsche and Heidegger*, tr. Thomas Harrison and Cyprian P. Blamires (Baltimore: Johns Hopkins University Press, 1993).

ADG: John Caputo and Gianni Vattimo, *After the Death of God*, ed. Jeffrey W. Robbins (New York: Columbia University Press, 2007). Vattimo's essay in this volume, "Toward a Nonreligious Christianity," first appeared in G. Filaramo, E. Gentile and G. Vattimo *Cos'è la religione oggi?* (Pisa: ETS, 2005), 43–61.

BE: *Belief*, tr. Luca D'Isanto and David Webb (Stanford: Stanford University Press, 1999).

BYI: *Beyond Interpretation: The Meaning of Hermeneutics for Philosophy*, tr. David Webb (Stanford: Stanford University Press, 1997).

DDWT: "Dialectic, Difference, Weak Thought" in *Graduate Faculty Philosophy Journal* 10 (1984), 151–164

DN: *Dialogue with Nietzsche*, tr. William McCuaig (New York: Columbia University Press, 2006).

DR: "A 'Dictatorship of Relativism'?," tr. Robert Valgenti. *Common Knowledge*, 13 (2007), 214–218.

EM: *The End of Modernity: Nihilism and Hermeneutics in Postmodern Culture*, translation and introduction by Jon R. Snyder (Baltimore: The Johns Hopkins University Press, 1988).

EWT: "Ethics without Transcendence," *Common Knowledge* 9 (2003), 399–405.

Abbreviations

FR: Richard Rorty and Gianni Vattimo, *The Future of Religion*,
        ed. Santiago Zabala (New York: Columbia University
        Press, 2005).

GPO: "Gadamer and the Problem of Ontology" in *Gadamer's
        Century*, ed. J. Malpas et al. (Cambridge, Mass.: MIT Press,
        2002), 299–306.

HNAP: *The Hermeneutic Nature of Analytic Philosophy: A Study of
        Ernst Tugendhat,* by Santiago Zabala, tr. S. Zabala
        and Michael Haskell. Forward by Gianni Vattimo
        (New York: Columbia University Press, 2008).

NE: *Nihilism and Emancipation: Ethics, Politics and Law*, ed.
        Santiago Zabala, tr. William McCuaig (New York:
        Columbia University Press, 2004).

NI: *Nietzsche: An Introduction*, tr. Nicholas Martin
        (Stanford: Stanford University Press, 2001).

OPN: "Optimistic Nihilism," *Common Knowledge,* 1 (1992),
        37–44.

RDV: *Religion*, ed. J. Derrida and G. Vattimo (Stanford: Stanford
        University Press, 1998).

TS: *The Transparent Society*, tr. David Webb (Baltimore:
        The Johns Hopkins University Press, 1992).

WTRV: "'Weak Thought' and the Reduction of Violence:
        A Dialogue with Gianni Vattimo" by Gianni Vattimo and
        Santiago Zabala, tr. by Yaakov Mascetti. *Common
        Knowledge* 8 (2002), 452–463.

Secondary literature

WP: *Weakening Philosophy: Essays in Honour of Gianni
        Vattimo,* ed. Santiago Zabala (Montreal and Kingston:
        McGill-Queens University Press, 2007).

(Throughout the book, I have generally cited the available English translations. On those occasions when I thought a retranslation was useful, I cite both the Italian and the English texts).

Introduction

I was a student in Rome in the 1970s when, attracted by the unusual title, I purchased *Il soggetto e la maschera* (*The Subject and the Mask*) by Gianni Vattimo. Although my knowledge of Italian was limited, I picked my way through the pages, fascinated by the author's remarkable interpretations, still redolent of the European political debates of the late '60s and of Nietzsche's attacks on the bourgeois subject. Although the book crossed my mind from time to time, I went onto the study of theology and did not again quickly return to Vattimo's work. Years later, a former student kindly sent me a copy of Vattimo's reflections on his faith, *Credere di credere* (*Belief*), thinking I might have an interest in the philosopher's direct engagement with Christianity. That book rekindled an interest in his thought, especially since I had been absorbed in examining aspects of the dialogue between religion and postmodernity.

I have always found Vattimo a beguiling writer, interested in the most significant philosophical questions and representative of the widespread contemporary struggle with religious claims. Most importantly, he insistently addresses enduring issues (the nature of truth, of interpretation and of secularization) that are important to Christian theology and to religious thought in general. Precisely because of this interest, I was enthusiastic when T&T Clark first spoke to me about writing a book about Vattimo's philosophy that would serve both as a general introduction to his work as well as a theological dialogue with him.

It should be noted that Vattimo publishes prodigiously, not only on philosophical matters but also on global and European politics. In this way, he exercises, in Italy in particular, the role that Jürgen Habermas fulfills in Germany as a public intellectual who also undertakes general cultural commentary. His work is well-known on the Continent where he has served in the European parliament and has been an outspoken leader on many issues. In the English-speaking world, however, Vattimo's thought is only

1

recently becoming better known. Richard Rorty has said of the Torinese's work that his "writings are among the most imaginative contributions to the tradition of philosophical thought that flows from Nietzsche and Heidegger" (*WP*, 149). Given the continuing influence that these two thinkers have, both philosophically and theologically, one can better understand the interest Vattimo carries for both the general reader and for the theologian.

Gianteresio (Gianni) Vattimo was born in Turin in 1936. After graduating from the university there, he went on to Heidelberg, studying with K. Löwith and H.-G. Gadamer. From the early 1960s onwards, he has been a professor at the University of Turin, with specialties in hermeneutics, Nietzsche and Heidegger. He has also been a visiting professor at several American universities, including Stanford and Yale. He has amassed an impressive array of publications, with scores of volumes and hundreds of articles both in professional journals as well as in general-interest newspapers and magazines. Vattimo has continued to engage the thought of Heidegger and Nietzsche (with his work on the latter sustained and even ground-breaking in some respects) and is the Italian translator of Gadamer's *Wahrheit und Methode*. More recently, his work has centered on the role of religion in contemporary life and thought as well as the possible convergences of postmodernity with the Christian faith. He was elected to the European parliament in 1999.[1]

I cannot claim to have read everything that Vattimo has ever written, nor is it my intention to cite every one of his published works. Nonetheless, I have read a great deal of his work, in all of its various genres (books, articles in learned journals, speeches, interviews and magazine pieces) including many of his columns in the prominent Torinese newspaper, *La Stampa*. In this volume, however, I have concentrated on his seminal philosophical books and his most significant scholarly articles. As with all thinkers, Vattimo consistently returns to certain central themes (even to certain texts of both Nietzsche and Heidegger) and it is with these core claims that I am mainly concerned. Secondary literature on Vattimo also continues to grow. There is one major *Festschrift* on his thought available in English, *Weakening Philosophy* (McGill-Queens University Press, 2007), which carries an extensive bibliography of both primary and secondary works.

Introduction

This volume intends to serve two purposes: (1) an accessible introduction to the philosophy of Vattimo whose works have been steadily translated into English but whose thought is known sketchily, if at all; and, (2) a dialogue and creative conversation between the philosopher, who maintains a continuing interest in Christianity, and the grand tradition of theological reasoning. Thankfully, theology today is ecumenical in scope. I am interested, then, in an engagement with Vattimo's thought that takes account of the richness of the entire Christian tradition and, indeed, at least to some extent, the entire patrimony of religious reflection. While Vattimo's idiom is largely Christian (and, particularly when speaking of the church, Roman Catholic), he intends his work, undoubtedly, as exemplifying a Christian diffusion into universality. I write, then, as a theologian with a serious interest in both ecumenical and inter-religious dialogue.

While I am hardly an apologist for Vattimian thought (and often disagree with his conclusions) I hope I have exercised, as all interpreters should, a *pietas* before his work, a "fraternal disposition" before the "other" seeking to understand him both fully and fairly. Only this kind of interpretative fidelity to the text protects the unique individuality of the "given form" thereby adhering to the classical hermeneutical axiom, *Sensus non est inferendus sed efferendus.* At the same time, I am interested not only in hermeneutical charity, but also in penetrating to the truth of the matters under discussion, *die Sache selbst.*

Of course, significant questions present themselves right from the outset: Can a man such as Vattimo, whose entire philosophy is soaked in Nietzschean nihilism, truly enter into dialogue with theology? Is his work nothing more than Dionysus hammering insistently at the gates of the City of God? Can his thought illuminate the Christian tradition, offering resources for theological thinking? Or is his attempt to reformulate the nature of Christianity nothing more than a catalogue of heresies, resulting in a badly misshapen faith? What are we to make of a man who calls his philosophy "optimistic nihilism" and who insists that "postmodern nihilism constitutes the actual truth of Christianity" (*FR*, 47)?

At the same time, despite any initial theological reservations we may harbor, should we not also frankly admit that Vattimo, the philosopher and cultural commentator, has his finger squarely on the pulse of our tumultuous times? Is it not true that large swaths of society are convinced that, in a world of countless interpretations about the meaning of life, the nature of truth and the existence of God, what actually counts for religious truth is tolerance and charity toward the "other"? Do not many accept the proposition that the passion for religious truth leads, all too often, to smug intolerance? And that aggressively held dogmatic beliefs are the cause of violence, both spiritual and physical?

How, then, can religion intellectually support a multivalent culture of tolerance? Does Vattimo's philosophy provide legitimate support, from a Christian and religious perspective, for just such a position?

Chapter 1

An overture to Vattimo's thought

Postmodernism . . . once again

Is there anyone not tired to the point of exhaustion by the word "postmodernism?" Hasn't the word been hammered to pieces by overuse? Is it so wide and polyvalent in meaning as to have been rendered useless, trotted out in order to defend some imprecise academic vagaries? Wildly different points of view are now labeled postmodern, a panoply of positions themselves occasionally at odds, making it impossible to render a succinct and accurate definition. And even with all of this, isn't almost everyone now willingly *post*modern, with modernity itself, the very epitome of bloodless rationalism, having fallen into deep academic disrepute? Postmodernity and religion were at first taken to be enemies with the former indicating some form of relativism at best and of anarchy at worst. But presumed animosity is hardly the case today, with some courting this line of thought as offering the best chance for the Christian message to be clearly heard. Since the narrative of postmodernity is important to Vattimo, some broad features of this concept, as well as his particular use of it, should be briefly sketched.

The term "postmodernism" refers, in general, to the continually growing critique of Enlightenment construals of rationality. *Modern* rationality is understood as attempting to pin down reason to the limited canons of empiricism, positivism or some equally narrow form of thinking and knowing. In the *postmodern* construal, modernity is equated with a reductive attempt to reduce truth to methodology, particularly those methods and canons associated with scientific inquiry. Heidegger, one of the architects of the movement, has charged that the rationality of modernity led inexorably to an accent on science and technology, to the reduction of legitimate philosophical wonder, to the equation of thinking with mere *techné*.

If the "modern" placed a pronounced stress on the homogeneity of thought, culture and practice, the postmodern response has been to celebrate discontinuity and pluralism. It has argued that modernity, in its rush to canonize the "foundationalisms" of positivism and empiricism, has failed to account for essential dimensions of actual historical life such as our embeddedness in determinate societies, cultures and practices, our traditioned and situated reason, our contextualized knowledge, our historicity and finitude. As such, postmodernity exhumes from Enlightenment obsequies notions such as alterity and difference, rupture and breach. By "presencing" precisely those horizons rooted in everyday existence—our social location, our ideological determination and our paradigm-bound rationality—postmodernity has become a call to arms against reductive, universalizing tendencies. In sum, postmodernity argues that there is more in heaven and earth than modern conceptions of human reason can hope to understand.[2] This pronounced stress on the finite and fragmented nature of thought sometimes leads to postmodernity being characterized as "relativist" in kind. In fact, its primary concern is to make clear that we are all theory-laden (to invoke Thomas Kuhn's famous term), that we live in a world that is subject to many different interpretations, with each interpreter harboring vastly different presuppositions which themselves reach down to the very marrow of thinking and knowing.

Vattimo is certainly a representative of this school of thought, willingly endorsing postmodern philosophy insofar as it attempts to surpass the reifying and constricting thinking of Enlightenment positivism. But Vattimo adds his own twist: Even though many try to make postmodernism a late 20th century affair, it is Nietzsche's manifesto, "God is dead" that marks the real passage from modernity (*EM*, 167; *NE*, 51). Why dragoon God into this discussion? Because insofar as we live in a world that is itself the result of very divergent interpretations, God is no longer "ready-at-hand" as a warrant for truth, order and objectivity. "God is dead" means not that God is inexistent, in the sense of a flat-footed metaphysical pronouncement (*AOC*, 11; *PD*, 21). It suggests, rather, that the "objective world" can no longer be built on a transcendent foundation. God is no longer available to us as the unchanging and immutable first principle who now serves as the basis for morality and truth, as a warrant for stable and fixed "metaphysical" positions. In the postmodern age, we must live with endless contingencies rather than with secure and available foundations. And this contingency and provisionality includes the affirmation of a "God" who himself does not escape interpreted existence. Our understanding of God is, and relentlessly so, also an interpretation. So, Vattimo says, "when Nietzsche teaches that God is dead, he doesn't only mean that there are no longer supreme values, he also means that a multitude of values has taken their place at the ruined foundation . . ." (*WTRV*, 462).

Despite his sympathy with postmodernism, and the isomorphism of many of his salient themes with this way of thinking, Vattimo also gives the impression of not being entirely comfortable with this term lest it appear that he fails to appreciate the actual *achievements* of modernity, particularly modernity's intense accent on human freedom, a liberation from suffocating class structures, hidebound traditionalism, idolatrous superstition and a constraining "natural" law. In all of these matters, Vattimo is, indeed, a defender of modernity. And it is precisely Vattimo's hesitancy about "overcoming" modernity, as well as his continuing appreciation of it, that leads us to introduce a term important to the entire Vattimian corpus: *Verwindung*. This word, with roots in Heidegger, etymologically refers to "twisting," to "convalescence" and to "alteration."[3] The term is important to Vattimo because it serves as a kind of code word to indicate that we cannot simply jettison or overcome (*Überwindung*) the modern era that has preceded us (just as Heidegger said we could not simply overcome the prior tradition of "Being"). Rather, our task is one of healing, which is also a kind of twisting and even deformation, because modernity must be disciplined and rethought in our own epoch and culture.

But why settle for a mere *Verwindung* instead of an *Überwindung*, a convalescence/deformation rather than an "overcoming"? The reason, Vattimo says, is because the term "overcoming" gives the unfortunate impression that we can somehow start all over again, right from the beginning, thereby establishing a new "foundation," as if we are not deeply determined by that which has preceded us (*DDWT*, 158). The proper image for postmodernity can never be of erecting a totally new "foundation" or "system" (which is to fall again into the trap of rationalist modernity). Rather, we should envisage the relationship between the modern and the postmodern by way of circular images, with a certain synergy between them, even if postmodernity rejects the notion of progress and the easy periodization of history that sometimes characterizes the modern (*NE* 49–50).

Modernity is the place where the "new" becomes the supreme value. "*Il faut être absolument moderne!*" becomes the fashionable maxim. But this leads to a kind of progressive, developmental view of life. History is always on the march toward some final goal; there is always some clearly determined *telos* in view. Postmodernity, on the other hand, displays "as its most common and most imposing trait" the effort to free itself from the logic of overcoming, of development and of innovation (*EM*, 105). Vattimo argues, in fact, that "overcoming" is itself a modern category since the very definition of the "modern" is the exchanging of the "old" for the "new" (*EM*, 167). One may even understand Nietzsche's doctrine of the Eternal Return, a notoriously difficult stumbling block for interpreters of his thought, as an unmasking of the failed logic of modernity, of the notion of unilinear, temporal, progressive development. The Eternal Return is best understood as a post-modern strategy, the unmasking of a facile periodization of history, with its allied notion of the inexorable march of temporal development (*DN*, 179).[4]

Pensiero debole or weak thought

Closely allied to Vattimo's *Verwindung* of modernity is that species of thinking known as "weak thought." Even those who know virtually nothing about Vattimo's philosophy may have heard the term *pensiero debole* or "weak thought." For this is the Torinese's signature phrase, much as one may connect Nietzsche with nihilism, Kant with transcendental thinking, Heidegger with Being or Gadamer with hermeneutics. Indeed, *pensiero debole* is a general philosophical style which pervades all of the Vattimo's thinking and is imparted to everything he has written. Insofar as he wishes to undertake a "convalescence-alteration" of major philosophical themes (of Being, truth, interpretation and secularization), a central step in his *Verwindung* of these notions is a weakening of their strong, aggressive claims to truth (*pensiero forte*), diluting them by means of large doses of contingency and provisionality. How, then, should weak thought be precisely understood?

It is perhaps best to speak of "weak thought" as an attempt to reconstruct rationality in a postmodern, postmetaphysical way. By this I mean that Vattimo intends to move contemporary construals of rationality away from purely modern notions of reason, with their aggressive assertions about the "certainly true," the "really real" and "absolute objectivity," with their insinuations that evidence and warrants are unproblematic concepts, readily available to settle questions of interpretative adequacy and with their concomitant affinity for an unchanging transcendental subject. Weak thought, on the contrary, holds that the world is not simply "given" to us as pure, uninterpreted, unmediated reality.[5] If contemporary philosophy has taught us anything, (and here Vattimo adduces not only Nietzsche, but Heidegger, Wittgenstein, Gadamer, Rorty and Kuhn), it is that the world is known by subjects who are already deeply enmeshed in history and tradition, who are themselves entirely theory-laden. Vattimo is convinced, then, that the world is "given" to us as an *always-already interpreted reality*. And precisely because of this, we must avoid strong thought with its blinkered claims to truth, finality, objectivity and absolute knowledge, with its concomitant avoidance of historical contingency. There exist no ultimate, normative foundations that are available to us "outside" of interpretation. There exists no "evidence" that is not already deeply implicated in determinate forms of life and in already elaborated interpretative structures. Consequently, we have no clearly available *archai* or *Gründe*, undisputed first principles or warrants, that could "settle" matters finally, that could offer definitive notions of truth which would escape perpetual provisionality (*DDWT*, 155; *PD*, 18).[6]

The internet serves as a good example of what Vattimo is driving at. As any casual user of the web can attest, the internet displays to us a profligate interpretative bazaar.

What is the nature of humanity?
What is the good we should pursue?
Which values are ultimate?
Is there a God?
Do we know anything about him?

In the answers proffered to these questions, we have the multi-valent, infinitely interpretable world on full view. The internet makes patently clear that we reside in a world of competing and proliferating interpretations without a defined center. And precisely this is Vattimo's point. Our world is without Archimedean levers that offer us "evidence" to decide these fundamental questions. In fact, it is just on the fundamentals that we see an array of highly variable answers. Strong thought insists on its objectivity and final truth; it insists that it has irrefutable "evidence" to buttress its case, to make final decisions, to offer clear answers. As such it tends toward positivism, aggression and intolerance. Weak thought, on the contrary, recognizes that all claims to adduce definitive "evidence" and indisputable "warrants" are themselves riddled with theoretical commitments, prior suppositions and background assumptions. No final or uncomplicated "givenness" is to be found in evidence itself. Weak thought, in a word, recognizes the always deeply interpretative nature of human life and discourse. And such recognition ineluctably weakens and "lightens" our sense of the finality of Being and truth.[7]

Vattimo, of course, is hardly the only thinker to insist on the primacy of interpretation or on the hermeneutical nature of human experience. One hears with growing frequency these days the pithy claim that "it's interpretation all the way down." This maxim, cited by several recent authors, finds its *fons et origo* in Nietzsche's assertion that: There are no facts, only interpretations. And this, too, is an interpretation![8] This passage, cited frequently by Vattimo (*BYI*, 26; *DN*, 74; *NE*, 155) is meant to remind us that we are embedded and conditioned observers, that we "perform" within different language-games, that there are no self-justifying criteria of legitimation, no universal or unambiguous warrants for truth. All warrants, rather, are deeply embedded in specific forms of life, in contingent cultural circumstances. This claim— that all knowledge is, necessarily and without exception, rooted in interpretation—helps us to see more clearly what *pensiero debole* means. It means that there exists a multiplicity of interpretations, none of which is self-justifying by virtue of appeals to universally available first principles or "evidence." We should understand, rather, that evidence and criteria are not unproblematic concepts. "Evidence" varies from community to community, from person to person. For example, while the believer may see the world as attesting to God's goodness and wisdom, a nonbeliever may see only a variety of biological, chemical and material causes. This is something of what Nietzsche meant by the phrase "God is dead." God cannot serve as an unproblematic first principle for objectivity as if "God" is not also an interpreted reality. Nietzsche's point about the inextricable interweaving of facts and interpretations constitutes one reason why Vattimo resists lumping him together with Marx and Freud. It is true that they were all "masters of suspicion." But Nietzsche was no subscriber to the "rationalization" thesis, the claim that idea of God will inevitably decline as education advances. Unlike Marx and Freud, Nietzsche mocked scientific positivism as a hopelessly utopian imposter; science gives us no more access to "truth" and "objectivity" than does religion.

Speaking broadly, then, Vattimo is part of that marked movement in contemporary philosophy and theology emphasizing that, as human beings, we are deeply shaped and conditioned by the intricacies and thick practices of our societies, cultures and languages. Human rationality is profoundly contextualized and circumscribed, rather than autonomous and neutral. As such, we only know ourselves and the world in and through antecedent norms and suppositions; there exist no pre-linguistic givens. We should avoid speaking, then, of "universal reason" or of "autonomous reason" as if there subsisted some pocket of reality not deeply defined by all of these interlacing emphases.

This insistence on human embeddedness in culture, language and tradition finds support in a broad variety of philosophical perspectives. For a long time now, Hans-Georg Gadamer and his disciples have been involved in unmasking the worldless, traditionless, Cartesian subject of the Enlightenment, with its truncated understanding of historicity, tradition and the nature of interpretation. Gadamer himself was hermeneutically developing many of the themes first broached by Martin Heidegger in *Being and Time*, especially the latter's jeremiad against those ignoring our enmeshment in the "worldhood of the world," the profound embeddedness that *Dasein* is always tempted to bury in the unremitting search for absolute and unencumbered certitude and first principles. Wittgenstein, too, reacting against an untenable positivism, stressed our culturally constituted norms and language-games, hoping to press the point that reality is always linguistically and socially mediated, i.e., meanings are determined by forms of life and particular practices rather than by neutral, autarkic, universal standards. Thomas Kuhn's highly influential manifesto, *The Structure of Scientific Revolutions*, introduced many of these same themes into the philosophy of science: we are profoundly theory-laden; different standards lead inexorably to incommensurable paradigms; words are not attached to objects in ways that are unproblematic and there is no neutral, sub-linguistic way of describing evidence. All of these thinkers, of course, are responding to and against the pretensions of Enlightenment modernity, with its positivistic notion of rationality, with its imperious Cartesian/Kantian subject taken as the *fundamentum inconcussum* for knowing and with its naïve and insolent claims to unsullied objectivity.

This view, deeply accenting our contingency and "situatedness," our immersion in a thick tradition, culture, history, society and language, has served to expose the inadequacies of positivism and radical empiricism, to overturn the Enlightenment notion of unconditioned reason and to dethrone the idea that human rationality is exercised "apart" from a world of historical contingencies. It is precisely this stress on human embeddedness that, as noted, has given rise to the phrase: "it's interpretation all the way down." By this is meant that one never has bare facts or *facta bruta*; reality, rather, is always interpreted reality, every seeing is an appropriative "seeing as," there exists no purely neutral level of observation, nor any unconditioned exercise of human rationality. Kuhn, one of the foremost proponents of the maxim, interpreted it in a very strong sense, arguing that, since every interpreter is deeply theory-laden, we cannot know the world "in itself." The phrase "in itself" was, in fact, meaningless, Kuhn contended, because there was no "higher viewpoint" or neutral Archimedean platform surpassing the theory-ladenness and embedded status of actual observers. Insofar as the scientist has access only to interpretations, he or she is dealing with the world as a constructed entity, that is, the world as it appears rather than the noumenal world itself.

Vattimo, with his program of "weak thought" or *pensiero debole*, similarly wishes to accent that we have no uninterpreted notion of truth, reality or Being. Nietzsche formulated this with the most brio when he wrote that there are no facts, only interpretations, that we live in a world that is created rather than "given." Vattimo adds that because we live in a deeply interpretative world, our claims to truth must themselves be hesitant, always marked by toleration and *caritas*. Weak thought, with its profound doubts about "objective reality" and "absolute certainty" serves, for Vattimo, as a way of liberating *human freedom* from those who would stifle emancipation and creativity with bellicose claims to certitude and finality. Weak thought allows the human being to seize fully his or her own life, to mold and shape it in new ways, apart from predetermined structures and assertive prejudices. As such, he is insistent that "weak thought" cannot be taken simply as a specious and rootless call for greater tolerance; it is intended, rather, as a fully developed philosophical program, as our later discussion will make clear. In fact, Vattimo says he is calling for a "strong theory of weakness" (*WTRV*, 453), a theory which is not simply aware of thought's limits, but traces the diminishment and withdrawal of Being in this epoch at the end of metaphysics (*BE*, 35).

Postmodernism, religion and *pensiero debole*: The retrieval of *caritas*

In light of Vattimo's unique interpretation of postmodernity, as well as his own program of "weak thought," what does he have to contribute on the question of religion and religious truth? While the pallid universality of the Enlightenment tended to regard religion as an emotive intrusion on the canons of strict rationality, postmodernity allows religion to re-enter contemporary discourse. This has caused some thinkers to hail postmodern thought on the grounds that it has freed theology from needing to adhere to Enlightenment canons of truth and rationality.[9] After all, there is little room for religion in the man of the Enlightenment, the *Aufklärer*. If religion *is* admitted into the societal parlor, it is consigned to an obscure corner, considered as belonging to the realm of the affective but cognitively empty, and, often enough, regarded as suffocatingly repressive and authoritarian. As Vattimo says, the modern West was increasingly founded "on the self-assurance of scientistic and historicist reason that saw no limit to increasingly total domination . . ." (BE, 56). And, of course, a spate of recently popular books claiming to defend atheism on the grounds of scientific discoveries shows that this trend is not altogether moribund. Some still long for a recrudescence of a "modern" spirit which occludes religion.[10] Vattimo, however, regards this kind of militant atheism to be as much a phenomenon of "strong thought" as is religious fundamentalism, noting that the end of modernity is also the end of positivist science and Marxist historicism with their aggressive claims to have mastered the deep, underlying structure of the universe and to have destroyed religion in the process (BE, 28). Vattimo is convinced that faith in the progress of Reason (and even faith in objective truth) has now broken down. Atheist manifestos, then, even with all their *Sturm und Drang*, their anti-religious huffing and puffing, are arriving at the scene in need of an oxygen tank, badly out of theoretical breath.

With the wide recognition of the hermeneutical character of all thought, the breakdown of algorithmic positivism and the *dépassement* of modernity, a new age has begun, one that finds religion readmitted into serious philosophical discussion. The insolent and imperious claims of modernity, to a truth founded on and limited to empirically verified facts, has almost entirely broken down. Calculative, technocratic reason can no longer pretend that it stands unaffected by a congeries of factors indicating the historical embeddedness of all rationality. Consequently, modernity's "philosophical prohibition of religion" has been eliminated (RDV, 81). Modernity can no longer assert, as it once did, that the rise of education and reason will lead ineluctably to unadulterated cultural progress and to the end of faith. The once potent Enlightenment *Abbau* of mythology has itself been demythologized. Alluding to this new postmodern temper, Vattimo concludes, "there are no longer strong, rational reasons for being an atheist" (ADG, 97). And again: the death of metaphysics, of strong thought, of an unmediated, uninterpreted world has, in the process, liquidated atheism (*AC,* 17). Given this account of postmodernism and weak thought, it is no surprise that religion has, indeed, been invited back into the drawing-room by Vattimo. After all, if all truth is of itself deeply historical and contingent, why prohibit religion? Of course, further questions immediately present themselves: What kind of religion is now readmitted to polite society? And by what manners must it now abide?

And just there's the rub. For if modernity can no longer be self-assured and imperious with "strong" claims to truth, then neither can religion. Consequently, while Vattimo thinks postmodernity and weak thought make room for religion, it is religion of a certain type and shape. We cannot simply "return" to religion, as if our eyes have not been opened by further reflection, particularly the contributions of Nietzsche and Heidegger (*BE,* 32).[11] The rediscovery of religion (and of Christianity in particular), then, must occur within the shadow of the theoretical overcoming of "objectivistic-dogmatic philosophies." Precisely how Vattimo understands this will be elucidated below. For the moment, it is enough to say that he seeks a kind of *via media* between the Scylla of a constraining positivistic modernity and the Charybdis of a narrow, literalist ecclesiality. Consequently, "dogmatic and disciplinary Christianity. . . . has nothing to do with what I and my contemporaries rediscover" when speaking of faith (*BE,* 61). Indicating his chosen path between the *Aufklärer* and the "fundamentalist," he adds that we should not be separated from Christ either by the scientistic positivism of modernity nor by ecclesiastical authoritarianism which "seeks to fix, with finality, the meaning of Revelation" (*BE,* 59). Neither modern scientism (with its apriori methods) nor premodern ecclesiality (with its precipitous enclosing of truth's boundaries) duplicates contemporary construals of faith. The return of religion depends "on the dissolution of metaphysics, that is, on the dismissal of all doctrines which claimed absolute and definitive values as the true description of Being's structures" (*AC,* 19).

Religion, therefore, can rely on no strong body of doctrine. Dogmatic assertions, with their claim to know reality, the *ontos on,* with certainty and finality, represent precisely the kind of objectifying, metaphysical thought that has been discredited by the deeply hermeneutical character of existence. Christian faith itself must now be understood in light of the multivalent contingencies that distinguish contemporary thought and life. And this leads Vattimo to his own interpretation of the essence of Christianity, an interpretation that finds its *raison d'etre* in *pensiero debole*.

Absent any strong claims, any belief or doctrine that can isomorphically mediate the world, any revelation that can tell us, in some sense, "final" and "objective" truth, then what is, to use an unfortunate phrase, the "cognitive yield" of Christianity? For Vattimo, the theoretical resolution of Christianity is found only in the notion of *caritas*, charity. As he says, "The Christian inheritance that 'returns' in weak thought is primarily the Christian precept of charity and its rejection of violence" (*BE,* 44). Here we see what Vattimo calls the happy convergence between the weak thought of contemporary philosophy and the fundamental teaching of Christian faith. He even speaks of the "transcription" of Christianity into weak thought, thereby announcing the theoretical embrace of postmodernity and Christian belief, a profound conjunction of (postmodern) faith and reason: Both faith and reason now renounce strong, dogmatic assertions which allegedly offer access to the logos-structure of reality, the *ontos on.* Both are equally implicated in the "twilight of Being," in the "lightening" of the solidity of reality that is the necessary residue of the dilution of objectivity.

This helps to explain why Vattimo is fond of citing the well-known dictum rooted in Aristotle's *Ethics: Amicus Plato sed magis amica veritas* (*BYI,* 40; *DR,* 218), a noble sentiment indicating that truth must take priority over friendship, even an intimate one. But he uses this phrase with a purpose, showing how, in our day, it has been contravened. He observes, for example, that when one sees large crowds coming out to cheer the pope, this is *not* an instance of "*amicus Plato.*" No one at all is claiming that the huge throngs of well-wishers that usually greet the pope's arrival agree with him on many disputed matters; no one is affirming that this man speaks the truth on controversial issues. Rather, one is applauding his universal call to charity, to friendship, to common understanding among all peoples. What is at stake here is *caritas*, charity, not some determinate principle of moral or dogmatic "truth." Vattimo notes that after the celebration of the Jubilee Year (2000) in Rome, with its large gathering of young people, the ground was found littered with condoms, thereby confirming that the preeminent sentiment was hardly "*magis amica veritas*" (*ADG*, 96).

In all likelihood, Vattimo would reverse the ancient axiom to read: *Amica veritas sed magis amicus Plato*. Such reversal would be legitimate on the grounds that, in comparison with charity, "there is no truth worth affirming" (*DR*, 218). He adds that we must construct an ethos based on charity to free us from our last idolatry, "the adoration of truth as our God" (*DR*, 218). For Vattimo, as we shall see, the very notion of truth is evanescent and ephemeral, ultimately dissolving into multivalent interpretation. To the claim that rival, conflicting interpretations can ultimately be decided by evidence, Vattimo would again point to the fact that all "evidence" is itself deeply riddled with theoretical commitments and presuppositions. One cannot now prefer truth to friendship or to charity because the death of the moral-metaphysical God to which Nietzsche referred means "that there is no 'objective' ontological truth that might be upheld as anything other than friendship, the will to power, or subjective bond" (*AC*, 105).

Is the truth then, as Nietzsche had it, that there is no truth? Vattimo certainly tends in this direction, as we shall see. For he is convinced that, in relationship to truth, a concept leading inevitably to strong, insolent and imperious thought, one does well to retrieve the Christian notion of *caritas* which is, with its emphasis on tolerance of the "other," deeply convergent with the claim that metaphysics (any system of thought insisting on absolutes) has now been dissolved into *pensiero debole*. Religion, then, must ultimately be understood as charity, in the sense of tolerance and openness toward other interpretations of reality. As such, it cannot "harden" into doctrine; it cannot make any final claims. To be a Christian, indeed to be a religious person, is to recognize that all thinking is "weak," that all knowing is interpretative, that "metaphysics," with its assertion of absolutes, must always be diluted into tolerant charity. And Vattimo regards *this* religious thought as following the dominical injunction to read the signs of the times, which offer to us no other command than *caritas*, the "commandment of love" (*BE*, 66).

A recent illustration of "weak thought" at work may be found in Vattimo's critique of a speech made by Josef Cardinal Ratzinger on April 18, 2005 after the funeral of John Paul II and just prior to his own election as bishop of Rome. Ratzinger denounced the "dictatorship of relativism" as the greatest intellectual deficiency of our time, with moral and doctrinal truth now regarded as entirely contingent and, therefore, as non-binding. In an article dedicated to this talk, Vattimo wondered aloud if it is, indeed, relativism that is the central problem with contemporary civilization. Which is preferable, he asks, charitable tolerance toward a variety of positions and lifestyles or perhaps the dogmatic claims one finds, for example, in the zeal of Crusaders, in the American theocons with their exportation of war to Iraq, or with the scientific certainty of a Hitler? (*DR*, 216). Is relativism really the worse choice? Is the tolerance of non-committal thinking really our problem? Or, rather, is it a surfeit of surety?[12]

Kenosis as paradigm

Given his claim that the retrievable part of Christianity is its accent on *caritas,* it is no surprise that Vattimo is deeply taken with the biblical notion of kenosis, an image that figures prominently in his thought. For the kenosis of God, the Incarnation, helps us to see why charity (tolerance toward interpretative plurality) is the living fruit of Christian faith. A central passage of the New Testament attesting to God's self-emptying is that described in Philippians 2.6-8: "Though he was in the form of God, Christ did not consider equality with God something to be grasped at; rather, he took the form of a slave, being made in the likeness of men. He humbled himself becoming obedient unto death, even death on a cross." This passage, one of the few biblical citations adduced by Vattimo, indicates a "weakening" of God, a renunciation of power and authority, a self-abasement which is the "dissolution of divine transcendence" (*AC*, 27). In the story of the Son of God become man, Vattimo sees the self-emptying of divine transcendence, a vulnerability now unexpectedly convergent with the "weak thought" of Heidegger who teaches the end of objectifying metaphysics and of Nietzsche, who argues for the death of the moral-metaphysical God.

In the kenosis, God has renounced power and authority—just as contemporary philosophy has renounced its claims to finality and truth. Both theology and philosophy, then, harbor deep currents tending in the same direction: both are concerned with overcoming strong claims, whether philosophical (I now have certitude about the stable structure, the final system, the *ontos on*) or theological (determinate biblical, doctrinal and moral teachings are absolutely and universally true). Vattimo even tells us that this convergence provided a solution to his personal philosophical-religious puzzle that seemed too good to be true (*BE*, 41). This is why he can say, in a truly revelatory statement, that "Christianity is a stimulus, a message that sets in motion a tradition of thought that will eventually realize its freedom from metaphysics" (*ADG*, 35). In other words, the kenotic action of God preached by the Christian faith has come to *fruition* in philosophy's renunciation of strong, objective structures; contemporary thought thereby confirms the fundamental message of the Gospel: what is enduringly important is charity, *caritas*, rather than any hard claims to final truth. The "end of metaphysics" as proclaimed by Nietzsche and Heidegger is simply a philosophical transcription of the New Testament's message of charity and love. Rather than being sworn enemies, the beating heart of Christian faith and *pensiero debole* are deeply and inextricably related. God's kenosis in Jesus Christ teaches us that God manifests himself as the vulnerable one who willingly "renounces" authority, as one who thereby undermines, given his own pronounced accent on vincibility, strong claims to truth. It is precisely in this kenotic Christianity that Vattimo discerns the root and paradigm of secularization.

Kenosis and secularization

Secularization is a word with which everyone is familiar. It usually denotes the gradual moving away from a sacral construal of society and cultural life to an understanding of human and social interchange in which God no longer plays a part, at least not significantly or publicly.[13] As with all aspects of his thought, Vattimo hopes to perform a *Verwindung* on the concept of secularization. Again, this is not an "overcoming" (hopeless in any case), but a reinterpretation that is both a convalescence and an alteration. As part of this *Verwindung*, Vattimo rejects two common understandings: (1) those who see secularization as a "loss of the center," i.e., the privation of a relationship with God and so a demonic disfigurement of the human and (2) those who advocate a triumphal scientism thinking that religion must be confined to the private realm and kept far from public discourse. In both cases, Vattimo concludes, secularization is understood as "emancipation from God" whether this is considered as a positive or negative development (*OA*, 210). His own intention, on the other hand, is to advance beyond both the premodern reactive and Enlightenment triumphal notions of secularization with their eulogistic or dyslogistic claims that God has, indeed, been eliminated from public life.

Vattimo's own contention is that religion should see secularization not as a development to be decried and reversed, but as a *triumph* of Christian belief, as a beneficent and propitious impulse given life by Christianity itself. In fact, when we come to understand that *the real fruit of religion is charity (caritas)* and that charity is rooted in God's kenosis (which is itself a parable of the renunciation of power and authority) we gradually come to see that secularization is not the opponent of religion, but one of its *vibrant fruits*. Secularization is, in fact, the gradual realization in history of the kenotic self-abasement of God; it is the result of kenotic *caritas* working its way through history. Rather than an adversary of the Christian message secularization is, on the contrary, an *essential component* of it. As Vattimo says, "Christianity's vocation consists in deepening its own physiognomy as source and condition for the possibility of secularity" (*AC*, 98).

Why is continuing secularization the fruit and not the deadly foe of fervent Christian (and, indeed, all religious) belief and practice? One reason is because secularization, properly understood, means precisely that there is "room" for everyone, no matter his or her belief (or lack of belief), in the public square. No one is excluded from equal participation in the realm of public life and discourse. Secularization is the legitimate fruit of religious charity because it opens society to every point of view, thereby rejecting an aggressive religiosity that degenerates into fundamentalist ideology, seeking to exclude those viewpoints not conforming to the "prevailing wisdom." On this reading, secularization is the recognition that the world is a festival of interpretative plurality with no one claiming privileged access to the *ontos on*. And this view, with its marked epistemological and ontological humility, is entirely convergent with the Christian understanding of kenosis, the self-renunciation of the power and authority of God. This is why Christianity's *actual* achievement does not consist in its determinate claims, in its system of dogma or doctrine; its stunning achievement, in fact, is the secularized truth of *caritas* which has led to the modern understanding of rights, to the humanization of social relations, to the dissolution of class structures. *These* achievements represent Christianity's historical, societal triumph. It is precisely these "secularized" accomplishments that represent the positive way in which modern civilization has responded to the announcement of the Christian tradition (*AC*, 26). Indeed, the West acknowledges its proper self-constitution by realizing that it is nothing other than secularized Christianity (which is, in fact, kenotic *caritas* unfurled in history). Vattimo concludes, therefore, that secularization must always be viewed positively by the Christian faith, indeed, be considered as one of its greatest successes. Consequently, the contemporary missionary task of Christianity is *not* to strengthen its own doctrinal, moral and disciplinary specificity (for this would be a return to a discredited "metaphysics" and would hardly make sense in a world deeply riven with religious strife), but to accent its unique contribution to world culture which consists in the opening of the secular, "lay" sphere of wide interpretative plurality, an opening rarely found in other cultures or religions.

Kenosis, then, as the outpouring and diffusion of the divine into the human, becomes *the very model for secularization*. In kenotic Christianity, religion finds its actual vocation, the weakening of its strong, metaphysical claims in service to the greater flourishing of interpretative pluralism. And this kenotic interpretation is not limited to society; it also has a place within the church. For the Bible, too, must be subject to a "secularizing interpretation" (*BE*, 86), an interpretation which necessarily entails the resolution of biblical claims into charity. This is to say that the fundamental meaning of the biblical message is God's love for humanity as well as God's self-renunciation of power and authority. And this divine self-emptying leads straight to the position of *pensiero debole*, of weakening, of secularization properly understood. How could it be otherwise? For how could one insist on "strong thought," how could one defend apriori natures, universal essences, literalistic biblical and doctrinal hermeneutics, all of which necessarily lead to exclusion and monochromatic interpretation when Christ himself appeals to us as "friends" and Scripture insists that the greatest commandment is love?[14]

The "natural sacred"

As we have seen, one reason why secularization should be understood not as the opponent but as the actual fruit of Christianity is the end of homogeneity and the consequent acceptance of interpretative plurality within society. A second reason why secularization should be beneficently welcomed is that, in the process of a societal "drifting away" from a sacral core, Christians are reminded that, by God's kenotic action, Christianity renounced those elements which merely *appeared* as sacred in the *natural order* (such as divine omnipotence) but which have no part in biblical religion. Secularization, then, is the way in which God's kenosis continues to realize itself in history, overcoming, in the process, *the originary violence associated with the natural sacred (BE, 48).* What precisely does this statement mean? Why is a central part of Vattimo's eulogistic analysis of secularization rooted in a polemic against the "natural sacred?"

Vattimo relies heavily here on the thought of René Girard who, in a plethora of studies, has argued that Christ's death and resurrection fully unveils the "scapegoat mechanism" that is part and parcel of the naturally sacred. A cultural anthropologist as well as a philosopher, Girard observes that, throughout the whole of human history, societies have retained their unity and social cohesion by identifying various persons, groups or classes as "evil ones," i.e., as causes of social and cultural dissension. Only when violent action is taken against the malefactors, when they are humiliated or wounded/killed, is society thereby "cleansed and healed," with cohesive social unity now fully restored. It is Girard's brief that the violence against Christ, leading to his ultimate death, finally unmasked this "scapegoat mechanism" as belonging to the "naturally sacred," that natural cycle of violence and cleansing has now been exposed by the New Testament (and, indeed, by aspects of the Old Testament as well) as illegitimate and anti-human.[15]

Vattimo is deeply taken with Girard's point that the death of Christ unmasks the violence of natural, sacrificial religion. He says, in fact, that his reading of Girard led him to thinking about secularization (the drifting away from natural religion) as a positive development. For secularization is the realization that divine self-abasement undermines the *naturally* "sacred core" of societies, particularly those exclusionary actions committed in the name of religion. Secularization is a Christian triumph precisely because it moves societies away from the exclusionary tendencies of natural religion toward the essence and core of true biblical religion which is charity itself. For if God did not hesitate to humble himself, if God willingly took the form of a slave, then how much more should men and women be willing to renounce not only strong thought (with its quest for certitude) but also natural religion, with its skewed understanding of God's identity and action in history?

The kenosis or self-emptying of God, then, indicates a divine self-manifestation that undermines our "primitive" conceptions of religion. But Vattimo goes beyond Girard, offering his own list of exclusionary (and therefore violent) characteristics which are manifestations of the "instinctively sacred," needing to be unmasked. He says, for example that the great scandal of Christian revelation, the kenosis, constitutes "the removal of all the transcendent, incomprehensible, mysterious and even bizarre features . . ." traditionally assigned to God (*BE*, 55). The "natural" conception of God is one of authoritarian law-giver, the transcendent and capricious one who rules the world with an iron hand; he is the moral God, the God of the philosophers to whom Pascal referred (*AC*, 15). Other elements of the primitive, unredeemed sacred not yet purified by Christian *caritas* include: the refusal to ordain women to the priesthood in Roman Catholicism (*AC*, 47; *FR*, 15); the many dogmatic and moral positions of the church ". . . . bound up as they are with the absolutization of . . . contingent historical events . . ." (*BE*, 55); the church's opposition to the distribution of condoms in the AIDS crisis in order to avoid ". . . the impression that Christian morality and doctrine may be weakening" (*BE*, 57; *FR*, 79); and, the condemnation of homosexual activity, on the grounds that this is sick or disordered behavior (*BE*, 73).[16] Even the ancient "just war" thesis may be an example of the natural sacred insofar as it consists of the church arriving at a compromise with powerful state interests (*BE*, 72).

All of these instances smack of a "primitive" notion of God, rooted in precepts of exclusionary violence, far from the kenotic charity in which God has manifested himself as "weak," as "friend," and as "love." Such positions try to pass off a historically embedded and contingent situation as identical with a "universal and perduring nature," devolving into the claim of an easily discernable human "essence." They represent elements that, not having been "cleansed" by the Gospel's central message, are, therefore, deeply corroded by the violent, exclusionary sense of native religion.[17] For Vattimo such elements represent the sacred as read through the lens of "nature," rather than accenting the God revealed in the kenotic message of the Gospels, the God who appears "after metaphysics." So, the Torinese can assert that he has rediscovered the doctrine of kenosis and "salvation as the dissolution of the sacred as natural-violent" (*BE*, 61).

We must learn to interpret both Scripture and church doctrine in light of this kenotic charity which entails the dilution and weakening of primitive religion. Secularization, rightly understood (as the corrosion/healing of the naturally sacred) is, in fact, "the very essence of Christianity" (*BE*, 49–50). By this Vattimo means that insofar as secularization is identical with kenotic Christianity, then all Scripture and doctrine must be interpreted *in light of caritas, in light of love, in light of God calling us friends,* rather than in light of a "natural" religion, with its tendency to adopt constraining tenets. And freedom from the naturally sacred leads, inevitably, to *liberty and emancipation* since humanity is no longer bound by authoritarian, exclusionary laws, by metaphysical universals and apriori essences, by irreversible moral and doctrinal statements, by strict precepts that have now been exposed by the Gospel as the antitheses of Christ's ultimate message of charity and friendship.

Vattimo's attack on the "natural sacred" here echoes (and supersedes) Heidegger's well-known comment about overcoming the God of metaphysics, the *causa sui* before whom one can neither dance nor pray, the biblical God who is quite different from the "transcendent One" of natural religion.[18] In this sense, one can say that Vattimo legitimately tries to "release" the biblical God from an overweening "natural" deity, the god of onto-theology who is not performatively disciplined by faith.[19]

Chapter 2
Interpretation, Being and truth

Vattimo and hermeneutics

For Vattimo, as we have seen, all thought and language is deeply bound up with particular conventions and customs. All human reason, therefore, is embedded, situated and "traditioned" in varying cultural, social and linguistic webs. Precisely because of this embeddedness, one should avoid the kind of aggressive rationality that insists on its own "particular truth." For just such insistence on the truth of one's claims, on one's own point of view, has led to intolerance and totalitarianism. Vattimo intimates, in fact, that the world has moved toward exclusionary violence in direct proportion to each particular group, nation, religion, culture and society pressing its own "way," its own "truth" as the fundamental and essential path to "reality," to the *ontos on,* the really real. But to insist on the truth of one's own socially determined group, nation or religion is to fall into the grip of a "strong thought" (*pensiero forte*) that is untenable. Such thinking is no longer defensible because we acknowledge today that the world is an interpretative bazaar, that so-called "evidence" conclusively proving the accuracy of particular positions is itself deeply determined by singular and idiosyncratic forms of life.

As earlier noted, the internet is the perfect exemplar of the current situation. The web offers an unlimited variety of choices explaining the nature of human existence. Of course, this vast interpretative plurality extends to religions as well. For religions are simply varying interpretations of reality, different "rewritings" of the world, themselves deeply conditioned, socially, culturally and linguistically. We live, Vattimo argues, in a world without a center, a Babel-like plurality, with an irreducible number of differing *Weltanschauungen.* This kind of pluralism necessarily "weakens" and "lightens" our understanding of Being, truth and reality

And such "lightening," clearly enough, displays the very meaning of *pensiero debole*: it is the recognition that the world is a festival of multivalent plurality, that no one can claim privileged access to the *ontos on*. This is the essence of Nietzsche's intermingling of facts and interpretations. Vattimo urges us to see that no interpretation, no particular disclosure of Being, is final or ultimate, thereby escaping a deeply inscribed contingency and provisionality. In the past, Enlightenment modernity (but surely not only the Enlightenment) has presented itself as the last word, the final truth; but the Enlightenment itself has been unmasked, as have all claims to privileged interpretation. What takes place over time is a continual "rewriting" of the world. No one has access to universal structures, to absolute and immutable essences. One meaning of the "death of God" is that there exists no final, encompassing vision of the world. This is why Vattimo is so taken by (and frequently repeats) Nietzsche's parable, "How the World Became a Fable" from *The Twilight of the Idols*.

In this parable, the "true world" was first available to the wise and virtuous man, the follower of Plato. But, gradually, the "true world," the "really real" became successively more unattainable. It was *promised* to the Christian who committed himself to living an ascetical and virtuous life; then, the true world became entirely unknowable and unattainable in Kantian and idealist philosophy, wherein the noumenal world escaped humanity's cognitive grasp. Finally, the idea of the "true world" no longer even served a purpose. It became a superfluous notion, best abolished. The "true world" in fact, no longer even exists![20] It is no surprise that Vattimo is deeply attracted to this passage, citing it in many of his works. Nietzsche's point (and Vattimo's) is not only that we have no universal, self-justifying warrants which give us access to "reality" but that, in fact, reality itself *is constituted* by the interpretations we offer. The world *is*, in fact, simply a *play of interpretations* (*BYI*, 7; *WP*, 402). Productive interpretations should not be understood as *discovering* pre-existent Being; precisely this point of view is the outdated notion that must be superseded—the claim that we only need to discover the *right* philosophy in order to understand the world that is desperately waiting to be discovered. Interpretations should be construed, rather, as *generating* Being, as new ways for Being to announce, disclose and manifest itself (*AC*, 67).

Being itself is here understood as productive interpretation, a notion we shall elucidate below.

It is important to recognize, then, that Vattimo is not simply arguing that we have no universal warrants available to us in order to choose among competing positions given our contingent, historical, embedded knowing. His is not simply the repetition of the widespread claim that there exist no ironclad epistemological foundations, no ultimate criteria that ensure the authenticity of our interpretations. Nor is Vattimo's position the Kantian one that our access to the noumenal world, the *ontos on*, is severely limited due to the transcendental structures of subjectivity. (One sees precisely this Kantian position derided in the retelling of Nietzsche's parable of the world as fable.) Vattimo's, rather, is the more insistently Nietzschean claim that the world is *created* by our interpretations; there exist no ontological foundations, no deep and enduring structures of Being. Any assertions about the world "in itself," the "true world" are deeply marred by their failure to account for the world's actual *constitution* by the creative subject. Reality itself (which always involves the subject who organizes and interprets it) is created by the observer; there is no "pre-existing" order in the world apart from interpretation. As Vattimo says, ". . . ontology must bid farewell to the idea of an objectified, external Being to which thought should strive to adequate itself" (*GPO*, 301). The Torinese eulogistically cites Nietzsche on this point: metaphysics basks in the premise ". . . that the chaotic and shifting world of becoming has a foundation in some stable structure, another world that is the true one. Faith in this structure is found in 'the unproductive who do *not desire to create a world* as it ought to be. They posit it as already available, they seek ways and means of reaching it. "Will to truth"—*as the impotence of the will to create*'" (*DN*, 18).[21]

Hermeneutical nihilism

Vattimo willingly embraces, then, two of Nietzsche's fundamental axioms: (1) there are no facts, only interpretations and (2) the world has become a fable. Such Nietzschean embrace helps us to understand why the Torinese speaks not simply of interpretation or of hermeneutics, as one might expect, but uses the more intense term, "hermeneutical nihilism." It also explains why one of his books is entitled *Nihilism and Emancipation*. One must not think that these two terms stand in accidental conjunction, as two fortuitously juxtaposed themes; on the contrary, they are intrinsically and essentially related. For Vattimo, nihilism (the end of belief in reality given in fixed, stable structures, accessible as a norm of knowing and acting) *is* emancipation (*DN*, 129). Emancipation precisely because nihilism recognizes the world for what it is: a multicultural Babel, an irreducible and complex polyvalency of vast interpretative plurality (*BE*, 29; *DN*, 128; *NE*, 54). As Nietzsche observes in the *Will to Power*, humanity is entirely deracinated, "rolling from the center toward 'X'".[22] It is just this decentering which teaches that reality is never given in fixed notions, never known once for all, never given as a final norm (*DN*, 129). This is also why Vattimo speaks of the "nihilistic vocation" of hermeneutics (*BYI*, 2). Interpretation takes place within the flux of historicity that cannot be undone by "hardened" claims willfully asserting the decisive structure of the world, whether this is cast as *ousia*, *esse* or *res cogitans*. Such assertive claims are ontologically naïve for we live in a world of infinite interpretability. Nietzsche and Heidegger have taught us that Being is continuing Event, that interpretation goes "all the way down," that there is no conclusive disclosure of "truth." Insofar as we bestow meaning upon the world in our Promethean freedom, nihilism is, indeed, the proper description. One lives his or her interpretation of the world without needing to believe it is "true" in the sense that it possesses some final ontological foundation (*DN*, 131). One does not, however, *grieve* the absence of foundations. On the contrary, Vattimo announces an "optimistic nihilism," an ability to celebrate a life of moderation and tolerance even if without the security of ultimate "knowledge."[23]

Vattimo is insistent, then, that hermeneutics cannot be tamed, cannot be fashioned into a docile instrument, a flabby and flaccid shibboleth in the hands of contemporary philosophers. Rather, we must straightforwardly thrust hermeneutics toward its proper fulfillment in nihilism, the frank acknowledgment of a vast array of cultural universes.[24] Vattimo uses the bold term "hermeneutical nihilism" to press his point that thinking not only occurs within a tradition (a point on which virtually all philosophers concur), but that such thinking cannot find some ultimate unity in history (as with Gadamer) nor in the discourse community (as with Habermas) nor can hermeneutics succumb to the ultimate and perduring "objectivist" temptation, regarding *itself* as the final, absolute, "metaphysical" answer. Hermeneutics, too, is part of the "play of the sendings," one particular *Geschick*, but not *the* definitive "solution" to perduring philosophical questions. Succumbing to that kind of metaphysical temptation would be both a performative contradiction and a significant philosophical error, identifying as final that which itself is, necessarily, contingent, provisional and transitory.[25] This is why Vattimo is often at pains to announce (Nietzsche-like) that he, too, is offering only an interpretation (*BE*, 44) rather than some final disclosure, some definitive answer, some true ground or absolute manifestation of Being. Even his decided accent on *caritas* cannot be an "ultimate" principle because it, too, would seek to establish itself as a final answer (*BE*, 64). And such an ultimate solution, he insists, is not available to us. There is no "winning" name for truth or for Being. Not even charity can claim this, for who knows how Being will be disclosed in the future? Who knows what manifestation will follow upon *caritas*? So, Vattimo can say that ". . . love, as the 'ultimate' meaning of revelation, is not truly ultimate" (*BE*, 65). For metaphysics (any belief in absolutes) can never be brought to an end by asking us to genuflect before some new, non–metaphysical "final" principle (*NE*, 94/95).[26] Nihilistic hermeneutics recognizes that there is no fundamental unity in history, that every attempt at this kind of periodization smacks of an Hegelian attempt to subvert the radicality of interpretative plurality (again, with the *Horizontverschmelzung* of Gadamer in mind). There should be no attempt to surmount the Babelic hermeneutical bazaar with yet more metaphysical strictures.[27]

The vast interpretative plurality that characterizes life and thought is not limited to the *Geisteswissenschaften*. Science, too, Vattimo insists, has become gradually aware of its deeply interpretative character (*BYI*, 26). Scientists do not simply describe the world "objectively"; they utilize a specific methodology which itself is culturally and historically determined (*ADG*, 28). Scientific knowledge, then, is never simply the "faithful mirroring of objectively defined fact" since there is always an embedded observer who defines, interprets, organizes and represents this knowing (*NE*, 137). Thomas Kuhn's *The Structure of Scientific Revolutions* is an acutely self-aware manifesto acknowledging the deeply hermeneutical character of science, the historicity of paradigms and the contingent cognitive yield of scientific inquiry. Methods, theories and axioms are always relative to determinate historical perspectives, to particular frameworks of meaning (*AC*, 6; *FR*, 51; *VFD*, 32). The rise and fall of paradigms are complex events, involving many factors other than simply "incontrovertible" scientific proof or allegedly undeniable "evidence." One sees in Vattimo the deep and lasting influence of Kuhn, with his insistence that there is no clear distinction between fact and interpretation as well as his assertion that while the scientist is able to solve individual "puzzles," knowledge about the deep structures of the universe is unyielding. Vattimo argues that even in science, truth has increasingly become an affair of consensus, of shared enterprise, rather than a conviction about perduring objectivity (*NE*, 35).[28]

End of metaphysics

Given the deeply interpretative character of both the natural as well as the historical sciences, Vattimo logically speaks of hermeneutical nihilism as the end of metaphysics; the dissolution of Being now ineluctably augurs the end of strong structures and finalities (*EM*, 156). How could it be otherwise? How could one insist on certitude about unimpeachably true structures when we are all embedded interpreters, when we are deeply inscribed within socio-cultural-linguistic traditions, when the manifestation of Being and truth is itself an evanescent historical Event? Hermeneutics reveals the historicity and finitude of the interpreter; the subject is no longer endowed with any stable human nature, whether ontologically or transcendentally conceived. Insofar as hermeneutics announces the deeply contingent nature of human life, it is, unremittingly, the end of metaphysics (*FR*, 45). Nietzsche hits the mark when he declares that metaphysics is "the science that treats of the fundamental errors of mankind—but does so as though they were fundamental truths."[29]

As with many contemporary thinkers, Vattimo wants us to acknowledge that there exist no first principles, no enduring "nature" inhering in substance or subject. But it is important to see that this position is affirmed both epistemologically and ontologically. It is not simply a matter, once again, of saying that no first principle is transparently available to us for the sake of establishing an incontrovertible foundation for knowledge. This position has, at least in certain philosophical circles, become something of a commonplace. Vattimo is also arguing that no first or final principles exist in themselves. For example, the idea of a stable human nature is not only inaccessible to us by means of clear and universal warrants; there exists no such reality as a universal nature. The very idea is a myth that has been destroyed by the corrosive acids of historicity and finitude. All of reality is inextricably and determinatively intertwined with history and culture. Once again, Vattimo has recourse to Nietzsche's insight on our contemporary decentered state: "man rolls from the center toward X, as in the Copernican revolution" (*EM*, 118).[30]

Nihilistic hermeneutics, then, is intended to open the door to a deep sense of the provisionality and contingency of all thinking, indeed, of all reality. This is what Nietzsche means by his claim that "God is dead."[31] It is not a constative proposition, an objective truth-claim, which would simply be a return to metaphysical, dogmatic thinking. It is, rather, the assertion that there is no ultimate, unmediated foundation for reality, no First Truth, no moral and metaphysical God upon whom everything else might be built (*AC*, 3).[32] "God is dead" reminds us that we have no access to a totalizing knowledge of the world. We cannot reach the *ontos on* (*OA*, 205). Indeed, the *ontos on* is created rather than simply "given." This is why one must untiringly expose every attempt to make final claims—the lingering Platonic and Kantian temptation to identify enduring essences. Hermeneutics exposes as untenable the claims of Platonic ideas, Aristotelian *ousiai*, Cartesian "cogitos," Kantian transcendental structures and Husserlian *Dinge*—all those permanent structural truths, those universally valid descriptions that pass as metaphysics. No interpretation can harden into finality, not even Vattimo's hermeneutical nihilism. For such thinking would simply repeat the mistakes tendered by Plato, Aquinas,

Descartes, Kant and Husserl, thereby ignoring the vicissitudes of history, the clarion affirmation that we live in a center-less, post-metaphysical epoch; it would ignore the ontological difference, the difference between Being and its determinate epochal manifestations (*ACT*, 16). By opening the door to contingency and provisionality, by becoming the new *koinē* of Western culture, hermeneutics has eroded the authority of "presence," the kind of *Gegenständigkeit* thinking that assumes that truth is a permanent possession. Of course, Vattimo wishes us to see that this profound interpretative plurality disarms every kind of fundamentalist ideology and so, the very possibility of physical and spiritual intolerance toward the "other."

But surely, one will legitimately protest, even in a world of vast plurality, one needs to adduce criteria to distinguish the better from the worst, the rational from the irrational. If we fail to do so, as Richard Bernstein has observed, we simply flee from metaphysics into anarchic relativism, which itself inevitably spawns a "fundamentalist," metaphysical reaction.[33]

Criteria for resolving interpretative conflict?

Vattimo is well aware that he intends to radicalize interpretative theory, to push it toward nihilism, to insist that hermeneutics cannot present itself as a new "meta-theory" solving all of our theoretical problems. And he is cognizant as well of the difficulties that attend such a program. As he says, the nihilistic conception of hermeneutics can "open the way to a conception of the world as a conflict of interpretations that seems dangerously close to a Nietzschean celebration of the will to power" (*BYI*, 28). For without clear criteria to separate rationality from irrationality, adequacy from inadequacy, then what evaluative norms beside power alone allow one interpretation to prevail over others? Does Vattimo offer any way out of the thicket? And to what extent can he do so given that "evidence" of any kind is already riddled with theoretical commitments, that warrants can never be universal, that facts are inseparable from interpretations? What possible criteria can be utilized if all evidence is "tainted" from the start?

Are there any critical principles that can be invoked besides the flabby relativism of universal tolerance?

Vattimo *does* say that accepting the significance of hermeneutical nihilism does not mean that "everything goes and anyone can say whatever he wants" (*ADG*, 33). He also tells us that not every interpretation is valid; it must be valid by way of consensus, by way of a community of inquirers (*AC*, 67). There are rules and criteria, then, even if rules themselves are relative to determinate forms of life, wedded to particular frameworks of meaning. Vattimo is claiming, in other words, that we do argue and seek to persuade but always and inescapably within certain forms of life, paradigms and theories that are themselves deeply embedded both culturally and linguistically. We "play" within rules of the game, without making further ontological claims as to whether the rules employed truly "describe" the world. Our arguments are necessarily tied to frameworks that are themselves provisional and conditional. This does not mean that we cannot proceed rationally. As Vattimo says, we may still proceed reasonably even when we forego the pretense of grasping an ultimate foundation. Our task is to build consensus in dialogue, without making any claims for absolute truth (*AC*, 5). Such is the case even within the philosophy of science. Kuhn, for example, has shown that rules have their "effective grounding in an historically and culturally determined public domain" (*EM*, 138). Consequently, Vattimo argues, one must always advance arguments for the adequacy of one's position rather than merely offering it as one option in the relativistic marketplace of the public square. Rationality does not become paralyzed by the loss of Cartesian foundations (*PD*, 10). At the same time, even while developing arguments for the plausibility and adequacy of a particular interpretation, one must simultaneously recognize its status *as* an interpretation (rather than an insight into the *ontos on*). Vattimo admits that he is trying to "propose arguments which, even if they do not claim to be definitive descriptions of things as they really are, seem to be reasonable interpretations of our condition *here and now*" (*BE*, 46).

Vattimo, clearly, is groping for what sounds like pragmatic, *practical criteria* for adjudicating between varying interpretations, between good and bad, better and worse—criteria developed within unique socio-cultural contexts. These are the kinds of practical, fallibilistic criteria that have been developed by various thinkers in the philosophy of science and elsewhere, and which include plausibility, explanatory power, fertility of explanation, puzzle-solving ability, fruitfulness and so on. These practical criteria are not intended to offer certitude with regard to competing positions—given that we have no theory-free "access" to reality, no God's-eye "higher viewpoint"—but to show that there do exist norms by which one can make judgments regarding the relative adequacy and plausibility of varying interpretations. We see such pragmatic criteria developed, for example, in the thought of Kuhn who argues that one can adduce practical norms as the basis for adjudication between competing scientific theories, even while eschewing anything approximating a "correspondence" between a theory and the world. Vattimo reaches for something like these criteria, but without any significant development of them, caused, most likely, by his claim that the *ontos on* is itself chimerical. One may, at any given time, offer a persuasive philosophical interpretation, but one must immediately add that any theory is itself contingent and highly changeable, never giving "access" to reality.

Ultimately, Vattimo's attempt to offer criteria for adequacy in resolving interpretative conflict is a thin area of his thought. And such sketchiness is not entirely unexpected. Since his main brief is advancing *weak thought*, since his theory warrants the name "hermeneutical *nihilism*," then seeking criteria, even practical, pragmatic principles, to adjudicate properly between competing truth-claims, will hardly constitute a priority.[34]

On the issue of interpretative adequacy, Vattimo mirrors his mentor Nietzsche by writing aphoristically and by continually reminding us of the maxim "There are no facts, only interpretations." Facts themselves are deeply implicated in interpretative patterns and preconceived ideas which color the "facts" themselves. And this is where Vattimo is truly Nietzschean and, as such, different from Habermas, and, to some extent, even from Kuhn and Gadamer, all of whom seek some via media on the issue of interpretative adequacy, hoping to develop practical criteria that have some purchase for adjudicating among competing accounts, even if not conclusively so. Vattimo fails to develop such warrants, mentioning them infrequently, an issue to which we shall return when discussing his understanding of truth.

Although Vattimo does not systematically develop criteria for adequacy in interpretation, he nonetheless calls his philosophy "optimistic" or "accomplished" nihilism (*EM*, 24).[35] This is to say that hermeneutical nihilism does not endorse anarchy or a violent will to power. Vattimo explains his optimistic nihilism by citing Nietzsche's comments found in his *Writings from the Late Notebooks* where he concludes, ". . . Who will prove to be the *strongest*? The most moderate, those who have no *need* of extreme articles of faith, who not only concede but even love a good deal of contingency and nonsense, who can think of man with a considerable moderation of his value and not therefore become small and weak. . . ."[36] Here, the *Übermensch* is unveiled not as the voluntarist monster created by Nazi ideology but as the one who avoids extremes, who deals with contingency and provisionality, who welcomes pluralism and multivalency, who understands the lack of final structures. This may not be the person who has clearly engraved criteria for interpretative adequacy, but is the one who can don many masks, live in many cultures, the one who can renounce foundations even while accepting the risk and historicity of human life.[37]

Concluding reflections

Vattimo's intent is to perform a *Verwindung* (a healing-alteration-deformation) on traditional notions of interpretation, nudging them toward nihilism, toward a capacious plurality and away from hermeneutics as a kind of encompassing philosophical "meta-theory." As with the notion of secularization, Vattimo will explicitly link his hermeneutical theory with Christian faith, going so far as to say that Nietzsche's claim that there are no facts, only interpretations represents the development and maturation of the Christian message (*FR*, 47). Why is this the case? Because in Nietzsche's hermeneutics (as well as in Heidegger's) we see a decided accent on the situated character of knowing, on the epiphanic manifestation of Being, disallowing any claim to "strong thought," to finality and certitude. In both Nietzsche's insistence on perspectival knowing, and in Heidegger's claim that Being is manifested only temporally, we see the Christian accent on weakness, on kenosis, on *caritas* (the beating heart of Christian faith) now come to theoretical fruition. In this philosophical movement toward *pensiero debole*, we see a happy convergence with the Christian emphasis on the vulnerability of God in the Incarnation, and thus, on the disarming of a strong, aggressive intolerance. Rather than being opponents of Christianity, as is sometimes thought, Nietzsche and Heidegger here become the champions of Christianity's *deepest and truest instincts*; they bring the dynamism and energy of the Christian faith, with its accent on kenotic sacrifice, to its theoretical fulfillment.

Before embarking on an extended theological dialogue with Vattimo, it is essential to examine more carefully his understanding of Being and truth.

Being and truth

Just as hermeneutical nihilism ineluctably corrodes strong thought, so too does the understanding of Being developed in the writings of Martin Heidegger. Heidegger's *Verwindung* of the metaphysical tradition, which issues forth in a new ontology, is another of the pillars of Vattimo's *pensiero debole*. How is this the case?

Heidegger opens *Being and Time* with a striking citation from Plato's *Sophist*: "For manifestly you have long been aware of what you mean when you use the expression 'being.' We, however, who used to think we understood it, have now become perplexed."[38] Vattimo, too, asks us to think about the proper use of "Being" language. How does Being appear in history? What does it mean to say that we live in an age characterized by a "weakening" of Being? Let us answer these questions by beginning with Heidegger.

As we have seen, Heidegger proposes not an *Überwindung*, in the sense of an absolute "re-founding" of metaphysics; such a position is philosophically untenable for "metaphysics cannot be abolished like an opinion."[39] In its place, he proposes a *Verwindung* of the discipline, which is not an annulment of the prior tradition, but its convalescence, retrieval and alteration.[40] What is the nature of this alteration/convalescence now proffered by Heidegger? The philosopher tells us, at the outset of *Being and Time*, that "our provisional aim is the Interpretation of *time* as the possible horizon for any understanding whatsoever of Being."[41] This is a highly significant statement because Heidegger intends to show that manifestations of Being and truth are themselves *deeply and inextricably linked to temporality*. As such, Heidegger is overturning metaphysics understood as permanent and fixed structures, as universally valid descriptions of human life, as manifestations of truth apart from historical contingency and finitude. *That* understanding of metaphysics represents the *forgetfulness* of Being that Heidegger is trying to overcome. Traditional metaphysics is always in search of perduring structures, essences and natures, seeking to *exorcise historicity*, to discover the final *arché* and *Grund* (*DN*, 112). Heidegger (with Nietzsche as precursor) wants to radically reinterpret the nature of what metaphysics really is. He argues that Being appears differently in the course of different historical epochs. Being manifests and discloses itself in varying ways that are themselves transitory and ephemeral. The definition of metaphysics is here reconceived, then, in light of the epiphanic nature of Being's appearance within time (*BYI*, 10).

Following and developing Heidegger's thought, Vattimo uses the term "metaphysics" (which always appears as a pejorative designation) as intending any philosophy or theory that offers some notion of the deep, fixed structure of the world or humanity. Under this definition, virtually every prior philosophical position elaborated in the West qualifies as "metaphysical" and shares in the defects of this approach. This includes Plato, Aristotle, Aquinas, Descartes, Kant, Hegel, Husserl, and so the list continues. Each of them offers a general theory about humanity and the world; each seeks some privileged description of the *ontos on*. But what each thinker actually offers is only one evanescent, determinate and ephemeral appearance of Being.

For Vattimo, the deeply traditional (and pernicious) accent on perduring and unchanging essences has become the *enemy* of human freedom and emancipation. Such structures, metaphysically conceived as mediated by *kosmos* and *nomos*, become the constrictive parameters within which "liberty" may be realized thereby constraining the absolute freedom of self interpretation, self-expression and self-realization. Human nature, for example, is construed as enduring and universal becoming, in the process, a synonym for arbitrary limitation. Humanity is thereby conceived within the confines of pure presence and so within the kind of *Gegenständigkeit* thinking properly attributable only to physical objects. Metaphysics seeks, then, to enforce an extrinsic, final norm, restricting human freedom, putting an end to the discussion of humanity's becoming in history, jeopardizing the liberty of human self-creation and ending the continuing conversation of historical consciousness. Of its very nature, metaphysics does not *promote* human freedom, but simply consolidates arbitrary and dominative authority (*ADG*, 43).

Human freedom is always compromised when one insists on apriori borders and parameters of an objectively given structure or nature. This is why Vattimo proclaims that the enemy of liberty is the one who preaches "final and definitive truth" (*NE*, 56). Emancipation, on the contrary, is precisely the overturning of objectivist attempts to define human nature, to place constraints on its attempts at self-realization. Richard Rorty's claim perfectly describes Vattimo's own position: We must overcome all efforts to establish an "unchanging, ahistorical human nature. This attempt to put aside both Plato and Kant is the bond which links the post-Nietzschean tradition in European philosophy with the pragmatic tradition in American philosophy."[42] And this comment, of course, helps to explain the importance of Heidegger. For Heidegger argues that the manifestation of Being is epochal and epiphanic, not final and enduring. This is necessarily the case given human finitude and its immersion in temporality, society, culture and language. Human life and knowing is characterized not by enduring essences, but by contingency and provisionality. There exist, then, no perduring *ousiai* which harden into fixed structures. There exist only those *Seinsgeschicke* which have occurred since Anaximander. It is no surprise then that Vattimo often speaks of Being as a sending or *Geschick* (*PD*, 22). This is to say that Being "appears" and "manifests" itself differently over time. It is Event rather than unchanging essence. And to say that Being is Event is to use the language of metaphysics to pronounce the death of metaphysics—a demise which is finally resolved in nihilism (*BYI*, 77).

Metaphysics thinks it offers an "objective" and "final" truth when, in fact, its practitioners are themselves deeply implicated in socio-cultural-linguistic webs of mediated knowing, thereby precluding any claims to finality or representational objectivity. The myth of objective knowing had its last recrudescence with modernity, with its positivistic claims to "truth." Postmodern and post-metaphysical thought, on the contrary, recognizes that all knowing is ineluctably interpretative in kind, offering no final or substantive claims to truth and reality, while always pushing us toward hermeneutical nihilism. Indeed, hermeneutical nihilism is what has beneficently replaced a metaphysics now exposed in its profound provisionality.

The influence of Heidegger continued

Heidegger recognizes that Being discloses itself as Event (*Ereignis*), as a sudden illuminative irruption or unveiling manifesting itself in history. This understanding is intended to overthrow the Platonic search for immutable essences, a search which replicates itself throughout the history of philosophy. One can observe the continuing attempts to categorize and isolate structures of being throughout history: as *ousia, esse, res cogitans, eidos* and so the list continues. But these varying attempts must be understood *not* as immutable, architectonic principles, but as provisional manifestations of the Event of Being in time. The abiding danger for philosophy is to mistake one "sending" of Being, one *Geschick*, for Being itself (*NE*, 6). As Heidegger has said, we can no longer adhere to the "illusion" that "the fundamental concepts of metaphysics remain always the same."[43] This is why Vattimo is insistent that understanding Being as disclosure, as Event, as illuminative irruption, as clearing (*Lichtung*) is the polar opposite of Being as stable and final structure.[44] Being is always in the process of revealing/concealing; it "comes to pass" in time and is differently "manifested" in varying historical epochs (*DN*, 189). What remains are successive modes of disclosure, continual and changing *Geschicke*, the unending "play of the sendings." It is no surprise, then, that Heidegger says that, in every age, "philosophy is a happening that must work out Being for itself anew. . . ."[45]

For Heidegger, Plato's forms, Aristotle's essences, Aquinas's *actus essendi* and Kant's transcendental categories are simply particular, epochal disclosures of Being. Philosophical thinking, however, must go beyond these individual "sendings" or "manifestations." It must step back into thinking about the primordial Ground from which individual "sendings" emerge. This is philosophy properly understood—the discipline which recedes from the individual *Geschicke*, from the different instantiations of Being in time, from the regional appearances of Being, to the Event which discloses itself in multivalent ways.[46] As John Caputo says, the real issue in Heidegger is not the distinction between Being and beings, but that which "grants" or "bestows" this distinction.[47] This is simply to observe that while the distinction between Being and beings works itself out in many different philosophers (one thinks, for example, of the distinction in Aquinas between the concrete *ens* and the *actus essendi*), philosophy worthy of the name involves asking about the origin of such a distinction. Vattimo insists that Heidegger does not want thinking to become "lost" in the truth of entities, of physical objects, of beings. This is not really thinking at all. Nor is thinking the claim that one finally has arrived at the very nature of reality, its essence, form or *eidos*. This, too, falls short of thinking. Philosophy *stricte dictu* must think the "disclosure," the announcement, the sending of Being over time, its "granting" as well as the concealment within history.

The Heideggerian understanding of Being places a marked accent on the provisionality and contingency of various "manifestations" given in the unending flux of temporality. And this insight fully converges with (and, indeed, inspires and supports) Vattimo's notion of *pensiero debole*. The world is constantly rewritten; the Event of Being is variously disclosed; there exist no determinative structures; the *ontos on* is "inaccessible."[48] Being is no longer understood as some "strong" structure, some objectively "present" reality. To insist on such perduring presence is precisely a forgetting of what Being really is, thereby confirming Heidegger's critique of *Seinsvergessenheit*. Consequently, Heidegger's *Abbau* of traditional metaphysics now makes room for hermeneutics and, indeed, for Vattimo's hermeneutical nihilism. The world is understood as the locus of endless rewritings, of continuing reinterpretation. To Vattimo's way of thinking, this *Destruktion* of metaphysics, this overcoming of immutable *archai* and *Gründen*, of the hardening of thought into pure presence, allows us to invoke and reappropriate once more Nietzsche's parable, "How the World Became a Fable."

Of course there are those, such as Derrida and Rorty, who think that speaking about Being at all must lead inexorably back to traditional metaphysics (*NE*, 28, 87). Vattimo, on the contrary, argues that while "being-language" is deeply rooted in the Western tradition, it requires, for just that reason, a *Verwindung*. This alteration-convalescence of the tradition leads not to a metaphysics *redivivus* or to some recrudescence of an alleged *philosophia perennis,* but straight to hermeneutics, to the claim that we live in inextricably intertwined socio-cultural-linguistic webs. Our thinking, consequently, will be ineluctably linked to contingent and embedded interpretations—and so to vast interpretative plurality. This is what Nietzsche meant when he said that philosophy heretofore has tried to solve every riddle, but thought in the future "must be carried on with a higher and *more magnanimous* basic feeling."[49] This is to say that thought will be "weaker," more tolerant, more generous, more reminiscent of Yeats's immortal claim, "the best lack all conviction while the worst are full of passionate intensity." *Pensiero debole* is precisely the recognition that there are many interpretations of reality, many historically dispatched messages, many understandings of the meaning of Being (*EM*, 175). Being, like hermeneutics, is now entirely aware of its profound contingency and conditionality.

The convergence of Nietzsche and Heidegger

As is already clear, Vattimo's two "patron saints" are undoubtedly Nietzsche and Heidegger. In different ways, both teach us about the necessity of philosophical reason abandoning its imperial pretensions, its claims to finality and certitude. Nietzsche's insistence on the interpretative nature of existence as well as Heidegger's announcement of the end of metaphysics, happily converge in their mission of corroding *pensiero forte*, giving birth, in the process, to both postmodernity and a new form of religious faith. If there is a Nietzschean-Heideggerian axis, it is this: there is no final, objective-dogmatic-metaphysical structure of the world; there exist no universal "natures" or "essences." As Nietzsche says, "it is of time and becoming that the best parables should speak: let them be a praise and justification of all impermanence."[50]

A typical Vattimian strategy is to draw together as closely as possible the thought of Nietzsche and Heidegger, despite the latter's claim that Nietzsche is the last man of metaphysics, the one who brings the Western tradition of ontotheology to a close. To his credit, Heidegger recognized that Nietzsche was not simply another nineteenth-century cultural critic, but an extraordinarily profound thinker of Being. Nonetheless, Heidegger's prosecutorial charge is that the "Will to Power" represents still *another* failed attempt at identifying the *one* final and comprehensive philosophical reality, thereby continuing the lamentable Western tradition of confusing one instantiation of being with Being itself.[51] Vattimo counters, however, that Nietzsche does not hold that the will of the isolated ego is now established as a new, unquestioned foundation. Indeed, the unconstrained will is precisely one of the subjective, metaphysical myths that Nietzsche wished to criticize (*DN*, 68, 133). The Overman, on the contrary, is the plural subject, the one who is able to live in a world of radically shifting interpretations, who can flourish without unquestioned first principles. Vattimo, therefore, forcefully rejects Heidegger's charge, insisting that *both* thinkers wish to show that "eternal truth" is itself deeply conditioned and contingent (*DN*, 186), even accusing Heidegger (as he had Gadamer) of taking a badly truncated view of Nietzsche's thought. Vattimo pushes the accusation further, charging Heidegger with refusing to admit openly his own deeply nihilistic tendencies. Insofar as Heidegger is teaching that Being has no stable, final structure, that there exists no moral-metaphysical norm, his thought is entirely identical with Nietzsche's, even if a different route is taken to the same conclusion. Vattimo further insists that Nietzsche "purifies" Heidegger in this sense: he stops him from lapsing into a kind of poetic mysticism or negative theology, reminding Heidegger (and us) that there exists only the play of interpretations, the continual rewriting of the world, thereby dismissing any possible lapse into aesthetic Romanticism. This is why Vattimo says his own reading of Heidegger may be labeled that of the Heideggerian Left, distinguishing it from any attempt to turn Heidegger's thought into a mystical or apophatic theology (*BYI*, 13). Heidegger's work cannot be understood simply as a deferral of complete presence, a theme easily and eagerly endorsed by negative theology. It should be read, rather, through a Nietzschean prism as a strong affirmation of the existing world as a play of "manifestations" and interpretations, none of which is finally and determinatively "true."

Both thinkers, Vattimo insists, have the same project in view: the dissolution of any foundations whatsoever, whether epistemological or ontological. Taken together, Nietzsche and Heidegger fully endorse a weak notion of Being and truth. As such, they have brought to philosophical fruition the principle of *caritas* announced in the kenotic Christianity of the Incarnation. This is why Vattimo can boldly say, "the Nietzsche of the death of God and the Heidegger of *Ereignis* [the Event of Being] are the most radical heirs of the anti-metaphysical principle that Christ brought into the world" (*AC*, 109). All three have renounced objectifying, dogmatic *pensiero forte*. All three are the forerunners of Vattimo's own "weak thought."

Vattimo and truth

Given this confluence of the Heideggerian/Nietzschean notion of Being, we may ask: what understanding of truth is at work in Vattimo's thought? Nietzsche tips us off: "Truth is the kind of error without which a certain species of life could not live."[52] This is a sentiment not far from Vattimo's heart. And how could it not be? For what is *pensiero debole* if not the renunciation of claims to universal truth, of the idea that there is a stable order to reality, a fixed order of essences? Vattimo has renounced these metaphysical claims as ontologically untenable, as myths exposed by postmodern thought, unmasked by the horizons of temporality, otherness and difference. On the contrary, we dwell in an entirely contingent and deeply provisional web of society and culture. We have no experience of "truth" that is not itself deeply interpretative, reflective of all these socio-cultural determinations. Precisely for this reason, Vattimo tells us that we must construct an ethic based on charity, freeing us from our last idolatry "truth as our God" (*DR*, 218). And it is why Vattimo can say, echoing Nietzsche, that "there exists no order, truth or stability outside the will itself" (*DN*, 19).

Given these assertions, how may we speak of a truth that is universal, transcultural, transgenerational and even, in some sense, final? Vattimo says we cannot. But does this response necessarily herald a plunge into anarchy? Many contemporary thinkers argue, like Vattimo, that metaphysical and transcendental thought does indeed calcify and betray our socio-linguistic embeddedness. At the same time, they seek not to demonize "truth," to claim that the very word is idolatrous, but to develop notions of truth and rationality fully adjusted to our finitude and contingency, even while simultaneously seeking to avoid falling prey to Nietzschean relativism. Many of these thinkers argue that what is needed is not the "end of truth" or a concomitant collapse into irrationality or random pluralism. What they seek, rather, is an ontologically *appropriate* notion of truth, one that is in accord with our socio-cultural-linguistic situation, one that recognizes that any notion of truth claiming to inhabit a realm beyond contingency is entirely untenable. The task, then, is to develop supple and flexible veridical understandings that recognize historical provisionality, that are not bound by "Cartesian anxiety," that move beyond ahistorical matrices and Archimedean levers, but that do not fall into the opposite error, the relativism of "anything goes." It is precisely this attempt that characterizes the work of several prominent thinkers.

Just here, for example, one thinks of the aforementioned work of Hans-George Gadamer, Jürgen Habermas and Thomas Kuhn, all of whom seek to develop "phronetic" notions of truth (relying on Aristotle's notion of *phronēsis*) that they deem ontologically appropriate.[53] Each has developed some variation of what is commonly called "fallibilism." As Richard Bernstein has aptly written, philosophical fallibilism is "the conviction that knowledge claims are always open to further rational criticism and revision."[54] It is not that there exists nothing worthy of the name "truth"; it is that we cannot claim to know this truth with certainty. The pronounced accent here is on epistemological humility, an accent with which Vattimo would certainly agree. Because fallibilists are acutely aware of the embeddedness of all knowledge, they share with Vattimo the general proscription against epistemological "foundations"—

understood as impregnable first principles abstracted from history and culture—now serving as a bulwark for justified knowledge.[55]

Vattimo is certainly not insensitive to the truth question, saying that it must be addressed in order to forestall "the widely held suspicion that the philosophical position of hermeneutics is relativist, anti-intellectualist [and] irrationalist . . ." (*BYI*, 75). And, at times, Vattimo does, indeed, sound like a fallibilist, especially when he talks about interpretative adequacy and when he speaks about the necessity of avoiding irrationalism and mere aestheticism (*BYI*, 104–106). He states for example, that any particular interpretation must "strive to articulate, develop and advance arguments for itself" (*NE*, 94). That is, a particular interpretation cannot simply offer itself as one version "displayed on a shelf in the supermarket of free opinion." It must develop "persuasive arguments in order to justify not just its own specific content but also and primarily its own status as an interpretation." What Vattimo is groping for here is some type of via media between fallibilism and full-blown relativism, what might be accurately termed a "soft fallibilism." One must advance arguments for the adequacy of one's position, rather than simply offering it willy-nilly in the relativistic "marketplace" as one among many possibilities. There appears here to be no sanctioning of a pure perspectivism in which we simply accept without question vastly different interpretations, wherein no one interpretation is better than another. As Vattimo says, rationality cannot remain paralyzed by the loss of Cartesian luminosity and stability (*PD*, 10).

At the same time, one develops this kind of supporting argument even while recognizing its status "as an interpretation" (rather than as a unique insight into the *ontos on*). And this interpretation must present itself as "the outcome of vicissitudes and supply a precise reading of them" (*NE*, 94). Vattimo wants to make clear that, even though we argue for our interpretations, trying to show their cogency and plausibility, the interpretations themselves can never be presented in a "metaphysical" sense, as "representing" the truth of Being, which, in any case, is always open to rewriting. All interpretations are themselves the result of contingent, changeable processes; they are creations of the spirit, constructions of reality. Contemporary philosophy recognizes this when it speaks of knowledge less as a state of affairs and more as the "plausibility and persuasiveness that is linked to a set of premises" (*AC*, 50). Moreover, all of our arguments, no matter how plausible, are always ineluctably embedded in localized rules, frameworks of meaning and textured and layered forms of life which make them both contingent and context-specific.

Vattimo's argument, then, is that we must avoid the temptation, all too common (and his subtly stated objection against Gadamer and Habermas) of asserting either "hermeneutics" or "fallibilism" as the final answer. This would be to succumb to the metaphysical temptation which has haunted the history of philosophy. Fallibilism itself, then, with its seemingly modest claims, cannot be construed as offering some final word or ultimate method. Vattimo, it appears, skates close to fallibilism even while shying away from the term and insisting that both Gadamer and Habermas need a strong dose of nihilism: for the former, to temper his romance with hermeneutics; for the latter, to release him from the throe of transcendentalism still clinging to the ideal speech situation.[56] Ultimately, Vattimo offers his own via media "beyond objectivism and relativism" (to borrow Richard Bernstein's title). Objectivism, of course, entirely misunderstands the nature of Being as fixed and stable, while unvarnished relativism cannot avoid the question of plausibility and, most importantly, must take account of *caritas*, the Christian contribution of inclusionary non-violence, thereby dismissing all those interpretations which are exclusionary and intolerant by nature. Vattimo's via media, then, *is* found in hermeneutics of a certain (nihilistic) type, but a hermeneutics that cannot present itself, any more than metaphysics, as the "final" name of Being and truth.

In evaluating Vattimo's notion of truth, one inevitably thinks of Nietzsche's tale from *Thus Spoke Zarathustra*. Speaking of some passing priests (who serve as placeholders for the morality and doctrine of Christian orthodoxy), he says,

> I am moved by compassion for these priests. I also find them repulsive. . . . He whom they call Redeemer has put them in chains; in chains of false values and delusive words. Would that someone would yet redeem them from their Redeemer! . . . They thought they were sleeping on an island, but it was a sleeping monster. False values and

delusive words: these are the worst monsters for mortals. . . .
Eventually the monster comes and wakes and eats and
devours what built huts upon it. Behold the huts which
these priests built![57]

Nothing can be built on the "island" of "dry land," which is to
say that no theory has access to the *ontos on*. No "way of life" can
reach down to the foundations of "truth." And this is the case with
hermeneutics and fallibilism as well; both should realize they result
from the vicissitudes of history. Both should recognize that the
world has become a fable. At times, then, Vattimo does indeed
come close to endorsing the classic notion of *phronēsis* rationality,
i.e., "hitting the best thing attainable by action" as defined by
Aristotle.[58] But Vattimo also wishes to push fallibilism away from
the lingering scent of metaphysics and toward Nietzsche's subver-
sion of every claim to truth (*DN*, 195) where even the "unmasking attitude is unmasked" (*WP*, 402). And in this Vattimo is distinct
from others who are attracted to both fallibilism and to the deeply
hermeneutical nature of human existence. For Vattimo wishes to
make certain that neither hermeneutics nor fallibilism *harden into
a final theory,* as has previously occurred during the entire history
of Western philosophy. Truth, like Being, is an Event, an irruptive
flashing up that is ephemeral and evanescent, a "clearing" that is
manifested differently in various epochs; it is a rewriting that takes
place anew in every generation and which vitiates any claim to
finality—even the modest claims of fallibilism itself.

For Heidegger as for Vattimo, art serves a paradigmatic role in
manifesting this irruptive and illuminative nature of truth. For art
unsettles conceptual systems by "deranging" ordered roles, throw-
ing objective, representational thinking into turmoil (*DN*, 117).
Art moves in the direction of Nietzsche's Dionysian spirit,
celebrating imagination, festivity and freedom, while unsettling
the dominative social practices that metaphysical systems seek
to instantiate. Positively, the truth disclosed by art allows for
the "flashing up" of insight, those irruptive occurrences that are
foreign to discursive or propositional thought. Works of art offer
glimpses of truth—although even these glimpses are transformed
and altered as the works speak to new generations in different
and varied ways. Stanley Rosen has disapprovingly observed that

"there can be no doubt that the thesis that art is worth more than the truth is the dominant principle of our time."[59] But this comment, I think, misses the essential point. What Heidegger and Vattimo argue is that art reveals an *appropriate*, indeed, paradigmatic understanding of what truth is—the *kind* of truth that is actually available to us. The truth offered by art does not "harden" into the pure and perduring presence characteristic of an object or a "thing"; each generation "appropriates" the truth in differing ways, precisely insofar as the work of art reveals unique dimensions of Being. Art, then, serves to illustrate that truth itself occurs in epochal, temporal manifestations, allowing the very notion of truth to escape from the merely discursive and correspondential.

Heidegger's well-known example of the disclosive power of art is Van Gogh's painting of a peasant woman's boots.[60] This work, in its very simplicity, manifests and discloses an entire existence, an integral world wholly different from any yield offered by a discursive analysis of the boots as objects. As Gadamer says, "The whole world of rural life is in these shoes. Thus, it is the work of art which is able to bring forth the truth of this entity."[61] The emergence and disclosure of the profound truth available in Van Gogh's shoes far surpasses any kind of calculative *Vorhandenheit* thinking. This is why Gadamer can add that Heidegger's essay invoking Van Gogh ". . . supports his central philosophical concern to conceive Being itself as an Event of truth."[62] We might say the same if we saw a painting of a rowboat by an old lakeside shack. The painting opens up a complete way of life, a relationship to nature and society, a truth that no mere "scientific" analysis— manipulative and measurable—could ever offer. The polyvalent truth of Being here presents itself in a way that goes far beyond the scientific, the methodical, the propositional.

Art and its truth, Vattimo notes, is also adduced by Gadamer in order to overcome the modern prejudice for scientific method (*VM*, 6–8).[63] It is not that science is rejected; modern science is not, however, the paradigmatic model for illustrating the nature of truth or knowing. This is why Heidegger insists in *Being and Time* that truth as correspondence is always secondary and limited in kind. Vattimo follows him here, saying that the most original sense of truth is the "opening within which every conformity or deformity can occur" (*BYI*, 16). This is to say that only within the greater horizon of epochal disclosure or manifestation can one speak of the "lesser" truth of correspondence. Truth occurs in a more primordial way than mere congruence and it is precisely this primordiality that the philosopher must think.[64] Vattimo, once again, links his philosophical *Verwindung* of the notion of truth with kenotic Christianity. Both shift away from a "hard" conception of *veritas* understood as final, objectifying representation, toward *caritas*, conceived as the kind of interpretive plurality that dilutes and corrodes "metaphysics" even while allowing for the irruptive flashing of insight, for the evanescent and epochal disclosure of Being.

Chapter 3

Can a Nietzschean speak to theology? Some historical considerations

To this point, I have straightforwardly recounted several crucial elements of Vattimo's philosophical thought. In the following chapters, his work will be subjected to a more extensive analysis by way of a theological dialogue, asking about the extent to which his work may be utilized by religious, and in particular Christian, faith and thought. Before evaluating Vattimo's work, however, I think it wise to recount briefly that venerable theological tradition which has always sought to find truth in all thinkers, even those inimical to traditional Christian faith and belief. This section should be understood, then, as a kind of proleptic response to those who might ask: Why enter into dialogue with Vattimo, a thinker whose Nietzschean romance purveys the logic of heterodoxy?

Some historical considerations[65]

Tertullian's famous inquiry resounds throughout the Christian tradition as a perennial challenge: "What does Athens have to do with Jerusalem, the Academy with the Church?" Precious little, Tertullian thundered: "Away with all attempts to produce a mottled Christianity of Stoic, Platonic and dialectical composition! We want no curious disputation after possessing Christ Jesus, no inquisition after enjoying the Gospel!"[66] Tertullian's comments have led some to suspect Christians of anti-intellectualism, of a desire to avoid the astringent winds of critical reason by fleeing to the unwavering certainties of tranquil faith. In fact, Tertullian's well-known query invites reflection on the proper relationship between Christianity and human reasoning. What role does philosophy have in contemporary Christian thinking?

The school of thought represented by Tertullian's probing wished to make clear not that Christian faith has little room for serious inquiry or for critical self-examination, but that, with the advent of Jewish and Christian revelation, philosophy has been demoted as an ultimately illuminating path of contemplation and reflection. Revelation represented the "true philosophy"—as so many early writers called it—thereby marginalizing the normativity of Greek thought that had been bequeathed to the Western world. Of course, if the early Christians had been aware of the wisdom emanating from the Far East, their remarks would have remained unchanged. For the revelation of God in the history of Israel and in Jesus Christ definitively surpassed any other system of thought no matter its antiquity or the distinction of its lineage. At the same time, most of the early Christian thinkers did not wish simply to dispense with the philosophical heritage of the ancient world. They sought, rather, to incorporate its best insights for the precise purpose of further explaining the faith, of making it more intelligible. In some matters, certainly, they saw contradictions with Christian truth—and in such instances the older approaches were to be quickly jettisoned. In other cases, however, they saw a general coherence between faith and philosophical reasoning, with the latter expressing incompletely, or in an ancillary manner, what revelation had entirely fulfilled.

As Christianity moved from its Palestinian matrix into the world of Hellenistic thought and culture, many of its early converts were philosophically trained. Justin Martyr, for example, a Greek thinker living in the middle of the second century, had been deeply schooled in Platonism. It is no surprise, then, that in his explicitly Christian works one finds distinct influences from particular dialogues, such as the *Timaeus* and the *Phaedo*. Greek thought receives a positive valuation from Justin on the grounds that all intelligent beings share in the universal Logos or Reason who is Christ. Indeed, Abraham and Socrates are properly called "Christians before Christ" [*Apol.* I, 46] and all men and women, insofar as they are created in God's image, have some share in the *logos spermatikos*, the seed of truth that enlightens humanity

[*Apol.* II, 8]. Even while endorsing a certain relationship between Christianity and Hellenic metaphysics, Justin is nonetheless careful not to trim religious faith to the parameters of pre-existing insights. The adjudicatory norm of true wisdom is neither Platonism nor Stoicism, but biblical truth.

While Justin defends a certain congruency between philosophical acumen and Christian faith, it is Origen who is the preeminent thinker on the issue of properly correlating them. He says in his treatise answering the philosopher Celsus, who had severely attacked Christianity: "We are careful not to raise objections to any good teachings, even if their authors are outside the faith, nor to seek an occasion for a dispute with them, nor to find a way of overthrowing statements which are sound" [*Contra Celsum*,VII, 46]. In his *Letter to Gregory*, Origen offers a typological accounting for this procedure: "Perhaps something of this kind is shadowed forth in what is written in Exodus . . . that the children of Israel were commanded to ask from their neighbors and those who dwelt with them, vessels of silver and gold . . . in order that, by despoiling the Egyptians, they might have material for the preparation of things which pertained to the service of God." Origen continues: "With the spoils taken from the Egyptians by the sons of Israel were made the movable Holy of Holies, the arc with its cover . . . and the vessel of gold to hold the manna, the food of angels. These objects were truly made from the most beautiful gold of Egypt."[67] Under Origen's influence, "spoils from Egypt" gradually became the major image sanctioning the use of "secular" philosophy in Christian thought. At the same time, Origen's appropriation of Greek wisdom is far from uncritical. He urges caution, aware that a lack of care will inexorably lead to abuses: ". . . Rare are the men who have taken from Egypt only the useful, and go away and use it for the service of God. There are those who have profited from their Greek studies, in order to produce heretical notions and set them up, like the golden calf, in Bethel." For Origen, the reciprocity between secular wisdom and God's Word is properly symbolized by the relationship between Abimelech and Isaac (Gen. 26). They are sometimes at peace, sometimes at war, for philosophy is neither opposed to everything in the Law of God nor in harmony with everything. In the last analysis, it is the Christian faith that must verify and judge all that is received from "alien" sources.[68]

In the East, the Cappadocians treated of the correlation between Christianity and secular wisdom at great length.[69] Basil, for example, has a profound but critical devotion to Hellenistic language and culture. One finds in his works positive references to Herodotus, Thucydides, Plutarch, Aristotle and, of course, the favorite thinker of early Christian writers, Plato. Basil's argument is unambiguous—we are in a contest for eternal life: "In preparation for it, [we] must strive to the best of our power and must associate with poets and writers of prose and orators and with all men from whom there is any prospect of benefit with reference to the care of our soul."[70] After all, Basil continues, Moses "first trained his mind in the learning of the Egyptians, and then proceeded to the contemplation of Him who is." But like Origen before him, Basil urges caution, invoking the metaphor of the bees: just as they neither approach all plants, nor seek the entire flower but only the honey, so we too should take what is suitable from pagan writers, even while passing over the rest.[71] Changing metaphors, Basil makes precisely the same point: we ought not to take everything without exception, but only such matter as is useful. After all, "a pilot does not heedlessly give over his ship to the winds, but steers it to harbor."[72]

More than a century after Origen, Augustine of Hippo repeats the Alexandrian's simultaneous endorsement of and admonition about the uses of philosophy. In a well-known passage he states: "If those who are called philosophers, and especially the Platonists, have said anything that is true and in harmony with our faith, we are not only not to shrink from it, but to claim it for our own use. . . . For the Egyptians had not only the idols and heavy burdens which the people of Israel hated and fled from, but also vessels and ornaments of gold and silver . . . which the same people appropriated to themselves, deigning them for a better use by the command of God" [*De doctrina christiana*, II, 40]. Augustine benignly cites his predecessors for availing themselves of just such instruction: "And what else have many good and faithful men among our brethren done? Do we not see with what a quantity of gold and silver and garments Cyprian . . . was loaded when he came out of Egypt? How much Lactantius carried with him? And Victorinus, Optatus and Hilary, not to speak of those who are living. How much Greeks out of number have borrowed. For what was done at the time of the Exodus was no doubt a type prefiguring what happens now."[73]

Augustine is the thinker who popularized the "spoils from Egypt" trope in the West. Precisely because of his influence, this image became a leading one among medieval theologians. The only way to deal with the treasures from Greco-Roman culture was to subordinate them to the wisdom of Holy Scripture. As John Rist suggests, Augustine's attraction to the Latin text of Isaiah (7, 9), *nisi credideritis, non intellegetis* (unless you believe you will not understand), implied that the wisdom of the Greek philosophers was incomplete because finally lacking the guidance offered by Christ, Scripture and the church.[74]

What is limpidly clear is that early Christian writers, reflecting on the relationship between revelation and the pagan thought that preceded them, did not posit a simple opposition between faith and philosophical reasoning. It is unsurprising, then, that Christians freely appropriated the vocabulary of antiquity, even while molding the meaning of words to accord fully with the Gospel. Terms such as "*ousia*" and "*hypostasis*," for example, surely had a classical heritage, but were now to be filled with the new wine of revelation. Along just these lines, Joseph Ratzinger has observed that in certain sectors of theology it has become fashionable to speak of the triumph, in the early church, of an Hellenistically inspired body-soul dualism, with the language of the "immortal soul" indicating just such a dichotomy. Ratzinger argues, however, that this alleged "hellenization" is badly inflated. Plato left no anthropological schema just "lying by the roadside." In fact, the current "textbook schematization of Greek thought" is nowhere to be found in Plato, Aristotle or Plotinus, each of whom defends a highly individuated and distinctive understanding of the soul/body relationship. On the contrary, Ratzinger insists, the teaching on immortality in the early Church was determined by its Christological center, wherein the indestructibility of the life gained through faith was guaranteed. Christian belief made assertive claims upon anthropology and these demands were not adequately met by any pre-existing philosophical concepts. Several Greek ideas were, indeed, placed at the service of the Gospel, but always by way of an appropriate transformation. Whereas Aristotle, for example, had seen the soul as totally bonded to materiality, the guiding Christian idea was that faith in Christ overcomes death, leading to the development of an original anthropology.[75]

Of course, the issue of the "hellenization" of Christian faith looms large here. Was the Christian message corrupted by its missionary thrust into the Mediterranean basin, which had its own tradition of philosophizing and conceptual thought? Did the church fly too close, Icarus-like, to this brilliant and glowing Hellenistic sun? Was the early Christian dogmatic tradition, as Adolf von Harnack famously charged in his *History of Dogma*, "in its conception and development a work of the Greek spirit on the soil of the Gospel"?[76]

One medieval friar who might have found at least some common ground with Harnack was Jacopone da Todi, who gave new voice to Tertullian's suspicions about marrying faith and philosophy: "*Mal vedemo Parigi che ne ha destrutto Assisi!*" With Paris now substituting for Athens and Assisi for Jerusalem, the friar's lament is clear enough: one cannot look kindly on Paris because it has destroyed Francis's city; critical analysis has undermined Christian spirituality. Jacopone's irritation was intensified, no doubt, by the spectacle of mendicant friars, formerly dedicated only to preaching the Gospel and collecting alms, now contending for theology chairs at Paris, a further sign of the dégringolade of the spiritual life. A relentless poet (and long thought the author of the elegant *Stabat Mater*), Jacopone versified his dismay:

> Plato and Socrates may contend
> And all the breath in their bodies spend
> Arguing without an end
> What's it all to me?
> Only a pure and simple mind
> Straight to heaven its way doth find
> Greets the King . . . while far behind
> Lags the world's philosophy.[77]

But Jacopone's protest was a relatively isolated one. By and large, the "spoils from Egypt" trope continued to exert significant influence in the Middle Ages. Thomas Aquinas, for example, was convinced of the synthetic unity of faith and reason, concisely exemplified in his axiom that grace does not destroy nature but perfects it [*ST,* I, 1, 8]. Elsewhere Thomas avers: "Although the truth of the Christian faith . . . surpasses the capacity of reason, nevertheless, the truth that human reason is naturally endowed to know cannot be opposed to the truth of the Christian faith" (*Summa contra Gentiles,* I, 7]. It is just this conviction that allows Aquinas to pursue unabashedly "spoils" from the ancient world.[78] At the same time, he continues to maintain the traditional caution: one can be in error employing philosophy if one "includes under the estate of philosophy truths of faith, as if one should be willing to believe nothing except what could be held by philosophical reasoning; when, on the contrary, *philosophy should be subject to the measure of faith* according to the saying of the Apostle (II Cor. 10.5), 'Bringing into captivity every thought unto the obedience of Christ.'"[79] Aquinas also makes clear that St. Paul's challenging statement, "I will destroy the wisdom of the wise," (I Cor. 1.19) should not be understood as rendering philosophy illegitimate, but as a proper reproof of those who trust only in their own erudition. Thomas even advances his own suggestive image replicating the "spoils" trope: those who use philosophical doctrines but subject them to the service of faith do not *mix* water with wine, but *change* water into wine [*De Trinitate,* q. 2, a. 3, ad 5].

Despite Aquinas's own intentions, the growing use of Aristotelian terminology in medieval Christian theology engendered profound concern about the continued purity of evangelical faith and doctrine. In response to such apprehensions, the statutes for the University of Paris, written in 1215, prohibited the teaching of certain books of Aristotle, such as the *Metaphysics.*[80] And Pope Gregory IX, in a stern letter to the Parisian theology masters in 1228, warned against an over-reliance on philosophical writings, cautioning them against weakening the Word of God with the fictitious tales of philosophers. Ultimately, of course, the fear of an unchecked radical Aristotelianism, with its incipient rationalism and philosophical imperialism, led to the condemnations of over two hundred propositions by Etienne Tempier, the bishop of Paris, in 1277.[81] Tempier's fear of philosophical dominance, preceded by Tertullian in the third century and Gregory IX earlier in the thirteenth, was further intensified by Martin Luther.

Luther's concern for biblical truth led to an unrelenting barrage of criticism aimed at "heathen philosophy"; at Aristotle, "the heathen philosopher"; and at reason itself, "Dame Witch."[82] Philosophy and scholasticism obscure the Gospel of grace, trading the Word of God for the magniloquent but vacuous discourse of pagan thought. Compared with theology, philosophy knows little about human existence because it misses life's origin and its ultimate *telos*. Philosophical reasoning has its place, certainly, but when juxtaposed with the rich texture of the Bible, it remains flat, formal and ineffective. Indeed, Luther even argues that reason is "blind and mad" because it can never begin to understand the Trinity, nor can it fathom that God's Son, the Incarnate Word, "assumed human nature and became flesh and blood with man" [22, 76]. This is why Luther can say, in a well-known passage, "Whoever wants to be a Christian must be intent on silencing the voice of reason. . . . To the judgment of reason they [the articles of faith] appear so far from the truth that it is impossible to believe them" [24, 99].

While Luther admits that "reason is the most important and the highest in rank among all things" and, in comparison with other human realities, "the best and something divine," nonetheless, in matters of faith reason easily becomes misguided [34, 137]. This does not mean that reason is always wrong for as the reformer insists, "We have to admit that philosophy and reason is not against us but for Christ . . ." [38, 250]. But one must keep in mind that while philosophy deals with matters understood by human probing, theology deals with issues apprehended by faith. Luther's rhetorical strategy is ultimately meant to remind Christians that those elements that are at the heart of the Gospel, the Incarnation and justification, "are above and beyond reason and philosophy." Faith entirely supersedes what is taught by merely natural sagacity. Luther, then, did not so much reject the "spoils from Egypt" typology as assertively remind the church that such thinking could only be successful if it avoided a decline into a Renaissance naturalism more influenced by classical thought than by the Word of God. His insights serve as a perennial warning to the church that unless Christianity is firmly rooted in Scripture, it can easily be led astray by *au courant* academic tastes, thereby subordinating the Gospel to temporary philosophical fashions. In the last analysis, one may say that Luther echoes—surely with unique accents—a comment of Aquinas, itself representative of the earlier tradition:

"In divine matters natural reason is greatly deficient" [*ST*, II–II, q. 2, a. 4].

Luther's powerful critique did not put an end to the "spoils" typology, even if it vigorously re-centered it on the truth of Scripture. This re-centering is reflected in the thought of John Henry Newman who sought, once again, to repristinate the traditional paradigm. Newman was particularly concerned about charges, largely from rationalist quarters, that the Gospels represented a farraginous stew of superstitious elements emanating from other religions (such as angels and demons) now piously commingled with stories about Jesus of Nazareth. To the claim that Christianity was simply a syncretistic mélange drawn from a wide variety of Eastern and Greek wellsprings, Newman responded with an image that duplicates the spoils typology. In his *Development of Christian Doctrine*, Newman does not deny that the church ingurgitates ideas from many sources; he argues, rather, that the church is a "treasure house ... casting the gold of fresh tributaries into her refiner's fire, stamping upon her own as time required it, a deeper impress of her Master's image."[83] The church, then, properly utilizes wisdom and truth whatever its parentage, but it does so by first casting any "spoils" into a cauterizing blaze, purging them of interlacing dross, then stamping the molten, newly purified substance with the image of Christ, in the process subordinating all wisdom to the ultimate truth of the Gospel. In a stirring response to those who claim that Christianity is merely an unfortunate amalgam of faith and philosophy, Newman asserts: "They [his opponents] cast off all that they find in Pharisee or heathen; we conceive that the Church, like Aaron's rod, devours the serpents of the magicians. They are ever hunting for a fabulous primitive simplicity; we repose in Catholic fullness. . . . They are driven to maintain, on their part, that the Church's doctrine was never pure; we say that it can never be corrupt."[84]

In the twentieth century, Christian theologians such as Henri de Lubac, Hans Urs von Balthasar and Karl Barth all have had something to say about the spoils trope. De Lubac, reprising Terence, insists that "nothing authentically human, whatever its origin, can be alien to her [the church]."[85] Cyril of Alexandria was on the right track with his use of Plato as was Ambrose with Seneca, Aquinas with Aristotle and Matteo Ricci with Confucius.

If the salt of Christianity is to maintain its tang, there must be an unending process of appropriation and bold thinking. It is not enough, then, simply to retrieve the Middle Ages or even primitive Christianity. The church can only revive the Fathers' all-embracing humanism and recover their dauntless spirit by a creative assimilation that is at the same time a transformation. De Lubac says that even thinkers who at first blush appear unalterably opposed to the Gospel (and here the adduction of Vattimo's work is apt) have much to offer: "Many ideas of a more or less Marxist, Nietzschean, or Positivist stamp may even find a place in some blueprint for a new synthesis, and neither its orthodoxy nor its value will be called into question on that account. In the church, the work of assimilation never ceases, and it is never too soon to undertake it!"[86] De Lubac was calling for a new dialogue with the existentialism, phenomenology and even Marxism that was sweeping Europe in the early twentieth century. Christianity could not ignore these movements as if there was nothing to be learned from them. At the same time, any appropriation of these ideas demanded that the Gospel fully transform them. To illustrate the relationship between theology and other disciplines, de Lubac liked to cite Augustine's recollection of the divine voice in the *Confessions*: *Non tu me in te mutabis sicut cibum carnis tuae, sed tu mutaberis in me.* (You will not transform me into you, as with your fleshly food; rather, you will be transformed into me.)[87]

De Lubac's voice was joined by that of Balthasar who offers a passionate *cri du coeur* calling for a recovery of the "spoils" approach in theology. Why did a Christian thinker like Aquinas devote himself to Arabic and Aristotelian philosophy? Why did Möhler avail himself of Hegel, Newman of Locke and Hume? "In all cases, they did so as to transpose natural philosophy to the supernatural order."[88] Pleading for a new openness to all human wisdom, Balthasar remarks that Aquinas had made full use of Plato, Aristotle and the Stoics, and surely, "if he had known Buddha and Lao-Tzu, there is no doubt that he would have drawn them too into the *summa* of what can be thought and would have given them the place appropriate to them."[89] Balthasar lambastes the "backwoods mentality" of certain Catholic philosophers who spurn the enrichments of contemporary thought in order to hold "rigidly fast to a medieval *status quo.*" Such an attitude, he insists, hands on the letter of the great scholastics while abandoning their inner spirit of "astonishing openness" to the *spolia Aegyptiorum*.[90]

Even thinkers seemingly at odds with Christianity, Balthasar adds, have something to offer the church. A fragment or stone may come from the bed of a pagan or heretical stream, but the Christian knows how to cleanse it until that radiance shines forth which shows that it is a fragment of the total glorification of God. At the same time, the Church can never tie down revelation to a frozen philosophical system, no matter its antiquity. Every concrete philosophy must be measured in terms of its "yes" or "no" to the supernatural order of revelation, to the one God appearing in Jesus Christ. For this reason, Balthasar insisted that the resplendent glory of the Lord could never be properly understood if the human spirit were taken as the yardstick of God's gratuitous love. The sovereign and free God cannot simply be assigned a post within a pre-existing system, as he is with Hegel's *Geist*, Schopenhauer's *Wille* and Schelling's *intellektuelle Anschauung*. Rather than be subject to systems vaunting themselves as absolute truth, the Word of God must demolish them. In the words of Mary's Magnificat, *deposuit potentes de sede*.[91]

Even Karl Barth, a contemporary of de Lubac and Balthasar and long regarded as the paladin of those resisting the blandishments of philosophy, does not entirely eschew the spoils typology. Despite his legitimate concern that philosophy not trim the Gospel to preconceived dimensions, Barth, in his discussion of the relationship between *eros* and *agape* offers these remarkable and well-known comments: "Is it a mere accident that the Gospel of Jesus Christ, this seed of Israel, took root in the perishing world of Hellenism? Has it been a misfortune that this origin has haunted its whole subsequent career? Is it merely in culpable self-will that we seek in soul the land of the Greeks, and cannot refrain from doing so even today, when we see so clearly that the necessary reformation of the Church cannot be the same thing as a renaissance of Greek antiquity? Is there not here something that is obligatory, and which it is better to see and accept than to ignore and deny, if we are ready and anxious to understand the Gospel of Jesus Christ in the full range of its content?"[92] A bit later Barth adds: "The violence displayed against Hellenism in recent theology is not a good thing. . . ." While St. Paul's theology of Christian love is not derived from Greek philosophy, "when he portrays the Christian living in love, he never uses barbarian or Israelite colors and contours but he undoubtedly makes use of Greek, thus betraying the fact that he took note of the Greeks and their *eros*."[93] Barth here sounds very much like Newman and de Lubac. It is not a matter of importing into theology unalloyed notions that will not themselves be purified and transformed by faith's own content. The chief point for Barth is that all philosophical affirmations must finally be redeemed in the light of God's Word.

A few years ago, in the encyclical *Fides et ratio*, John Paul II addressed the question of the faith/reason relationship, warmly endorsing the spoils trope.[94] The pope makes clear, however, that such endorsement is not born of naiveté regarding the Fall's effects. Reason, in fact, has been severely wounded—so much so that the path to truth has become "strewn with obstacles." Indeed, human reasoning is "distorted and inclined to falsehood." The encyclical endorses Irenaeus and Tertullian (to whose names we may surely add those of the great Reformers) who, following the Pauline warning that "no one take you captive through philosophy and empty deceit" (Col. 2.8), sound the alarm when confronted with a perspective seeking to subordinate the truth of revelation to the interpretation of the philosophers. It is only with these admonitions in mind, then, that one may sanction the utilization of secular wisdom. At the same time, the encyclical argues that Paul in the Areopagus (Acts 17.18) provides evidence that Christian proclamation was always engaged with the philosophical currents of its time. And the disciplining of Hellenic theory by faith is discernible throughout the patristic tradition. One must conclude, therefore, that the ancient Christian writers did not identify "the content of their message with the systems to which they referred." Tertullian's famous question about Athens and Jerusalem should not be taken as a reproach to a proper understanding of correlation, but as an indication of the critical discernment with which Christian thinkers first confronted ancient philosophy. This discriminatory caution is not limited to historical examples; the process is a continuing one. *Fides et ratio* singles out India's heritage for its potential enrichment of Christianity. And what is said of India "is no less true" for the great cultures of China and Japan and for the traditional cultures of Africa. The encyclical approvingly cites the bold assertion of Aquinas: "Whatever its source, truth is of the Holy Spirit."[95]

Given this warm Christian endorsement of "spoils" through the centuries, we may ask if Vattimo's postmodern thought, his emphasis on *pensiero debole*, interpretative plurality, the end of metaphysics and the triumph of secularization have something to offer Christian faith?[96] Robert Jenson has astutely noted that no philosophy can subvert the coherent drama of the Gospel, which is either the overarching story of the world or is pure myth. In Jenson's words, "We may press theology's claim very bluntly by noting that theology . . . claims to know the one God of all and so to know the one decisive fact about all things, so that theology must be either a *universal and founding discipline* or a delusion."[97] Jenson is entirely right. Either theology is the *founding* discipline or it is, as Heidegger insisted, simply an *ontic, regional science* much like chemistry and mathematics, leaving the truly primordial issues of Being and truth to philosophy.[98] Christianity, of course, understands Jenson rather than Heidegger as having the last word. Nonetheless, the church uses all forms of "wisdom," no matter their provenance, to illumine the claims of revelation. Vattimo himself appears unaware that there has been a long and intense tradition of theological reflection on the relationship between revelation and "secular" wisdom, but he at least recognizes the Christian provenance of his thought when he says: "I have a preference for Nietzsche and Heidegger in part (or perhaps above all) because . . . their thesis, based on one interpretation of their work, seems to be in harmony with a specifically Christian religious substratum that has remained a living part of me" (*BE*, 33). Still again: "And I probably arrived at this formulation of ontology because it was from those Christian roots that I began" (*BE*, 70). At least in theory, it is not *simply* a matter of running Christianity through the philosophical mills of Heidegger and Nietzsche.

In what ways does Vattimo's thought need to be performatively disciplined by faith, a process to which the entire Christian tradition bears witness, so that any silver or gold he may offer to theological thinking may be properly assimilated, without resulting in an accommodationist golden calf at Bethel? Can Vattimo's thought be cleansed and purified, so that his philosophy is able to reflect something of the glory of God? Or, to use the image adduced by Basil, should we, like Ulysses's men in the face of the Sirens, plug our ears with wax?

Chapter 4

Theological dialogue with Vattimo (I): Postmodernity and theology

Postmodernity

In evaluating Vattimo's project, one may recognize, right from the outset, the reasons for its widespread and growing popularity. Isn't everyone tired of aggressive claims to truth no matter the quarter from which they emerge? Do not such affirmations, whether found in a newspaper, a political party, an academic journal or a pulpit, lead to arrogant smugness and even intolerance? Doesn't Vattimo's thought legitimately seek to respond to the rise in extremism, in fundamentalism, in global animosity? Aren't people tired to the point of exhaustion of hearing tales of violence born of clashing ethnic and religious identities: Catholics against Protestants in Northern Ireland, Jews against Muslims in the Middle East, Sunnis and Shiites locked in perpetual struggle, thereby giving credence to the claim that strong religious belief leads inexorably to violence? Isn't this the basis for Vattimo's attraction—the contemporary desire to avoid hectoring fundamentalisms of every stripe, to elude the kind of passion (religious or otherwise) that fosters a crusade for truth apart from human dignity and freedom?

And doesn't Vattimo's thought have the ring of authenticity when he argues that in a world of competing interpretations, we should allow the actual truth of religion, its fundamental contribution to shine forth: the renunciation of aggressive truth-claims (*caritas*) and the diffusion of religious particularity into secularized universality, thereby fostering a sense of fraternity and solidarity among all peoples. Isn't this the most appealing part of Vattimo's argument which gains him an immediate reception—the priority of charity and fraternity apart from determinate truth-claims which, in any case, are themselves provisional and contingent interpretations of reality? Doesn't Vattimo have an innate appeal to large numbers of contemporary men and women who seek the face of God but find a significant stumbling block in the moral and doctrinal teachings of Christianity and, indeed, in those of virtually all religions? Vattimo often notes that Christ's reinterpretation of the Old Testament turns on compressing the entire Mosaic Law to the commandments of love of God and neighbor. He wonders if something similar will not happen, is not already happening, within contemporary churches, whereby a whole host of doctrinal and moral teachings are being reduced, or better, diffused, into *caritas*. Even Walter Kasper, the president of the Vatican's Council for Christian Unity, seems somewhat taken by the contemporary appeal to harmony and fraternal unity. He has said that while ecumenism is surely not synonymous with good natured humanism, "the most significant results of ecumenism in the last decades—and also the most gratifying—are not the various documents, but rediscovered fraternity: the fact that we have rediscovered one another as brothers and sisters in Christ. . . ."[99] While surely not duplicating Vattimo's thought, one hears in Kasper's message strong accents of fraternity and common understanding, quite apart from the differing doctrinal claims that separate Christian churches and different religions.

Then, too, Vattimo's attack on modernity makes for an attractive siren song. For who can disagree with his calls for a reintroduction of religious discourse into contemporary life or with his attacks on those who, on the basis of their own aggressive *pensiero forte*, would disenfranchise contemporary talk about God, thereby excluding religion from the public square? By railing against modernity's attempt to limit knowing to positivistic rationalism and instrumental scientism, Vattimo joins many other thinkers seeking to transgress the artificial limits on rationality imperialistically imposed by the Enlightenment. This *Verwindung*, as Vattimo styles it, is intended to overcome the bankruptcy of present-day atheism with its reductionistic rationalism and its univocal imagination, in the process pushing beyond the constricting straitjacket of rationalist modernity.

As a postmodern thinker, Vattimo invokes constitutive dimensions of human life and knowing now widely and properly
accepted as legitimate: the conditioned finitude of the subject; the
perspectival nature of thinking; the theory-laden status of the
inquirer; and so the list continues. This congeries of elements need
not indicate that truth does not exist, but they make clear that the
inquiring subject, in his or her search for truth, is, and profoundly
so, historically, socially, culturally and linguistically embedded.
Vattimo's is the claim, then, that we have no access to a neutral
standpoint or norm from which to establish a "foundation" on
which knowledge could be built. He abjures first principles of
any kind and regards all "evidence" as interpretatively riddled.
All such claims for epistemological "foundations" are themselves
provisional and contingent, governed by different language-games
and paradigms, unable to offer the kind of "ground" that founda-
tionalism has typically sought. This is the widespread argument,
then, that reason is always tradition-dependent, saturated with
prior participatory commitment. There exist no universal warrants, no all-encompassing definitions of rationality, to which one
may appeal. Thomas Kuhn expressed this peerlessly in the philosophy of science, arguing that sociology, in fact, has a significant
role in deciding which paradigms are accepted as true precisely
because the warrants adduced as "evidence" are already theoretically assimilated to determinate *Weltanschauungen* thereby obviating the possibility of a viewpoint "higher" than the always-already
embedded subject.

Many Christian thinkers have been attracted to this kind of
thinking precisely because it insists that there are no "higher"
or "broader" grounds, to employ spatial metaphors, from which
Christian belief may be judged, allowing Christianity itself, therefore, to be as "foundational" as any other invoked theory. Christian
beliefs are not subject, as they often were in modernity, to critique
by an alleged ahistorical rationality or by presumed positivistic
"evidence." This is reflected, for example, in John Milbank's representative comment that, in postmodernity, one cannot now contrast the alleged "particularist obscurantism of religion" with the
universality of the human.[100] Claims to "scientific" objectivity and
"rigorous" rationality are, in fact, as embedded and contingent as

the traditioned claims made by Christian faith. Christianity, then, cannot be placed in an alien Procrustean bed wherein it must adhere to rules set by "evidentialist" modernity. In this sense, Vattimo is certainly a strong ally of those hoping to show the marked limitations of modern epistemology.

It is important to remember that Vattimo wishes to accent a deep convergence between postmodernity and (what he takes as) the essence of Christianity. For Christianity not only benefits from postmodern thinking (by being allowed into those public precincts from which it had been banned), but philosophy benefits from Christian faith in that the latter conspires, by its accent on kenosis and *caritas*, in the general "weakening" and "lightening" of thought. This is why Vattimo claims that postmetaphysical philosophy is made possible by Christ (*FR*, 50). What he means, of course, is what he earlier referred to as the happy conjunction of Christianity and *pensiero debole*. Indeed, the West, as the land of the "twilight of Being," the place where the weakening of Being has occurred, is preeminently the land of kenotic Christianity, which, in its essential core, has the vulnerability of God at the heart of its truth. In this sense, the West, by its philosophical trumpeting of the end of metaphysics, indeed, of all strong structures, discovers its profound continuity with the central message of the New Testament, and, therefore, comes to understand itself properly as a "transcription" and "application" of the classical biblical message.

What is central in Vattimian thought is that kenotic Christianity, with the self-abasement of God, gives rise to the very possibility of postmetaphysical, postmodern philosophy. This is why Vattimo can say, in a revelatory statement worth repeating, "Christianity is a stimulus, a message that sets in motion a tradition of thought that will eventually realize its freedom from metaphysics" (*ADG*, 35). In this formulation, the kenotic action of God comes to fruition in philosophy's dilution of strong structures and in the advent of *pensiero debole*. This is why the Torinese can conclude that "postmodern nihilism (the end of metanarratives) is the truth of Christianity" (*FR*, 51).

If Vattimo were simply calling for greater toleration, for an end to aggressive and assertive truth-claims, for a "weakening" of fundamentalism and ideology, virtually anyone would willingly sign on to his project. But he has made clear that "weak thought" is not simply a call for greater tolerance, for a "weakening" of aggressive assertions; it is, indeed, a philosophical program. And it is this wider objective—for example his thought on the proper ordering of society—that gives rise to certain difficulties.

Society, violence and *strong thought*

A significant part of Vattimo's program is the claim that weak thought, *pensiero debole*, is essential for the proper functioning of a democratic society. Only the end of objective, representational, "metaphysical" thinking, allows for a proper democracy (*NE*, 83). Why is this the case? Because, Vattimo says, if there really exists an objective truth, "there will always be someone who is more in possession of it than I and is thereby authorized to impose its law/obligation on me" (*ADG*, 37; *CRO*, 52).[101] This is tantamount to saying that strong thought (objective claims of any kind), with its peremptory assertion of ultimate principles, vitiates the procedural and provisional dimensions of democratic societies, ineluctably leading to oppression and possibly to violence. Only Nietzsche and Heidegger, with their calls for weakening, with their recognition of Being as illuminative irruption rather than perduring structure, offer theoretical assistance to procedurally based democratic societies. Politically, then, there can never be any final or normative claims, any ultimate affirmations about the nature of humanity; all assertions must be discharged into the realm of the procedural. Such a position may have some purchase in purely secular matters (although even here one may observe difficulties—are there ever any actions that are always wrong?). Nonetheless, discharging specifically *religious* belief into the realm of the procedural makes little sense. Vattimo, however, regards any kind of strong thought, including strong religious thought, as necessarily indicating a crushing heteronomy that suppresses legitimate human autonomy and creative freedom. We recall once again that the proper linkage for Vattimo is nihilism *and* emancipation. Final, formal truths are constraining and confining; hermeneutical nihilism, limited only by the Christian contribution of *caritas*, is fully emancipatory. To the objection that without an ordering to truth, freedom degenerates into license or dominative power,

Vattimo responds that truth can never be fixed and human nature itself is a contingently constructed reality. He concedes, however, that it is precisely the contribution of kenotic Christianity, of *caritas*, that necessarily limits the will to power, thereby obviating the physical or spiritual violence spawned by certain versions of nihilism.

In the past, religion had to be theoretically excised from the public realm precisely because its claims could neither be softened nor publicly validated. This, of course, is the view that Jürgen Habermas still espouses today, clearly demarcating the public and private spheres, insisting that religion has no place in the political *agora*, even warning religion that it could impair its very essence if it seeks to enter the public estate by offering universally available warrants for its claims. Vattimo, on the contrary, severs the Gordian knot of religious and societal relations by claiming that every species of *pensiero forte* must be renounced and diluted into weakness. The proper ordering of society is built upon the abjuration of theoretical absolutes; it is created by the acknowledgment that no one is in possession of warrants that could finally resolve disputed questions. Religion, then, is willingly readmitted to the societal discussion with the proviso that it relinquishes its absolute (and ultimately coercive) claims.

Vattimo's comments on religious imagery are revelatory insofar as they illustrate just how devitalized and denuded of strong assertions the public square must be. He does not object, for example, to the crucifixes that are often found in the classrooms, courtrooms and other public buildings of countries with a Roman Catholic heritage. He does, however, object to the wearing of the chador by Muslim women. Is this a patent case of anti-Muslim prejudice? Not at all. Vattimo makes clear that the crucifix is acceptable precisely because it has *lost its assertive power*. It serves simply as a cultural accoutrement, barely more noticeable than the wallpaper. In other words, the crucifix has already, by its acculturation to secular society, grown "weak" and attenuated. The chador, however, is a powerfully aggressive symbol of strong thought, of an exclusionary truth-claim. As such, it must be banned from the secular sphere in order to allow and encourage interpretative plurality (*AC*, 95–97). The same point may be illustrated by comparing the ringing of Christian church bells and the Muslim call to prayer by the *muezzin*. Church bells have now faded into the cultural background, having already become "secularized," aestheticized and so "weakened," barely understood as a summons to prayer even by Christian believers, while the Islamic call to prayer, on the other hand, constitutes an aggressive, forceful assertion of (exclusionary) religious truth.

This contrast between the crucifix and the chador is revelatory because it indicates that, for Vattimo, no one with strong beliefs can truly participate in the public sphere. Believers must suppress their religious faith—or deeply reinterpret it—in order to engage in public life.[102] One wonders, however, if Vattimo, by taking this position, truly achieves his hoped-for *Verwindung* of modernity. If it is true that the Enlightenment excised religion from the public square isn't it also true that Vattimo is simply replicating this excision, but invoking Nietzsche and Heidegger rather than the positivistic rationalism of modernity? Is Vattimo, in fact, offering nothing more than the *laïcité* of the Enlightenment, the naked public square of modernity, but even more radically, because, while appearing to be mildly accepting of religion's contribution, he is, in fact, emasculating religion of its specifically cognitive content? Isn't *pensiero debole* simply the "privatization" and "marginalization" of religion by another means, the French Revolution absent the guillotine? Religion here only realizes its "supernatural" vocation when it is entirely secularized.

Of course, in Vattimo's native Italy and in Europe generally there is a long tradition of state religions in profound tension with the secular estate. Understandably, then, Vattimo opposes a kind of religious heavy-handedness, *integrisme* classically understood— with religion having authority over the authentically secular sphere—which *did*, in fact, limit human autonomy and which hardly encouraged religious pluralism. We might see an analogue today in the desire by some to impose Shari'a in certain countries now sanctioning legitimate pluralism. In this sense, Vattimo rightly appeals to the advances of secularization, to a "lay" sphere in which interpretative plurality of all kinds (including religious plurality) may flourish. One may even speak of a country such as the United States as having established such a secular sphere from the beginning, deciding forcefully against a state religion precisely in order to allow religious freedom and pluralism to flourish. But this did not imply the renunciation of strong claims; it meant, rather, that room needed to be created in order for strong assertions, including forceful religious claims, to coexist simultaneously and peacefully.

Ultimately, for Vattimo, Christianity's contribution to the public square can only be that open-ended tolerance which is rooted in the self-emptying vulnerability of the kenosis. But one must understand this tolerance *not* as the respect for varying, strongly held assertions. Vattimian tolerance means the abandonment of any authoritative claims to truth. It is the recognition that, in a world of vast interpretative plurality, with no "access" to the *ontos on*, no "strong thought" whatsoever may be purveyed. Religious citizens should never make assertions about the proper ordering of society on the basis of their own firmly held doctrinal or moral beliefs. Such societal intrusion cannot be sanctioned because all such claims are necessarily rooted in "metaphysical" principles. The *actual* contribution of Christianity to society is to take seriously its own commitment to kenotic *caritas*, and, consequently, to abandon strong claims to truth and morality even while welcoming a capacious plurality. Such a position would be a proper instantiation of Christianity's deepest instincts, the triumph of *caritas*. In the ensuing dilution of its own positions, Christianity would come to its own fulfillment as a procedural democracy abjuring absolutes. This is why Vattimo can say, only semi-facetiously: "I believe that the truth of Christianity is not the pope but democratic society" (*ADG*, 98).

In Vattimo's uniquely postmodern public ordering of society, Christians could hardly bring unique perspectives on issues such as abortion or embryonic stem cell research. Such "strong" (even theocratic) positions have no place in public discourse (even if their intrinsic viability could be "redeemed" by means of publicly accessible arguments). Vattimo would not allow, of course, the public redemption of arguments by appeals to a universally discernable *humanum* (a perduring human nature) since such arguments would necessarily invoke teleological claims which have been deconstructed by Heidegger. It is no surprise, then, that Vattimo finally throws down the gauntlet to the Christian faith without mincing words: the inescapable choice for religion is either to accept the destiny of *pensiero debole* (by becoming weak, abandoning strong truth-claims, discharging all into the realm of the procedural) or to insist on objective, metaphysical truth, thereby leading a life of social disruption, slowly devolving into a sect rather than a civilization, living a life indistinguishable from cultural senescence (*AC*, 97–98). As earlier noted, the choice Vattimo offers is far from a *Verwindung* of modernity; it is, in fact, virtually indistinguishable from the choice presented by the Enlightenment itself: either abandon firmly held truth-claims by becoming one highly tentative voice in the world of interpretative exchange or once again be privatized and rendered marginal by society and culture. In the final analysis, Vattimo cannot overcome his philosophical claim that true Christian doctrine and morality *is* secularization, understood as the adoption of *pensiero debole*. Christianity is not thereby deprived of a voice in the public square. On the contrary, the voice of "authentic," kenotic Christianity is best heard when it champions a fully secularized, procedural society devoid of strong truth-claims of any kind.

It is precisely at this point that one wonders why Vattimo has failed to consider an obvious alternative. If a central contribution of Christian faith is the expansion of *caritas* into the public square, i.e., the Christian recognition and endorsement of vast interpretative plurality, then why cannot hermeneutical pluralism coexist with strongly held beliefs? Why not recognize that secularized democracy has already, at least theoretically, admirably achieved one of Vattimo's goals: an open, tolerant, expository bazaar, an irreducible multiplicity of opinions, but without the renunciation of strongly held claims? Why not admit that Christianity, too, can share the goals of ending aggressive extremisms and fundamentalisms, of overcoming antagonistic identities which are deeply intolerant of the "other," of seeking a comprehensive, inclusive public ordering of society that does not degenerate into exclusionary violence (whether spiritual or physical) without renouncing its own principles and beliefs? Why not recognize that believers can positively inform public discourse with their own faith, without aggressively trespassing upon (and, indeed, by insistently defending) the dignity of others?[103] Vattimo, it seems, is too wedded to the notion that any strong assertion is indefeasibly authoritarian, intolerant and totalitarian; any claim of knowing the *ontos on*, even when such declaration is redeemed by persuasion, public argument and democratic election, still violates the canons of hermeneutical nihilism, necessarily leading to strictures on human freedom and so, to fundamentalist exclusion and ideological violence. Only "weak thought," far from metaphysical certainty, adequately protects human emancipation and societal autonomy.

But if strong thought is always a Vattimian instance of "metaphysics," one might put the question to him: How is metaphysics to be properly understood?

Being and metaphysics

In his noted Regensburg Address of September 12, 2006, Joseph Ratzinger, Benedict XVI, invoked a section from Plato's *Phaedo* where false philosophical opinions were the subject of Socrates's comments:

> It would be easily understandable if someone became so annoyed at all these false notions that for the rest of his life he despised and mocked all talk about being—but in this way he would be deprived of the truth of existence and would suffer a great loss. (*Phaedo*, 90, c–d)

Ratzinger cites this text for many reasons, one of which is for the purpose of explicating exactly why the language of "Being" has traditionally been important for theology. Vattimo, as we have seen, deeply influenced by Heidegger's epochal and evanescent notion of Being, seeks a *Verwindung* of the metaphysical tradition, continuing to use such language but in a manner now altered and healed by a thorough rethinking. So, despite his persistent use of the *language* of Being, Vattimo speaks freely of the *end* of metaphysics, of the "twilight of Being," of the termination of objectifying thinking. Such comments give rise to the question: does Vattimo's postmetaphysical understanding of Being have any theological purchase? And this converges with another query of long-standing Christian reflection: does the language of Being offer theological benefits, or does it simply distract from the Gospel message, mixing evangelical purity with an alien and debilitating Greek idea?

For a long time now, one would think that those proscribing the use of ontology, of Being language of any kind, were theologically ascendant. After all, who hasn't seen the legion of contemporary condemnations of "ontotheology," a word as slippery and contentious as postmodernism? With roots in Kant but popularized by Heidegger, "ontotheology" seems to indicate a quick and thoughtless marriage of "Being" and "God," with the former overshadowing the latter. But it is worth going to the roots of ontotheology and how objections to it penetrate to the heart of theological thinking. In the sections that follow, I propose to trace briefly: (1) Vattimo's understanding of Being language; (2) why his thought is convergent with some traditional objections to metaphysics; and (3) why some notion of metaphysics is essential to theological reasoning.

Reflections on God and Being

Heidegger tells us that ontotheology is the kind of thinking that takes Being as "ground" or "cause." God is identified within the horizon of causality as final principle or as pure act.[104] But this is the god who is badly confused with one particular appearance or disclosure of being in history, particularly the manifestation of Being as *energeia* and *actualitas*. This is the god before whom man "can neither fall to his knees in awe nor can he play music and dance. . . ."[105] It is the god of philosophy, not the God "after metaphysics," the groundless God beyond the appearance of one epochal sending at a determinate moment in history.

Vattimo, as we have seen, does not abandon the language of Being, but places a pronounced accent on Being as irruptive Event, as variously disclosed in the continual "play of the sendings." The god who appears as first principle, as supreme being, as *Esse subsistens*, represents the god conflated with one epiphanic appearance of being in history. When we speak of god and *this* notion of being in the same sentence, we are confusing the God of revelation with the god who is understood (by the ancients, medievals and early moderns) as identical with "ground" with "act," with "actuality." The problem here is that *one, particular understanding of being now becomes normative for understanding who*

God actually is. And this, for Heidegger and Vattimo, misunderstands *both* Being and God. For Being is given historically, by way
of epochal sendings, *Geschicke*—meaning that no one unique
"sending" should be taken for God himself. God must be beyond
any particular "sending" of being, and cannot, therefore, be confused with any traditional notion of *causa sui* or *Esse*. Such confu-
sion is precisely what it means to have forgotten the ontological
difference between Being and beings.

But there is another, more pertinent reason that Vattimo finds
the traditional language of Being to be entirely inappropriate
when speaking of God and revelation, even apart from Heidegger's
claim that such language wrongly encapsulates God in one epochal
sending. This second reason has to do with Vattimo's relentless
polemic against the "natural sacred." We remember here the pronounced influence of René Girard, who claims that cultural
anthropology reveals the "scapegoating mechanism," i.e., the
attempt by societies to achieve social cohesion by designating
a person or group as the "evil one" whose destruction heals the
various elements that have splintered a particular culture. Girard's
further argument is that the Christ-event both reveals and unmasks
this mechanism as a "natural" but brutal affront to human dignity.

It is precisely Girard's reflections that allow Vattimo to cast a
wider net in his attack on the "natural sacred," extending this censure to metaphysics itself. The "natural" is not simply limited
to Girard's "scapegoating mechanism" but is widened by the
Torinese to include many elements that *appear* to constitute the
"natural" social order. So, as earlier noted, Vattimo will claim that
various ecclesial condemnations of homosexual behavior, or the
limits placed by some churches on the ministerial roles of women,
or even elements of the "just war" thesis, are nothing more than
dimensions of "natural" religion that are untouched by, and therefore require purification and redemption by, the central message
of the Gospel which is charity, *caritas*. Charity alone, the very
heart of kenotic Christianity, rebels against "natural" exclusionary
violence by overturning every kind of intolerance and repression
issuing forth from the "merely apparently sacred." Just at this point
Vattimo invokes metaphysics as typifying primitive sacral culture.
For not only does traditional metaphysics miss the epochal and
transitory nature of particular sendings of Being, it also badly

confuses the *apparently* natural order of creation with a legitimate gateway for understanding the sacred. This is to say that metaphysics offers itself as a pathway to God when, in fact, the *natural world obscures and conceals rather than manifests and discloses the message of the New Testament*. Metaphysics inexorably leads to an understanding of God as purely transcendent, as first cause, as supreme being, as *ipsum Esse subsistens* and so on (*BE*, 49–50). But this natural notion of god entirely occludes the vulnerable, kenotic Christianity that is revealed in the Incarnation.

It is particularly in this Vattimian polemic against metaphysics and the "naturally sacred" that one sees a reprise (although clearly in a different key) of some of the traditional objections against "ontotheology" lodged by Protestant thought. Long before the term ontotheology became popular, Karl Barth had railed against being-language in theology, particularly the metaphysical roots of such discourse, the *analogia entis*.[106] The conjoining of *ontos* (Being) and *theos* (God) smacked of a significant and major error: the subordination of biblical truth to a prior philosophical theory and, therefore, the subordination of the transcendent God of the Bible to a human construction, to mere philosophy. The wider context for Barth's attack (which, of course, encircled liberal Protestantism as well) was the apprehension that elements from "outside" the Christian faith were illegitimately imported into theology in a severely misguided attempt to justify the "rationality" of Christian belief. The concern was that Christianity first needed to establish preliminary "rational" criteria in order to justify theological knowledge and discourse. And this attempt at justification manifested itself in both the "existential" philosophy of the Schleiermacher-Ritschl-Hermann school of liberal Protestantism and the continual attraction to metaphysics found in Roman Catholicism. Barth's legitimate fear was that faith itself could become secondary to a general antecedent system, to philosophical prolegomena that trimmed Christianity to the pre-existing contours of its own Procrustean bed. It is precisely for this reason that Barth took to task the Bultmannian-Heideggerian approach of "existential analysis" which looked to gain a preliminary understanding of Christian language and reality. What occurs with both existentialism and the traditional language of metaphysics is that one first develops a general anthropology or ontology, only secondarily making room for the affirmations of faith. Christian dogmatics and scriptural truth thus become subordinate to a more encompassing philosophical project. Barth succinctly states his argument when he says that the issue is "whether there really is an essence-context superior to the essence of the church and so a scientific problem-context superior to dogmatics."[107] Barth is fearful that the emphasis on Being, found in Roman Catholic claims that there is an *analogia entis* between God and sinful creatures, allows a profane "*es gibt*" (there is) to be applied even to God, thereby sanctioning an antecedent system ruling faith.[108] Barth states his position with sterling clarity when he says: "Prolegomena to dogmatics are possible only as part of dogmatics itself."[109]

Of course, the concern Barth voices is not his personal *creatio ex nihilo* but has roots deep within the Reformation. Luther's attacks on Aristotle, on Scholasticism and on philosophy in general are well-known. Luther was fearful, of course, that the straightforward Gospel of sin, grace and justification in Jesus Christ had become entangled with philosophical concepts and Aristotelian notions that not only failed to illuminate but that, in fact, entirely obscured and obfuscated the salvation won in Christ Jesus. Luther's theology was not intended to obviate the legitimate role of reason in explicating the Bible, but to call the church away from a theologizing that had become so enamored of certain philosophical concepts and distinctions that the central message of the New Testament was no longer clearly visible. It is the unquestionable primacy of the Bible that leads to Luther's withering comments, earlier noted, about "heathen philosophy" and about reason as "Dame Witch." Luther's critique is two-fold. Philosophy by its nature considers immanent categories and is, therefore, unable to tell us what is most essential about humanity, our relationship to God in Jesus Christ. While philosophical reasoning has its place, compared to the rich texture of the Bible, it is formal and ineffective. As we have already seen, in a famous passage Luther avers: "Whoever wants to be a Christian must be intent on silencing the voice of reason. . . .To the judgment of reason they [the articles of faith] appear so far from the truth that it is impossible to believe them."[110] Reason, for Luther, is *ultimately* impotent before the clarion affirmations of Christian truth.

Secondly, anticipating Barth (and reflective of deep currents within the tradition) Luther is fearful that philosophy taken as an antecedent system will deeply deform biblical truth. This does not mean that Luther is against either philosophical thought or human reasoning. But he is nonetheless extremely wary of those who mix theology with philosophy. So, for example, he speaks of third-century thinker Origen as one "who embittered and corrupted the Scriptures with philosophy and reason, as the universities have hitherto done among us." And he severely scores the thought of Pseudo-Dionysius, the Christian writer taken as a disciple of Paul who exercised such great influence on the later tradition, for his admixture of philosophy with the Gospel. Luther attacks Dionysius's *theologia negativa* because it prescinds from the cross of Christ and, as such, is inspired more by Plato than by the Gospel: "Nowhere does he [Dionysius] have a single word about faith or any useful instruction from the Holy Scriptures."[111] Luther's motto is *crux probat omnia*. Any philosophy is only useful insofar as it falls under, and is judged by, the truth of Christ crucified.[112] It is no surprise, then, that Luther, commenting on I Timothy 6.20-21, says: "The apostle condemns what the universities teach because he demands that everything not from Christ must be avoided. So every man must confess that Aristotle, the highest master of all universities, not only fails to teach anything concerning Christ, but that what he teaches is idle nonsense." Even Plato and Cicero "who belong to the better state" are not to be trusted; instead, "let us learn true wisdom is in Holy Scripture and in the Word of God."[113]

Luther's proper polemic, Hans Urs von Balthasar has noted, scores the illegitimate conflation of the form of the cross with the form of the cosmos. He rightly protests against an "analogizing semi-Pelagianism" wherein the world of beauty potentially overshadows the world of biblical glory. With this looming danger, Balthasar continues, one must wait for Luther "to bring the sharpness of the crisis to consciousness."[114] But even Balthasar might underestimate the extent to which the best of the earlier tradition, while having great respect for philosophical reasoning, nonetheless recognized its ultimate weakness in the face of divine revelation. In the words of Aquinas earlier cited: "In divine matters, natural reason is greatly deficient."[115] In this legitimate concern about metaphysics (and so about the natural) overshadowing the Gospel of grace, we see a certain convergence with Vattimo's thought (even if the Reformation would certainly abjure Vattimo's full-blown Heideggerian reading): religion and metaphysics are, at best, uneasy partners, warily circling each other as competing metanarratives. Vattimo decries metaphysics because he thinks religion's claims need to be "weakened," understood as "epochal" rather than structural or final, and because metaphysics yields only a natural understanding of God and a debased ontology (especially in its assertions about human nature and natural law). What metaphysics misses is precisely the kenotic Christianity of *caritas* that is the heart of the Gospel. The Reformers censure metaphysical thinking because of their belief that this kind of philosophizing offers its own full-blown narrative obscuring the story of the world that is inherent in, and peculiar to, the Gospel of Jesus Christ. Their apprehension, of course, is not limited to the sixteenth century but is found in contemporary Protestant and Roman Catholic thought as well.

A reprise of these earlier concerns may be found, for example, in the work of Colin Gunton, profoundly inspired by Barth, who condemns Pseudo-Dionysius for relying on metaphysical causality as a structuring principle of the universe rather than on the "temporally and economically structured biblical characterizations of God's action in the world."[116] Gunton's criticisms of Dionysius closely parallel those of Luther: the cross is subordinated to the beauty and grandeur of the cosmos; biblical truth has become secondary to a metaphysical vision of reality. This same idea—that philosophy obscures the Word of God—may be found in Gunton's reading of the 1998 encyclical on faith and reason tendered by John Paul II and entitled *Fides et ratio*. The pope speaks about the necessity of metaphysics for theology, although always in service to Christian faith. He says, for example, that for a philosophy to be of use to Christian belief, it must have a "genuinely metaphysical range." Only philosophies of this type are able "to confirm the intelligibility and universal truth of [theology's] claims." Even more firmly, John Paul II maintains that "any philosophy which shuns metaphysics would be radically unsuited" to the mediation and understanding of revelation.[117] Why this firm insistence on the role of metaphysics in theology? The pope's point is that, insofar as the *claims* of the Christian faith (embodied, for example, in the Nicene Creed) are universal, transcultural and transgenerational, then metaphysics offers the *kind* of reasoning (inasmuch as it deals with universal dimensions of humanity, for example) that substantiates in the philosophical order the logic of Christianity's assertions about universal and transcultural truth. In other words, philosophies that have a metaphysical range are appositely utilized by Christianity since they add a dimension of intelligibility to faith's *prior and always determinative* assertions. Gunton, however, expresses the strongly Barthian fear (entirely legitimate in its intention and traceable back to Tertullian in the third century as well as Jacopone da Todi and Etienne Tempier in the thirteenth) that for the encyclical "the Christian faith . . . requires foundation in a general philosophy of being." And this "runs the risk . . . that the particular will be constrained or even overwhelmed by the general."[118]

One sees this same fear of an undisciplined philosophy encircling and overcoming Christian faith in contemporary neo-Barthianism, particularly in the theological movement called "postliberalism." Postliberal theologians rightly point out that ways of thinking, acting and judging are deeply rooted in particular forms of life. Christianity, too, has its own form of rationality and justification; its truth warrants and criteria are to be found in the Christian community itself, not in universal standards that are imported and imposed from elsewhere. Christian claims are to be judged, therefore, according to the rules and warrants proper to the uniquely Christian form of life. Postliberal thinkers here echo the ancient Tertullianesque misgiving that a Christian "despoiling" (to return to Origen's trope) quickly becomes a fateful and degenerative step, falsifying revelation wherein philosophy imperialistically asserts its authority over God's own Word. As with Luther, Barth and Gunton, the legitimate and overweening fear is that Christian faith will become subject to the alien warrants of rationalist modernity, placed in the Procrustean bed of a foreign philosophical system. Postliberalism is apprehensive that Christianity, preeminently a *scientia de singularis* rooted in ancient Israel and reaching culmination in Jesus of Nazareth, will be overwhelmed by antecedent philosophical systems. But Christian truth-claims cannot be measured according to external norms; the church's assertions possess a unique rationality as well as warrants that are proper to itself alone. There cannot be imposed secular standards entirely unconnected with the "thick" house of faith. If alien warrants are imposed, then, just as Luther and Barth feared, the Gospel of grace becomes secondary to some prior unity and "foundation," some epistemological or metaphysical standard to which the Christian message must submit its claims. But, in fact, Christian theology is under no obligation either to offer "publicly accessible" arguments or to defer to any kind of extrabiblical adjudication. The very meaning of the turn to postmodernism (and here we may invoke Wittgenstein, Sellers, Kuhn and Geertz) is that we have moved beyond the universal and overarching standards of positivistic modernity and their attempt at the circumscription of every form of thought. Metaphysics, according to postliberalism, is simply another attempt to apply inapposite philosophical criteria to the Gospel.

Even though the fear of metaphysics has largely been developed through the prism of the Reformation, this idea is not absent from Roman Catholic thinkers, particularly contemporary ones. Jean-Luc Marion, for example, is deeply concerned about the calcifying effects of a narrative about God shaped more by the language of being than by that of the biblical economy. Of course, what is entirely apposite in Marion is a proper rejection of a baroque, encrusted, ontotheology, with *ontos* (Being) now overshadowing the dramatic narrative of God's self-manifestation. This is the kind of reified *Vorhandenheit* thinking (God as simply *causa sui*) that Marion (and Vattimo) strongly reject as conceptual idolatry. This was the primary point of Marion's early book, *God without Being*, in which he characterized the metaphysical tradition as sanctioning just this kind of eclipse of *theos* by *ontos*.[119] Marion argued there that being-language has no place whatsoever in the question of God. In service to protecting the divine Otherness, the language of being must be jettisoned; metaphysics, of its nature, offers only an enclosing and circumscribing horizon, an idolic rather than an iconic purpose, masking rather than disclosing the divine presence. As he says bluntly: "conceptual idolatry" has a site (metaphysics); a function (theology in ontotheology) and a definition (*causa sui*)[120] This thought has continued to appear in

Marion's work, even though he has cautiously emended his original polemic against metaphysics properly understood.[121] But Marion's early contentious language against metaphysics closely replicates Vattimo's polemic against *Gegenständigkeit* thinking, accenting the fact that the God of whom Christianity speaks can never be taken as a ready-at-hand object.[122] In this sense, then, we may see a convergence among Vattimo, Marion and a line of thought emanating from the Reformation: natural philosophy needs to be healed through the Gospel, otherwise the Gospel itself may fall prey to an alien system. Vattimo encapsulates this sentiment when he says: "the biblical legacy is that of recalling philosophy to what . . . we may call the event-like character of Being, encouraging it to recognize the violence inherent in the metaphysical essentialism of Greek origin" (*RDV*, 91).

The natural sacred and the logos-structure of reality

If Luther and Barth legitimately feared that philosophical systems could subordinate the cross to antecedently elaborated prolegomena, then this concern also led Protestant Christianity to be suspicious of accenting the truth and meaning of the universe, of the logos-structure of reality, one might even say of the "naturally sacred," independently of biblical truth. The obvious fear, once again, is that the drama of the gospel narrative is subordinated to the truth of the cosmos "apart" from the redemption and salvation imparted by Christ. As noted, Vattimo's polemic against the "natural sacred" lives under the aegis of Girard's insistence that, throughout history, societies have identified individuals or groups as "demons" who have borne the consequent brunt of criticism, opprobrium, intolerance and violence. Vattimo argues that this victim-based scapegoating is legitimately extended to the entire realm of the "natural sacred." We find it wherever we see exclusionary violence—whether physical, psychological or spiritual—and it is always erected on principles not purified, redeemed and healed by kenotic *caritas*, the central message of the Gospel embodied in the vulnerable self-abasement of the Incarnation. Of course, Vattimo has his own list of corrosive and degrading elements belonging to the *faux* sacrality of the natural order. But his point remains always the same: one cannot trust the natural order since it presents as "sacred" practices which may themselves be deeply exclusionary, far from the kenotic manifestation of God disclosed in Christ as "friend" and as love. Vattimo has little affinity, then, for the neo-Platonic claim that the theater of the world provides a locus for the mind's ascent to the Infinite or for the profound intermingling of metaphysics and mystery that such an ascent suggests. Such neo-Platonic thinking is deeply implicated in the notion that the *kosmos* itself properly mediates truth and beauty, reaching inexorably toward the Infinite.[123] On the contrary, the God who has appeared "after metaphysics," the God of the New Testament, offers an understanding that surpasses, purifies and, indeed, reverses, the purely natural, cosmological view. *This* God is not the God of the *kosmos* with its immutable laws and essences. He is, rather, the God who has revealed himself through his message of kenotic charity.

Once again, in Vattimo's insights, we may discern a distinct but *limited* convergence with the traditional Protestant distrust of seeing divine action in the unredeemed logos-structure of reality, a position related, of course, to the Reformation critique of metaphysics. For in their *classical* ways of understanding the nature/grace or creation/salvation distinction, Roman Catholics and Protestants have placed the accent somewhat differently. For Catholics, the two orders, ontological and soteriological, are distinct but in fundamental continuity. For traditional Protestantism, however, a wedge has been driven between fallen and corrupted nature and the healing work of the Redeemer. Broadly speaking, the entrance to evangelical theology is found either in the authority of Scriptures or in individual experience while Roman Catholicism has placed a marked accent on nature's own intelligibility, its inner meaning, as offering some glimpse of the Creator. It would not be surprising, then, if some quarters of Protestant thought find the call for a postmodern theology "after metaphysics" entirely legitimate insofar as certain sectors of Reformation theology have long resisted the idea that there exists an intelligible *form of the cosmos*, a logos-structure of reality itself, offering some understanding of God even "apart" from Christ and the Gospel of grace. Vattimo's attack on the "natural sacred" as well as the larger architecture of postmodern thought, finds here some convergence with traditional Protestant suspicions about the inner intelligibility of nature and being.

Of course, the root of the Protestant concern is that the "natural sacred" (and, therefore, the logos-structure of reality) is an idea that Christianity first adopted from the ancient world, then intensified during the late medieval rebirth of pagan learning. But the continually lurking danger is that the glory of the world is now confused with the glory of God, and, consequently, that the analogizing imagination overlooks—precisely because the world now mediates divine glory—God's harsh *judgment* on the world rendered dramatically in the cross of Christ. Once again, the insight *crux probat omnia*, the cross judges everything, is intended to challenge a facile elision of the majesty of nature with the glory (and judgment) of the God revealed in Jesus Christ. This pointed evangelical objection (which Vattimo shares in his own way) is aimed at every attempt to collapse the undeducible form of the crucified God into the form of worldly beauty and magnificence. Balthasar has rightly said that Luther and Barth remain important (among other reasons) because they keep the beauty of revelation from slipping back into an inner-worldly natural beauty.[124] The theological protest of the Reformation here is precisely a remonstrance against a metaphysical *theologia gloriae* that silently passes over the revelatory scandal of the cross's judgment on a sinful world.

One sees this kind of thinking concretely unfurled in the classical Reformation apprehensions about natural theology and natural law thinking, elements typically characteristic of Roman Catholicism. Both ideas rest on the notion of the form of the world, of the cosmos "alone" mediating something of God's truth even "apart from" historical revelation. Catholicism relies here on what may be called the "relative autonomy" of nature; this is to say that nature has its own autonomy (through which it mediates something of divine truth) even if this autonomy, needless to add, is always relative in kind, always found within the one estate of God's graciousness. Natural human realties, then, inexorably exist within the one supernatural estate of sin and grace. But they do possess some comparative autonomy inasmuch as they are constitutive of the *humanum*, the universal dimensions of created humanity itself. It is on this basis that Catholicism speaks of natural law

reasoning and of natural virtue, a reasoning and human achievement available to all men and women, even apart from specific
religious or Christian belief. An example of this kind of thinking
is offered by Robert Sokolowski who subtly expresses the kind
of autonomy that is proper to "nature" when discussing the *telos*
of human practices and actions: "We might also tend to look to
revelation for the more definitive communication of the true ends
of things . . . [And] it is true, of course, that revelation will often
declare certain natural human practices to be good and others
to be bad, but these things also have their *natural visibility*, and one
can argue more persuasively about them if one brings out their
intrinsic nobility or unworthiness, their *intrinsic* rightness or wrong-
ness, as well as the confirmation they receive from revelation."[125]
Sokolowski's point, a traditional Roman Catholic one (although
certainly with resonances elsewhere), is that meaning is mediated
on the basis of created nature, of the *humanum*, of universal human
realities which allow for a visibility in the natural order even if
this visibility is, of course, intensified, broadened and purified by
revelation itself. There is an order of nature and reason which,
although weakened by sin and in need of redemption, still, in its
impaired state, sees something of truth. John Paul II, in his 1995
encyclical *Evangelium vitae* reflects this line of reasoning when he
says that while the Gospel of Jesus Christ is intrinsically linked to
certain conclusions in the moral order, many of the same conclusions may be reached on the basis of arguments disengaged from
the context of faith. The encyclical continues that the Gospel of
life "despite the negative consequences of sin . . . *can also be known
in its essential traits by human reason.*"[126] This is not to make the
untenable claim that reason subsists within a *natura pura* outside of
the domain of God's grace; it is to affirm that arguments may be
made regarding the moral order which have a rational validity
even apart from full-blooded, intrasystemic Christian belief. Of
course, these arguments would surely be strengthened by belief,
but they are neither unintelligible nor lacking in cogency without
them.[127] In other words, the pope is saying that there exists only
one supernatural order of grace. But within this order, "natural"
arguments can be made on the basis of reason alone, i.e., arguments having a logical structure, a universal value and a rational
validity independent of faith, even though never independent,

ultimately, of the estate of grace. For just this reason, John Paul II, in his encyclical, *Fides et ratio*, firmly insisted on the autonomy of philosophy in its own realm, even while denouncing its self-sufficiency, indicating once again the endorsement of a "natural" metaphysics, imperfect surely—and always needing the light of revelation—but valuable nonetheless.[128]

Protestant theology, again classically, is more suspicious of reasoning on the basis of the natural capabilities of the "*humanum*" alone and is more likely to welcome (at least aspects) of those philosophical impulses seeking to de-center metaphysics, theological ontology or the logos-structure of reality, precisely in its faithfulness to the *theologia crucis*.[129] Vattimo reverberates with this suspicion of "natural law reasoning," with the claim that the logos-structure of reality reveals something of the divine will. For this is not only a reversion to a philosophically naïve and discredited metaphysical thinking, it is as well a misunderstanding of the central message of kenotic Christianity, which (happily converging with contemporary philosophy) calls into question any notion of fixed ontological natures. Further, by insisting on an objective, stable structure for both the cosmos and humanity, metaphysical theology necessarily inhibits *emancipatory freedom:* "As long as the Church can depend on some natural, rational ethical structure [natural law], they can try to enforce this ethics not only on believers but on everybody" (*ADG*, 92–93). Metaphysics, by its insistence on a universal human *physis* seeks to obviate interpretative plurality, thereby calling into question the very hermeneutical charity insisted upon by the Gospel and obviously tending toward exclusionary violence (*AC*, 117).

Deeply related to the issue of the logos-structure of reality is Vattimo's appropriation of Wilhelm Dilthey's argument that the advent of Christianity signals a marked turn away from "Greek," cosmological metaphysics toward the interiority of the soul's relationship with God.[130] One can discern in the Christian movement, Dilthey argues, a passage from Hellenic objectivity and intellectualism toward an emphasis on subjectivity and interiority. Christian interest in the internal life of faith, in the soul's relationship to God, slowly dissolves and corrodes the "metaphysical," cosmic dimension of Greek thought, a dilution that finally evolves into Kantianism. Augustine himself, Dilthey remarks, was caught between his neo-Platonic philosophical training and his new-found Christian interest in interiority. Insofar as the church of Augustine's time was forced by external circumstances to take the place of the State, thereby upholding the crumbling ancient civilization, the full implications of the Christian "inward turn" was not yet fully seen. It is only with Kant, Dilthey argues, that Christianity's predilection for the interiority of the subject comes to full bloom, with the cosmos no longer considered a significant mediator of meaning.[131] While accepting much of Dilthey's analysis, Vattimo adds that Kant still burdens us with transcendental subjectivity and with the existence of the noumenal world. It is not Kant who finally overturns the primacy of Hellenic thought, but only Nietzsche of the "death of God" and Heidegger of the *Ereignis* that embody the complete antimetaphysical philosophy initiated by Christ. The Kantian synthetic apriori, even with all of its emphases on the autonomous subject, must still yield before Nietzsche and Heidegger; only with them is the Greek world of clarion objectivity entirely eroded.

It is just here that Vattimo adds his own contribution to Dilthey's narrative. Vattimo tells us that Nietzsche and Heidegger, despite all of their advances, fail "to develop fully the implications of Christianity's antimetaphysical revolution" (*AC*, 111). Why is this the case? Because both thinkers have a complicated relationship with the Christian faith as evidenced by Nietzsche's rebellion against life in a Lutheran parsonage and Heidegger's distancing himself from his early Catholicism. As such, neither philosopher can clearly see that the antimetaphysical wave that Christianity begins is, when properly interpreted, fully congruent with his own "weak" thought; indeed, it is Christianity itself that gives the impetus to postmetaphysical philosophy. Further, philosophy *requires* a turn to the message of kenotic Christianity, *caritas*. For it is precisely with this philosophical deployment of Christian charity (uniquely understood) that Vattimo can drive home two related points. First, the accent on charity (over truth) fully unmasks the "*Amicus Plato*," thereby showing (with Heidegger and Nietzsche) the transitory nature of the *ontos on*. Secondly, charity serves as a normative limit to a reactive, violent hermeneutics. Only charity can ultimately constrain the violent possibilities inherent in a certain understanding of the Nietzschean will to power and in philosophical nihilism.

But is it true, as Vattimo contends, that metaphysics has no role in contemporary thought and, a fortiori, in philosophy? Does any attempt to develop metaphysical thinking violate Christianity? No doubt, Vattimo would respond that any such thinking must be subject to a *Verwindung*, an understanding of Being that is now epochal and transitory, not tied to the notion of enduring presence in which metaphysics traditionally trades. Just here it will be useful to examine both the role of metaphysics in theology, as well as why philosophy of any kind, metaphysics included, needs always to be performatively disciplined by faith.

Theology and (purified) metaphysics: A necessary union

Unlike Vattimo, Roman Catholic theology has tended to place a marked accent on the role of metaphysical thinking within theology. Why is this the case? And how has the Reformation, with its legitimate protests against overweening ontology, helped to discipline and purify any role that metaphysics might now play?

Some hints may be found in John Paul II's aforementioned encyclical of 1998, *Fides et ratio*. As we have already seen, the pope says that for a philosophy to be of use to Christian belief, it must have a "genuinely metaphysical range." And he insists that "any philosophy which shuns metaphysics would be radically unsuited" to the mediation and understanding of revelation. A more recent endorsement of metaphysical reasoning is offered by Benedict XVI in his much-discussed Regensburg Address of September 12, 2006.[132] The pope argues that the encounter between the biblical message and Greek thought was providential, as attested by the vision of St. Paul in Acts 16 wherein his path to Asia is blocked while, at precisely this time, a Macedonian pleads for his aid. Paul's vision may be interpreted, Benedict adds, as indicating a necessary and fruitful rapprochement between biblical faith and Greek inquiry. The pope recounts that the name of God revealed in Exodus 3.13 suggested to the Fathers of the Church the profound union of belief and thought, of philosophy and faith. The biblical name for God, "I am" is therein united with a philosophical idea, the notion of existence and Being. As the younger Ratzinger says in his *Introduction to Christianity* (explicitly invoked in a footnote to the Address), in this union one finds that "belief is wedded to ontology."[133] One should look very carefully, however, at this marriage between *ontos* (Being) and *theos* (God). It is decidedly *not* intended to allow the subordination of God to a philosophical idea—or to sanction the hegemony of the god of the philosophers over the *Deus revelatus* announced by Christ. Such subordination, as we have seen, was the legitimate fear of the Reformers and of more contemporary theologians such as Barth. What Ratzinger is suggesting, rather, is that in this marriage of faith and philosophy, one sees the commingling of the philosophical insight into the primacy of the existing real, of Being itself, with the revelation of the Lord of the universe manifested in the history of Israel and in Jesus of Nazareth. The "I am" of Exodus and again, of Isaiah 48.12, "I am He, the first and the last" and finally, the "I am" of John's Gospel (Jn 8.24; 8.58) all converge on just this point. The fullness of existence prized by ancient philosophy and the revelation of God's name in Exodus, Ratzinger argues, comes to fruition and fulfillment in the identity of Christ. Precisely here one detects the proper conjunction and transformation of philosophy by faith and revelation.

Again in the early church, Ratzinger insists, a choice was boldly made for utilizing and purifying the god of the philosophers, even while rejecting the gods of various mythic religions. Our God, the early Christian writers say, is the highest Being of whom your philosophers speak. Our faith is, in fact, the "true philosophy" as some Christian thinkers called it, a faith that embodies the fullness of the *logos*. This early Christian interest in the language of "Being" is in service to the claim that Christianity is concerned with the actually existing real rather than with the world of appearances and falsehood. For just this reason, Christians rejected the folk customs and *mythos* of ancient Greek *religio* in favor of the truth of Being, but this truth now expanded and *fully transformed* by the incomparably new wine of Revelation.

As important as the convergence is between the claims of biblical religion and the *logos* of ancient philosophy, such conjunction is not the only reason for a cautious unity between theology and metaphysics. Why are philosophies with a "metaphysical range" essential for theology even when Vattimo says, echoing Heidegger, that Being must be "lightened" and "weakened" and that the West finds its vocation as the land of the "twilight of Being?" One reason for the invocation of metaphysical reasoning is because just such thinking can help clarify and illuminate the universal, continuous, transgenerational and transcultural claims of the Christian faith. Christianity holds that the same truth of revelation, embodied, for example, in the Nicene Creed, is held by all peoples regardless of widely differing socio-cultural circumstances. Revelation itself, then, has a substantive and self-same aspect across all generations and cultures. This identity, to be sure, is highly nuanced and qualified, allowing for organic development and architectonic change, but necessarily displaying significant dimensions of continuity and duration as well.

The invocation of metaphysics, then, is intended to offer theoretical reinforcement *in the philosophical order* for the universal, transcultural, transgenerational claims of Christian faith and doctrine, thereby adding a further dimension of logical coherence to faith's claims. This adduction of metaphysics does *not* occur because the Gospel has deficiencies that need to be supplemented from another quarter, but because the unitary character of truth is such that the Gospel and proper human reasoning must necessarily cohere. The pertinent questions are these: If Christian affirmations are enduringly true amidst very different societies, cultures, worldviews and perspectives, then how does one philosophically support this doctrinal constancy and meaning invariance over the course of incommensurable cultures? How, in other words, does one find in the "natural" order a proper resonance with what the church holds by faith, viz., the substantial continuity and identity of Christian teaching in and through historicity, change, difference and socio-cultural "otherness"? The answer suggested by the appeal to metaphysics is that reason, in its own relatively autonomous domain, must be able to confirm certain aspects of the truth of revelation (such as the very *possibility* of the universally and abidingly true and the very *possibility* of meaning invariance) over the course of transient centuries and vast cultural, social and linguistic differences. If reason were unable to establish this, then

Christian doctrine and theology would appear irrational, thereby violating nature and transforming faith into merely authoritarian belief. Metaphysical thinking helps to explain, in the philosophical order, doctrinal constancy, universality and substantial perdurance (elements which stand at the very heart of Christian faith) in a world of incommensurable and highly variable customs, norms and mores. Metaphysics, then, is certainly not intended as the Hegelian erasure and sublimation of the finite by an overarching philosophical system. Its employment, rather, is *at the service* of the concrete truths of history offered by way of Judaeo-Christian revelation. The alternatives are either a non-metaphysical theology, which, by simply asserting the universal truth of Christianity absent correlates in the philosophical order has the scent of an irrational and authoritarian fideism or, conversely, the assertion that Christian claims are localized declarations, entirely malleable to times and cultures rather than universally and perduringly true.[134]

On the basis of his Heideggerian and Nietzschean narrative, Vattimo would certainly reject this kind of metaphysical thinking as failing to account for the profound ontological effects of historical contingency and socio-cultural embeddedness. Traditionally, one may see some of Vattimo's concerns (even if without the Nietzschean buttressing) reflected in the claim that there exists a deep and unbridgeable abyss between Hellenistic and Hebraic ways of thinking. This is the charge levied by Adolf von Harnack in his famous manifesto, *Das Wesen des Christentums*—a book which seems to find new theological and philosophical life in every generation. Harnack's claim is that the simple Hebraic message of Jesus of Nazareth, "God is our Father and all men are brothers" was badly distorted by Hellenistic philosophy, forcing useless speculation about the Eternal Logos eternally generated from the Father and about three *hypostases* sharing one divine nature. Historical fact, Harnack avers, is here drawn into the realm of "metaphysics," making the Christian teaching on the Trinity reek of philosophical obscurantism and overweening supernaturalism.[135] Having denied the claim that Christian faith assimilated and *transformed* Greek ideas *in service to* the Christian faith, Harnack can only conclude that the council of Nicea in the fourth century marked the triumph of the priests over the people, i.e., the Hellenistically educated clergy over an allegedly simple, uncomplicated and a-philosophical faith.[136] Of course, Vattimo's claims are more radical than those of Harnack. But we see in Vattimo's thought a distant echo of the Harnackian assertion that philosophy and metaphysics are deplorable Hellenistic imports that have only served to pollute the pure Hebraic tradition and to warp the fraternal *caritas* that is the central message of the Gospel.

But does metaphysics, in fact, simply deform Christian faith, denying ineluctable dimensions of human existence (such as historicity and socio-cultural difference)? Or does it, on the contrary, seek to penetrate to the depths of the real which is both complex yet unified, seeking eidetically (*eidos*) discernable dimensions of human life? More importantly, and of the interest to the entire tradition but acutely to the Reformers, how does the Gospel *performatively discipline* philosophy in general and metaphysics in particular?

The performative disciplining of philosophy by faith

Even if metaphysics is necessary for theology, we can agree with Vattimo that there must always be a *Verwindung* of metaphysical thinking, meaning by this an alteration and convalescence of philosophical thought. For to insist that philosophy in general and metaphysics in particular must be always purified and healed by revelation is to recognize the truth of the Reformation claim that evangelical purity must firmly discipline and transform thinking of any kind. And Vattimo, as we have seen, has a convergent theoretical point when he insists that the "naturally sacred" cannot be normative, especially if "natural" is understood as any notion not purified and healed by Christian *caritas* (even if Vattimo, *in actu*, offers a unique understanding of *caritas* itself). Luther had already said something like this when he asserted, "No one can become a theologian unless he becomes one without Aristotle."[137] The Reformer hopes to remind Christianity that neither Aristotle nor any other philosopher may be uncritically adopted without significant modification by Christian faith itself. The performative drama of salvation can never be subsumed under philosophy's essentialistic reflections.

Of course, Luther is entirely right about the performative disciplining of philosophy by faith. Philosophy can never become a "foundation" more axial than the Gospel; faith can never be accommodated to some latter-day bed of Procrustes. We have moved beyond modernity to theological postmodernity precisely to the extent that we recognize that "modern" philosophical foundations are inappropriate for proper Christian thinking. With the fundamental insistence of contemporary neo-Barthianism, then, one can entirely agree: given the primacy of revelation, all uses of philosophy (and other disciplines) must be transformed by the Christian faith. There can be no *uncritical* assimilation of metaphysics into Christian thinking since this would be to subordinate the Gospel to an alien narrative. A proper use of metaphysics in theology respects these Barthian concerns, rejecting any capitulation to secular, extrabiblical norms which now adjudicate the legitimacy and truth-status of Christian assertions.

But even while renouncing philosophy understood as an alien and predetermining norm, theology must nonetheless use metaphysics in order to explicate theology's universal and transcultural assertions—to show, in other words, why the claims of the Christian faith, precisely in their materially continuous and universal nature, find support not only in revelation, but *also in the natural, philosophical order*. This is hardly to subjugate theology to an imperious, alien form of thought. It is to show that the claims of Christian doctrine, and a properly disciplined metaphysics, conjunctively cohere. It is always a matter of maintaining a proper balance between the priority of faith and the intelligibility required in the philosophical order for the sake of illuminating faith's decidedly universal and materially continuous claims.[138] Such proper balancing is why theology must reject Heidegger's attempt to dragoon Luther for his own double-edged project, which has as its goal both to decouple theology from metaphysics, and to dethrone theology as the foremost mode of thinking. Heidegger, with his attempt to demote the absolute primacy of theology, cleverly tries to use Luther as an ally in the struggle: "Faith does not need the thought of Being. When faith has recourse to this thought, it is no longer faith. This is what Luther understood."[139] Of course, Luther's concern about the "thought of Being" was to keep Aristotelian Scholasticism from obscuring and eclipsing the

Gospel of grace, to remind Christians that the cross is the founding event of Christianity (and so of the world), not pure metaphysical speculation. But Heidegger alters Luther, twisting his thought in service to his own thesis that philosophy is the true *ontological* discipline, reflecting on the whole of reality (including, of course, the nature of Being), while theology is, like chemistry, an *ontic, regional* way of knowing that examines and reflects on only one aspect of existence, in this case, on "faith-filled *Dasein*."[140]

But Heidegger is wrong on both counts. Theology is, indeed, the narrative that is, in Robert Jenson's phrase, "the story of the world." Consequently, theology must firmly rebut Heidegger's claim that it is a regional ontic discipline, entirely unsuited to handle the primordial ontological questions that go to the heart of thinking. On the contrary, insofar as it is based on God's own revealing word, theology is the horizon within which all thinking must *ultimately* take place. At the same time, theology must refute Heidegger's decoupling of theology and metaphysics precisely because theology *uses* metaphysics in order to ensure that its claims do not have the scent of fideism, i.e., theological assertions without explicative support in the natural, philosophical order. It is precisely in that "natural" order that metaphysics *confirms* that the universal and materially continuous claims theology makes are not unintelligible on philosophical grounds. This is to say that the very possibility of truth that is both universal and materially continuous across generations and cultures must be theoretically defended.

Metaphysics, then, as with every kind of thinking appropriated by Christian theology, needs to be performatively disciplined by faith, even as faith utilizes every form of thought in service to the intelligibility of Christian truth. In one sense, then, we can surely say that Vattimo is theoretically correct when he places the accent on evangelical *caritas* (even if he interprets this in an idiosyncratic manner) and when he recognizes the shortcomings inherent in an adoption of Hellenic thought *en bloc*.[141] In this instance, we may discern a certain convergence between Vattimian and properly Christian forms of thought. But even if Vattimo's work finds a *certain* resonance with traditional Christian—and particularly Reformation claims—we must recognize that Vattimo is not particularly interested in trumpeting the Gospel as the "story of the world." Vattimo can only accept this understanding in a highly attenuated sense, meaning that the Gospel is the story of the world *if and only if* by this phrase one means not "exclusive" ontological claims about the God revealed in Israel and in Jesus of Nazareth but the secularizing message of hermeneutical nihilism which receives theological impetus from the parable of the Incarnation.

Chapter 5

Theological dialogue with Vattimo (II): Truth and interpretation

As we have already seen, Vattimo insists that there is no final, ultimate, metaphysical structure to reality. Because of this, truth is best conceived as Event, as ephemeral historical message. This is why Vattimo balks at the Aristotelian dictum, *Amicus Plato sed magis amica veritas*. Why stress truth over charity? For who really knows the truth about life or about God? Truth is evanescent and transitory, not stable and fixed. It is precisely a fixed understanding of truth that leads inexorably to claims of certitude, to limitations on human freedom, to exclusionary violence. This is why Vattimo insists that if there really exists an objective truth, "there will always be someone who is more in possession of it than I and thereby authorized to impose its law/obligation on me." He adds, reprising Kant, ". . . when it comes to religion, I say that truth does not matter. It is morals, ethics and charity that count" (*ADG*, 107).

How could the truth proper to religion be other than charity? *Pensiero debole* disallows any strong thought, any "representational" or objective claims, doctrinal or otherwise. Religion's "truth," then, must always be the truth of *caritas*, now understood as tolerance for widely differing interpretations of reality. Because of this capacious plurality, religions must refrain from insisting on the veridical status of their own particular set of assertions. Precisely here we do well to remember Nietzsche's parable "How the World Became a Fable" from *The Twilight of the Idols*. This story offers an important indicator of how varying claims to truth (both philosophical and theological) have gradually dissipated throughout history. Friendship and charity become the axial principles only when one leaves behind claims to objectivity and universality (*AC*, 111).[142]

Just here, a significant issue presents itself. If truth and Being are evanescent and transitory, without final, dogmatic, objective, "metaphysical" reality, then what is the status of the kenosis, the self-emptying of God which forms the central theological "pillar" of Vattimo's own thought, allegedly converging with (and, indeed, offering the paradigm for) the "weakening" philosophical insights of Nietzsche and Heidegger? At times Vattimo speaks as if the Incarnation of the Eternal Word is an objective, historical reality (*AC*, 60). But if Being is manifested, á la Heidegger, only within a transitorily disclosive horizon, can we affirm finally and objectively that the Eternal Son of God took flesh? And would this not constitute, under the strictures of Vattimo's philosophical program, the much-maligned absolutization of a contingent historical event? Would the Torinese admit that the kenosis is ontological bedrock, even if, needless to say, unprovable and so inaccessible by way of public arguments? Would he admit that this Event, the love of God revealed in the Incarnation of the Son, is a definitive, absolute, historical reality?

The argument may be made, of course, that Vattimo is only contending that the kenosis, like all events, is subject to highly divergent interpretations which themselves differ considerably precisely because of the historical and socio-cultural provisionality of the interpreting subjects, thereby disallowing any universally accessible warrant for its truth. But such a contention would be, at best, very old news. Christians have never claimed to have a universally conclusive warrant for the Incarnation other than faith itself. And everyone has known that the kenosis is an entirely contingent, historical event, indeed, so much the epitome of contingency that it was regarded as the *scandalum particularitatis* par excellence. Thus, the assertion that Vattimo wants us to think within interpretative contingencies, thereby avoiding "hard" epistemological foundations, has little philosophical purchase in a tradition which, on this matter, is entirely cognizant of them. In fact, Vattimo's whole philosophy is more radical than this. He has railed against objective truth-claims, indeed, against any strong thought whatsoever. He is hesitant even to speak of the *ontos on* since it is *created* by interpretations, not "given" to us or mediated by us. How, then, could one claim absolute, final, metaphysical truth, invoking here all of the Vattimian pejoratives, for the Incarnation itself? Why should this stand as ontological bedrock? As Vattimo himself tells us, ". . . by standing for freedom, this includes freedom from (the idea of) truth" (*ADG*, 37).

How, then, is the kenosis to be understood? I think that it is best conceived, in Vattimo's thought, not as an actual historical event or as an "objective" truth, but as a metaphor or a theological "cipher" (to invoke Karl Jaspers's terminology), indicating a belief which is itself purely symbolic or metaphorical, but which exercises an enormous influence (*Wirkungsgeschichte*) on an entire civilization. It is an interpretation which has become a bonding belief of the embedded community of Christian culture, but whose "metaphysical" truth, in the sense of a final, perduring description of the world, is never affirmed. Vattimo refers to the Nicene Creed in just such a manner—as an external "symbol" by which members of a community identify themselves, a kind of code or "identity card" destined to function as a sign of recognition (*BE*, 77). This, of course, is intended to dilute and dissipate the descriptive and ostensive elements of the Creed. The *Niceanum* is not meant to be an affirmation that is isomorphic with the world (even analogically); it is acknowledged, rather, as a communal identifier, something like a cultural name badge, but is not to be taken as objectively or representationally true.

In fact, Vattimo does finally clarify the ontological status of the oft-invoked kenosis when he tells us that Christian preaching on charity "is a call that arises from the historical event of the incarnation (*it is historical not in the sense that it is a 'real' fact but rather insofar as, in its* Wirkungsgeschichte *(effective history), it is constitutive of our existence*) and that speaks of the nihilistic vocation of Being" (*AC*, 112; *DC*, 118, emphasis added). The Incarnation, then, cannot be taken as an historical event, as a dogmatic, metaphysical fact. Nonetheless, we live, intensely so, within the long shadow of its *Wirkungsgeschichte*, its effective history. This term, popularized by Gadamer, reminds us that we exist, inescapably, within the horizon of the founding events and stories that define our culture. And Vattimo is arguing that the Eternal Son of God become man is one of the founding narratives of Western civilization, one of the major accounts which has established the horizon within which we exist. Asking about whether the kenosis "really" happened is to assume a pre-existing *ontos on;* it is to posit a fixed, ontological structure of the world beyond the ephemeral disclosures of the Event of Being. It is to misunderstand the essential point, which Vattimo pithily frames: *Wirklichkeit* is *Wirkungsgeschichte;* reality itself is constituted by the long shadow of effective history rather than somehow existing "outside" of it (*GPO*, 305).

This is why we should understand that when Vattimo speaks of kenosis, it cannot be taken in the sense of an objective, representational, "metaphysical" truth. Such thinking would violate the entire philosophy of *pensiero debole.* At the same time, one detects in the Torinese a palpable struggle. There exists a contest between his attraction to kenotic Christianity, to the event of the Incarnation as the central affirmation of Christian faith—and his Nietzschean-Heideggerian nihilism which entails the claim that the Event of Being is never disclosed finally nor encapsulated objectively or dogmatically. But these differing vectors—the actuality of Christ's Incarnation and the Nietzschean-Heideggerian nihilistic-epiphanic notion of Being and interpretation—cannot finally be reconciled. And Vattimo clearly understands this, making his choice accordingly. This is why all Christian doctrine must ultimately be diluted by secularization. Even the kenosis itself, the very symbol and cipher of charity, must be immolated on the altar of "secularizing" thought. In a stroke of irony, the Incarnation is here both priest and victim, the very epitome of vulnerability which presides over the dissolution of every claim to truth—and the potent symbol which must, in the last analysis, take even its own "historical" life.

Vattimo's option forces us to ask: if Christian kenosis cannot be taken as ontological bedrock, then why bother with a contingent and provisional symbol, even if it is deeply embedded culturally, casting a very long shadow of effective history? More to the point: why should the *symbol* of kenotic Christianity serve as a brake on the nihilistic will to power? Can we really believe that such *mythos,* severed from forceful ontological roots, has the power to constrain violence? Does *caritas* have any purchase if Christianity and its central truths have themselves no metaphysical force? How long can society live off expended Christian capital? Can the symbol of kenotic Christianity really stop the ultimate implications of nihilism, the Hobbesian *bellum omnium contra omnes?* One inevitably thinks of the words of the novelist Flannery O'Conner commenting on the Eucharist, "If it's a symbol, to hell with it."

A dynamic very similar to Vattimo's thought on kenosis may be found in his understanding of God. Does Vattimo believe in God? He has, of course, fully endorsed Nietzsche's "God is dead." But this can legitimately be taken simply to mean that any notion of God is an interpreted one—that God's existence, therefore, cannot serve as a neutral epistemic foundation on which to build a universal system of knowledge. This position is unexceptional and has been adopted by any number of thinkers. More interesting is Vattimo's claim: "I do not say that God exists or God does not exist, as if it would be a matter of stating a descriptive proposition of the realistic, metaphysical type." And again, "Affirmations such as this are possible only if one adopts your [he is referring to an interlocutor] descriptive realistic position, which is already internal to a scientific objectivism . . ." (*AOC*, 11). Traditionally, of course, Nietzsche's claim "God is dead" underlines the impossibility of absolute moral values, of "metaphysical" finalities. But Vattimo thinks a bald assertion of God's inexistence is a simplistic reversion to metaphysics. This is why he avers, "I am a believer, but I believe in the 'God of the Bible.' The Bible is the basis of a tradition to which I belong and without which I cannot possibly think of myself. I know nothing of Buddhism or Hinduism. I do not contest the legitimacy of these religions . . ." (*AOC*, 11).

In these passages, we have the strong sense that "believing in God" for Vattimo is simply a matter of recognizing that we dwell within the horizon of a determinate tradition, an effective history (*Wirkungsgeschichte*) in which the term "God" is impossible to escape. "God" is open to an infinite number of interpretations, but the term itself cannot be erased from our history. It can be erased neither culturally, because it is so deeply embedded in our historical civilization nor can it be erased theoretically because atheism has itself been unmasked as the residue of a now discredited positivism. Living within the "horizon" of God, acknowledging that God is ineluctably a part of embedded Western existence is, in fact, what "believing in God" means for Vattimo. It does not intend the affirmation of God's "objective" existence (which remains a pitfall of *pensiero forte*). This is the reason that Vattimo often cites an essay by the historian Benedetto Croce entitled "Why we are unable not to call ourselves Christians."[143] Croce's point, but more insistently Vattimo's, is that Christianity is so deeply embedded in the socio-cultural fabric of the West (and of Italy, surely) that it would be unthinkable to "construct" his personality without it (prescinding, of course, from the question of whether Christianity describes a "state of affairs"). This is why Vattimo can serenely say, "I do not believe that religious experience is still linked to the metaphysical conviction that 'God exists' and that it is our obligation (as Christians) to help others take account of this" (*AOC*, 15). For the Torinese, we should recall, truth is our last God; we should not be seduced by the imagined enchantments of the *Amicus Plato*. On the contrary, charity and friendship are the heart of the Christian message to which we should give allegiance. This is why Vattimo can say, in a statement without ambiguity: ". . . in relation to love, everything else associated with the tradition and truth of Christianity is dispensable and may rightfully be called mythology" (*ADG*, 41).

Like the Incarnation of Christ, the existence of God should not be construed in an ontological sense. Vattimo's is the strong Nietzschean claim that the world has become a fable, that the *ontos on* is created, that Being is disclosed to us only in deeply historicized manifestations. "God" as well as "Incarnation" are names given to historical irruptions of insight which can never be taken in any final or objective sense. We cannot, then, be wedded to constative propositions, "God exists" or "Jesus of Nazareth is the Eternal Son of God." At most, there has occurred an Event, an irruptive "lighting up," an illuminative force, a dynamic disclosure, revealed in Christ and Christianity. But to offer "metaphysical" statements, perduring assertions about the Incarnate Logos or the Trinity or even simply about God, is to engage in illegitimate "objectification" seeking to fix by absolute affirmations the unending flux of historicity. One can neither close down effective history nor try to stop the flow of temporality, the continual "play of the sendings." This is why Vattimo can eulogistically cite Bonhoeffer's claim, "*Einen Gott, den es gibt, gibt es nicht*"—a God who is given, is not given.

We must remember that for Vattimo the world is continually rewritten by new interpretations. We stand in one place in history; new interpretations will succeed us, as will new disclosures of Being.

Metaphysical systems (with their unslaked thirst for absolutes) hope to nail down Being with dogmatic certainty, to bring historical *Bewusstsein* to an end. But this attempt is doomed to failure. This is why representational thought of every kind must be diluted by hermeneutical nihilism.

Christian doctrine

Given the preceding comments on both kenosis and the Godhead, it is not difficult to discern Vattimo's thought on Christian doctrine. Isn't doctrine the worst representative of absolute claims, of objectifying thinking? As usually conceived, doctrine tends to congeal and harden the Event of Being, to "freeze" the disclosive manifestations that appear in time. Christian doctrine (and creeds preeminently) try to seize the flux of history, announcing that, finally, the Event of Being has been "captured" in a proposition. Vattimo asks: "What exactly do I believe about Christian doctrine?" He answers, "I consider myself a half-believer because I cannot answer this question conclusively" (*BE*, 76/77). He tells us, rather, that he does not hold a "metaphysically conceived faith" and that the creed is an external "symbol" by which members of a community identify themselves. He further avers that the Word cannot be "enclosed and hardened within the authoritarian boundaries of dogma" (*AC*, 82).

Vattimo, of course, and legitimately so, wants to call into question a "frozen" view of dogma, one that equates doctrine simply with propositional truth and which eviscerates the vital, personalistic, engaging elements of religious experience. This is why he insists that the postmodern recovery of faith has "nothing to do with the acceptance of strictly defined dogmas . . ." (*AC*, 8–9). What Vattimo understandably rebels against here is the *Gegenständigkeit* notion of religion, with doctrine offering simply a "representational" understanding of truth. He is surely right, then, (echoing theologians without number) when he says that the Bible is not primarily a book of moral commands. And he is equally accurate in his implication that the "strong thought" of Christian teaching cannot be reduced to a clenched fist whereby human beings are deprived of their legitimate freedom.

But Vattimo's philosophy, with its pronounced accent on hermeneutical nihilism, disallows even a humble notion of Christian doctrine, one which speaks enduringly (although certainly not exhaustively) about God's inner life and work. In the Torinese's view, this is precisely to fall back into fixed, objectivist thinking, confining and limiting Being in its authentically disclosive power. Consequently, a proper *Verwindung* (alteration-deformation) of Christian doctrine, one that respects the demands of *pensiero debole* must abandon the notion of continuous and perduring presence that is ineluctably implicated in Christian creedal and confessional claims.[144]

Ultimately, Vattimo would resolve and compress all strong Christian assertions into charity, *caritas*, now understood as the acknowledgment of the world as a vast interpretive bazaar, and with the concomitant recognition that strong claims to "truth" lead inexorably to exclusion, intolerance and violence. *This* notion of charity is the essential message of Jesus Christ and of the New Testament, overcoming in the process any species of thought claiming to offer definitive, doctrinal teaching. This is the meaning of Vattimo's pertinent comment: "The Christian inheritance that 'returns' in weak thought is primarily the Christian precept of charity and its rejection of violence" (*BE,* 44). This resolution of doctrine into *caritas* (which Vattimo contends, is not far from Christ's own compression of the entire Old Testament Mosaic Law into the two great commandments), delivers a double blow: it puts to an end the philosophical attempt to harden Being into any particular manifestation and it theologically deconstructs the kind of divisive violence that congealed dogma naturally creates. The dilution of doctrinal truth-claims into the *caritas* of pluralism recognizes that the vulnerable, kenotic self-abasement of God is paradigmatic for the entire life of the church. Why should the church be concerned with the authority of its doctrinal message when a vulnerable God has himself renounced such authority? This is why Christian doctrine, for Vattimo, is itself a manifestation of the *natural sacred*—it, too, has not yet been cleansed, purified and healed by kenotic Christianity and so clings to the "older" form of "natural" religion.

Of course, much of what Vattimo says here has been already discussed at length in Christian theology and, indeed, has been done so for centuries. What kind of truth does doctrine mediate? How can finite, limited concepts mediate something of the One who is himself unlimited? How can doctrinal statements achieve a proper balance between the *Deus revelatus* and the *Deus absconditus*? These questions force us back, ultimately, to the very concept of revelation, a notion, unsurprisingly, not discussed by Vattimo and an idea that would itself be ultimately denounced as not only philosophically erroneous—insofar as it fails to recognize the evanescent nature of disclosure—but also as theologically misguided insofar as the very concept smacks of exclusionary violence and so reeks of the primitive sacred.

Christian faith holds that God has entered into a loving, personal, intimate relationship with his creation and freely manifested something of his own inner life. This life is revealed to us preeminently in the history of Israel and in Christ's teaching as preserved in the Scriptures. The great councils of the church, Nicaea, Constantinople and Chalcedon, offer authoritative interpretations of the biblical text in light of the performative life of the church, its worship, exegesis and spiritual-theological insight. One element that is surely common to the Scriptures, the early Christian writers and the great councils is this: the teaching tendered is not proposed as a transitory or evanescent solution. It is proposed rather as God's own Word, a Word communicated personally to men and women for their salvation, for the sake of leading them to eternal life. It is precisely this sense of teaching, as the scripturally and ecclesially articulated presence of the self-manifestation of the Triune God that continued with the Schoolmen in the Middle Ages and with the great teachers of the Reformation. And this understanding of the Gospel of Jesus Christ has led to the defining characteristics of doctrine as universally and continuously true.

Luther accurately summed up this understanding when he said, in a well-known statement, *Tolle assertiones et Christianismum tulisti*.[145] And it is no surprise that Vatican II, in its dogmatic constitution, *Dei Verbum*, insisted that there is an element of revelation that Christians consider to be universal, normative, self-same and eternal. For example, the Christian dispensation, as the new and definitive covenant, will never pass away (no. 4). And, "God has seen to it that what he has revealed will abide perpetually in its full integrity and be handed on to all generations" (no 7) One can see from such statements the significant investment that the Christian church has staked on its ability to know God's self-manifestation with dimensions of clarity, objectivity and perpetuity. These watchwords are not the invention of contemporary theology; they characterize a long tradition of reflection upon the meaning of Christianity and the very nature of the affirmation that God has "revealed" himself. Recent theologians have strongly echoed these convictions. Wolfhart Pannenberg, for example, says that "dogmatics has always accepted this task [confirming its own truth] in connection with the divinely grounded universality of its content which embraces the reality of the world from its creation to its eschatological consummation."[146] This is, of course, simply to say that the Christian narrative is the objectively true story of the created world, from beginning to end. Gerhard Sauter similarly states that "dogmatics . . . says what must be said as credible unconditionally and under all circumstances. God has revealed to us who he is." Sauter later adds: "Dogma states that which has unassailable validity."[147] And Robert Jenson's astute claim, reflective of the entire theological tradition, bears repeating: theology knows the one decisive fact about all things "so that theology must be either a universal and founding discipline or a delusion."[148]

All of these theologians, together with Vatican II, clearly press the claim of the universal truth of dogmatic assertions. Christian doctrine, in its most authoritative statements, linguistically articulates God's self-manifestation both universally and enduringly.[149] And it is precisely on this point, of course, that Vattimo and theology must part company. For the Torinese, as for Heidegger, Being and truth must always be understood as limited, evanescent disclosures. As irruptive manifestations, they can never be "captured" in dogmatic formulas, nor may Christianity itself claim any absolute finality. It is worth remembering, just here, that Heidegger speaks of theology as a "regional" manifestation of Being, like chemistry and mathematics, reflecting on faith-filled *Dasein*. It is not the discipline that thinks the nature of Being itself. Heidegger's transparent point is that theology cannot think *prima philosophia*, the manifestation and withdrawal, the givenness and concealedness, of Being over time. Theology may claim to offer "answers" but only philosophy understands how these "answers" are themselves "granted" and subsequently "withdrawn" within the overarching horizon of historicity. By this maneuver, Heidegger wishes to dethrone theology—and just as surely Christian faith and doctrine—from any pretensions to ultimacy. Theology offers responses that are themselves deeply historicized (taking one manifestation of Being as ultimate), while philosophy recognizes more clearly the unending historical dialectic of presence and absence, givenness and withdrawal. It is precisely for this reason that Heidegger, in his *Introduction to Metaphysics*, verbally slashed Theodore Haecker, a Christian who had written a book entitled *What is Man?* Heidegger vigorously polemicized against Haecker that he already "knows" the answer to this question on the basis of his Christian faith. But how can such a response be seriously called thinking when Haecker has recourse simply to one historical manifestation of Being?[150]

Vattimo adopts and intensifies Heidegger's position. The world itself is "created" and "rewritten" over time, by new disclosures of Being, by differing interpretations of the meaning of life. Those who think they have finally "discovered" the structure of the world, or that they are in the process of arriving at some final and determinate conclusion, have not understood the deepest insights offered by contemporary philosophy. They have not understood, therefore, that the postmodern rediscovery of religion can never be confused with a return to a premodern, doctrinal Christian faith. Of course, Vattimo makes points that are clearly true, even if well-known to all theologians. (Indeed, one often wishes that Vattimo would investigate the labors of contemporary theology with its nuanced crafting of issues.) No theologian would argue that Christian doctrine is exhaustive or conclusive or absolute in the sense that it could not be perfected with greater insight or sharper formulation. And calling into question the fact that God's truth cannot simply be equated with propositions is very old news, indeed. As Aquinas said in two pithy formulations that are still entirely correct: "*Actus autem credentis non terminatur ad enuntiabile, sed ad rem*" (*ST*, II–II, q. 1, a. 2, ad 2), indicating that the act of faith terminates not in the proposition but in God himself; equally important, Thomas describes the article of faith as *perceptio divinae veritatis tendens in ipsam* (*ST* II–II, q. 1, a. 6), indicating that the statements of faith *tend* toward divine truth without grasping it fully.[151] More recently, Avery Dulles has stated that "the symbolic language of primary religious discourse can never be left behind if the dogmas and theological formulations of Christian faith are to be rightly appreciated."[152] There has been, in fact, a great deal of reflection on the socio-cultural-linguistic embeddedness of all theological assertions, including those of Christian doctrine. But from such delimited embeddedness one cannot apodictically conclude, as Vattimo does, that doctrine is itself simply an historicized formulation that can be entirely diluted by *caritas* for the sake of erasing its representational, metaphysical and, therefore, exclusionary dimensions.

Eschatological and analogical language

Vattimo is on a bit firmer ground when he insists, again following Heidegger, on the essentially eschatological dimension of Christian doctrine. He astutely notes that in a 1920 lecture, Heidegger severely criticized "representational" and "objectifying" theology, claiming that this kind of thinking gave free rein to "metaphysics" betraying the teachings of the New Testament in the process.[153] In his exegesis of certain Pauline passages (such as those from the second letter to the Thessalonians), Heidegger points to the uncertainty surrounding the letters, the sense of judgment, of *parousia*, of eschatological expectation, that saturate the epistles.[154] But this eschatological and even apocalyptic biblical attitude is soon buried under the weight of Hellenic thinking (once again the Hebraic/Hellenic split) which turns away from the genuine Pauline attitude toward the fixed, the representational, the always-already present and, thus, toward the "ontotheological." Metaphysical thought, imported Greek thinking, buries and overcomes the experience of authentic instability that characterizes the New Testament itself. The biblical portrayal of historicity and eschatology are "forgotten" under the influence of a hardened *ousia*. Heidegger will drop the religious language when he publishes *Being and Time* seven years later, but his concerns will remain the same. Under pernicious post-Socratic influences, Being is thought of as that which is present, as ready-to-hand, rather than as irruptive and illuminative, as eschatological and temporally disclosive.[155]

Vattimo, of course, wishes to utilize Heidegger in order to drive home his own thesis that Christian doctrine, when understood as fixed and final, betrays the teaching of the New Testament. And, the Torinese argues, this *Verwindung* of doctrine has the support of the Scriptures themselves: Being and truth are biblically revealed as ephemeral and fleeting rather than stable and certain. This is why Vattimo can conclude that "what in the end becomes clear is that after its origins, the history of Christianity forgot the authentic meaning of eschatological waiting, and therefore *can be taken as the history of the Antichrist*" (*AC*, 131–132, emphasis added). The Antichrist is invoked because Christianity, seduced by an alien philosophy, "hardens" its notion of truth into magisterial tenets. But the authentic message of the New Testament resists such doctrinal sclerosis in favor of the continuing attitude of expectation and uncertainty. Only when the Christian faith is separated from the Antichrist of representational thought, can it begin "... the task of thinking of faith without 'substance,' perhaps without dogma, and without theology as a science" (*AC*, 134).[156]

For Vattimo, the "dogmatic" part of faith, faith as "*scientia*," must be diluted into secularized, inclusive charity, into a "lightening" of Being. This explains Vattimo's interest in Heidegger's early exegesis of determinate Pauline passages: Christian existence involves waiting for the Lord's return, "leaving aside the substantive elements" of revelation (*AC*, 135). Insofar as the Christian's life is "radically historical and, therefore is determined by the vital cultural frameworks into which he is thrown," this existence should abjure any positive content, resisting all definition (*AC*, 135). In Vattimo's telling, proper Christian life is entirely coterminous with *pensiero debole*, a thinking that refuses to congeal into "objective" statements. The Torinese closes *After Christianity* wondering if, by leaving behind the philosophical stumbling block of metaphysical objectivism, we might still be able to find a new, productive vision of Christianity.

If Christian theology must reject Vattimo's assertion of an entirely non-dogmatic faith, it can nonetheless agree that his (and Heidegger's) accent on the eschatological vision of Christian thought is surely warranted. So when Vattimo says that we must be on guard against the "compelling power of the simply present"

(*RDV*, 92), when he insists that Being is permeated with the future as well as the past, when he rebels against truth simply "hardening" into unrelieved presence, when he insists on the productive effects of historicity, theology can unhesitatingly endorse his thought. For structuring theology eschatologically means recognizing that the "present" is, indeed, a shadow of the fullness of truth, that God cannot simply be assimilated to pre-existing forms, that the naming of God is not subject to idolic reification, that now we see in an anticipatory mirror, only later shall we see *facie ad faciem*. As Pannenberg rightly says, insofar as we are "riveted to historicity . . . the knowledge of Christian theology is always partial in comparison to the definitive revelation of God in the future of his kingdom."[157] Christian doctrine, while abidingly mediating the truth of God's self-manifestation, does so only partially and incompletely, in the decided interplay of presence and absence, making no claims to exhaustiveness or to ultimate adequacy which always remain eschatological ideals. Vattimo seeks to show that divine truth is not subject to mere *Vorhandenheit* thinking, that revelation itself resists an easy conformity to any pre-existing philosophical form. In this sense, he rightly copies Kierkegaard, the paladin of those who resist every kind of flattening positivism and abjure every attempt to assimilate the divine to an apriori philosophy that has not itself been "shattered" by the truth of revelation. With these accents in Vattimo, virtually all theologians would be in agreement, but without similarly concluding that only a non-doctrinal faith legitimately protects such concerns.

And what is true of eschatology is also true of apophatic thought. Vattimo clearly does not want religious truth reduced to a representational, objectifying notion of God, the kind of humdrum claim that would reduce the Lord of all to "ready-at-hand" status. His fear is that Christian doctrine, with its ostensive and descriptive dimensions, falls precisely into this trap, placing God into pre-existing horizons, failing to find a language and a *way of thinking* that surpasses the kind of "metaphysical" forms now available to us. In these concerns, as earlier noted, one finds convergences between Vattimo and the oft-expressed pejorative comments about metaphysics scattered throughout the works of Jean-Luc Marion, especially in *God without Being*. But, here too, Vattimo is generally unaware (as was also the early Marion) that there is a very long tradition of Christian thought which stands on restive guard against reifying theological thinking. Eastern thinkers such as Gregory Nazienzen, Pseudo-Dionysius and John Damascene are all outstanding in this matter. Aquinas sums up much of this tradition in his careful work on the attribution of human language to God. Thomas was convinced, as was the tradition both before and after him, that revelation, and, a fortiori, Christian doctrine, allows for a certain degree of cognitive penetration into the Godhead, thereby enabling us to say something formally and substantially (*formaliter et substantialiter*) about God's own life. But such affirmation is concomitantly balanced with the recognition that divine unveiling and manifestation lives together with significant elements of mystery, unknowing, otherness and nescience, a profound hiddenness rooted in both the finitude of the knower and the infinity of the known that entirely abjures modern Cartesian certainty. Aquinas's thought, therefore, is always an oscillating, dyadic movement between the two poles of presence and absence, of knowing and unknowing. Vattimo's continual jeremiads against "objectivity" would be acceptable to Aquinas to the extent that, when speaking of God, objectivity itself can be invoked only within the highly delimited strictures demanded by analogy itself.

Thomas's understanding of the predication of names to God is such that human discourse never tries to encompass the divine within a totalizing, univocal understanding of reality. On the contrary, Aquinas is entirely sensitive to the postmodern (and pre-modern) admonition that when one deals with God, one treats of the primordially "Other." At the same time, he defends revelation as concerned with God's self-manifestation—God's decision to enter a salvific dialogue with his creatures—even while stating that "in this life, we cannot grasp what God is, but what he is not and how we are related to him" (*SCG*, I, 30). At virtually every cardinal theological juncture, Aquinas does not simply adopt the pre-existing language of Being found in the prior philosophical tradition. When speaking of God, for example, as *Ipsum Esse subsistens*, Aquinas issues several warnings about the analogical use of such terms, indicating the ways in which such language must be rethought given the infinity of its referent.[158] Indeed, despite his clear accent on the actuality of revelation, Aquinas makes clear how little we actually know of God insofar as the attributes of love, mercy, goodness and wisdom subsist in the Godhead in a manner that is almost entirely unknown to us.

Some theologians, particularly those from a Reformation background, have questioned the reliability of analogical language, based as it is on the analogy of being (*analogia entis*). As noted earlier, Karl Barth was fearful that the *analogia entis* established an apriori Procrustean bed, subordinating the Word of God to a pagan theoretical narrative, subsuming God under a general metaphysics. In Barth's wake, theologians such as Eberhard Jüngel, Robert Jenson and Wolfhart Pannenberg have cast a wary eye at the possibility of using analogy in order to explain the cognitive yield of God-language.

Pannenberg's later comments are cogent here, indicating the importance of analogy, even while acknowledging that it is not without its own difficulties. With the earlier tradition, he avers that all talk about God begins and ends with his inconceivable majesty which transcends human concepts. At the same time, "only by analogy can we attribute positive descriptions of God to the divine essence"; this element of truth remains "notwithstanding all the objections that can be brought against the idea of analogous predication."[159] It should also be remembered that Roman Catholic theology, while leaning on analogical language (and so on the *analogia entis*) in order to explicate the dyadic interplay between God's manifestation and hiddenness, between the *Deus absconditus* and *Deus revelatus*, could still insist on this extraordinarily apophatic teaching at Vatican I:

> the divine mysteries, by their very nature, so excel the created
> intellect that even when they are handed on by revelation
> and received by faith, these mysteries remain covered by the
> veil of faith itself and, as it were, shrouded in darkness, as long
> as in this mortal life "we are away from the Lord for we walk
> by faith and not by sight". (2 Cor. 5, 607)[160]

Vattimo himself does not discuss analogy. He does counsel us in this fashion: "What we really need to do, and this does not necessarily conflict with Christian religiosity, is to say farewell to claims of absolute truth" (*NE*, 56). Of course, as it stands, Vattimo's statement is ambiguous. No theologian has ever claimed knowledge of *absolute* truth, understood as comprehensive knowledge of God. Epistemological humility is deeply entrenched throughout the entire tradition of Christian orthodoxy, as our discussion of eschatology and analogy has indicated. *Deus semper major:* the truth about God always exceeds our conceptualizations of him; we have no "essential" knowledge of God as the teaching on analogy seeks to convey. Further, as many theologians have observed, even the most formal doctrines of the church, such as the teachings of the early ecumenical councils, convey only beginnings rather than endings to disputed questions, setting the broad parameters within which further investigation may take place. As Karl Rahner insisted in his spirited dialogue with Hans Küng, even the most authoritative doctrines may be one-sided, historically restricted and open to correction, but still true.[161] What is asserted here, of course, is that there *always* exists a significant dimension of provisionality and contingency in the formulation of Christian doctrine (for how can the mystery of God ever be fully comprehended?) even while maintaining a certain representational dimension as well. So when Vattimo speaks of the church bidding "farewell" to Absolute Truth, he must understand that the Christian church has never embraced such a notion. In his polemic against this kind of thinking, Vattimo must be careful that his conception of theological truth is not itself guided by the very Cartesian compulsion he wishes to overthrow. Theology has a highly nuanced understanding of the cognitive claims of biblical and doctrinal statements. Reducing this to a desire for "absolute" truth or to a bald "objectivity," to an unyielding presence without absence, to a "strong thought" without humility is to become captive to veridical notions that have long been eschewed by the theological tradition. It is to fall into a theologically incongruent either/or: either absolute knowledge or the theological unknowing of *pensiero debole*. But this is an either/or which fails to recognize the careful attempt of the Christian faith to balance revelation and mystery.

Revelation and truth

It is highly unlikely that Vattimo would be pacified by the Christian acknowledgment of a strong degree of theological nescience.

For Christianity, despite its renunciation of comprehensive truth about God, still insists that it possesses a final truth that is, indeed, the truth of the world, a truth that is (surely as the very word implies) valid for all generations and for all cultures and that, on certain points, is irreversible. Vattimo here would likely echo the Nietzschean sentiment of John Caputo: no one is hardwired to the Secret; no one has knowledge of the absolute (*ADG,* 117). And Vattimo would likely invoke his own condemnation of the "violence implicit in every finality, in every first principle that would silence all further questioning" (*BE,* 65; *CC,* 63). Of course, this comment, too, is deeply ambiguous. Of theological questioning there is no end. But Vattimo can countenance no form of religion which violates the epiphanic and transitory nature of Being, which calls into question hermeneutical nihilism, which insists on access to the *ontos on,* which, in a word, is not entirely and without remainder *pensiero debole.* In *certain* ways, as noted earlier, Vattimo comes close to the principle of philosophical fallibilism enunciated by many contemporary thinkers. For example, the aforementioned American philosopher, Richard Bernstein, reacts to "strong" religious thought when examining the assertion of John Paul II that "people seek an absolute . . . something ultimate . . . a final explanation, a supreme value . . . a truth which confers a certitude no longer open to doubt."[162] In response to the pope's comments, Bernstein states a position that would, with significant modifications, also describe Vattimo's: "A variety of philosophers have questioned the very idea of such an absolute and final truth." Such questioning is not relativism, he continues, but fallibilism, "the conviction that knowledge claims are always open to further rational criticism and revision. Fallibilism does not challenge the claim that we can know the truth, but rather the belief that we can know that we have attained the final truth with absolute certainty."[163] With Bernstein's defiance of the claim that there exists an "absolute and final truth" or that we may justify our positions with certainty, Vattimo would be in complete agreement (even while harboring reservations about fallibilism's own methodological truth-claims).[164]

There is no final, "metaphysical" truth—as Heidegger's reflections on the epiphanic nature of Being have indicated—just as there are no universal warrants which would allow us to justify our positions with certainty. These assertions are at the very heart of *pensiero debole*. The claims advanced by Christian revelation are simply *one more interpretation* of the world, one more construal in the interpretative festival that is thinking. "Revelation" may never be understood as a "privileged" locus from which other narratives may be judged, nor can it intend itself as final or "absolute," even in the carefully circumscribed sense sanctioned by theology. Indeed, we recall that for Vattimo, the very *contribution* of kenotic Christianity is that it renounces the truth of its narrative, "secularizes" it in the interest of allowing interpretative plurality to flourish. How could there exist "revelation," a term which in itself denotes dimensions of ultimacy, objectivity and perpetuity, when knowledge of the *ontos on* is precisely what must be unmasked, when the very idea of revelation reeks of representational and metaphysical ways of thinking?[165] The claims of Christian revelation, then, including its fundamental doctrines, may exist as one of the many "rewritings" of Being. But revelation cannot assert—by pointing to apodictic divine origins—an end to the historical flux of temporality, to the epochal presencings of Being, to the continuous flood of interpretations, of which there is no end in sight.

And this, of course, amounts to a very significant difference between historic Christianity and Vattimo's postmodern interpretation of it. For Christianity insists that revelation, while a profoundly multi-faceted reality, also and necessarily has an irreducibly cognitive dimension, a dimension entirely absent in Vattimo's thought. For what can we actually "know" when the manifestation of truth and Being is profoundly tied to temporality and historicity, when perduring and final knowledge is proscribed, when hermeneutical nihilism is the cognitive "yield" of interpretative plurality? In Vattimo's thought, religion is *caritas*, humility, self-abasement, the abandonment of power, the advance of the secular, the flourishing of interpretative plurality. But it is *never knowing* which would, if taken in any strong sense whatsoever, violate the cardinal principles of *pensiero debole*. Vattimo confirms this when he again insists that Christianity is about freedom and this includes freedom "from (the idea of) truth" (*ADG*, 37). And again, he avers, the way out of violence and conflict "does not lie in choosing one of the truths or styles in conflict and postulating that it is the true truth that will set us free" (*NE*, 58).[166] Revelation, then, particularly its crystallization in Christian doctrine, will necessarily be understood as authoritarian, exclusionary and violent. Once again, we see here a reprise of Heidegger's aforementioned attack on Christianity found in his polemics against Haecker's book, "*What is Man?*" Christianity claims to know the answer in advance. But this is not serious thinking. The problem is that Christianity takes one *manifestation* of Being as final and definitive, thereby missing the epochal disclosure of Being in time.[167]

How, then, does Vattimo, who entitles one of his books *Credere di credere* (believing that one believes) understand the idea of revelation? It surely can have no cognitive content, if this is understood as involving dimensions of perduring truth. One cannot, then, ask about the reality of the Incarnation or of the Trinity. Such questions brush too closely to representational thinking; Vattimo endorses instead only the idea that we live in a "embedded" and "traditioned" world saturated with the ideas of Christ and of God even if we can make no commitment to the ostensive truth mediated by them. For Vattimo, the "revelation" of Christ is found precisely in the symbolic importance of the Incarnation which theologically underwrites hermeneutical nihilism. *This* is the meaning of the vulnerable self-emptying of God that is characteristic of the kenosis. The kenosis serves as a cipher or symbol of the essential message of the Gospel which is "love" and "charity" toward the other, especially charitable tolerance toward other interpretative "styles." The revelation of God is that there is no revelation besides the creative will to power—limited only by the exclusion of violence toward the other (thus, Christian *caritas*). Does Vattimo truly achieve here his hoped-for *Verwindung* of the traditional notion of revelation? Or is his simply a post-Heideggerian retrieval of G. E. Lessing's ring parable, which, by its assertion that the true ring (the true religion) is beyond knowing, relativizes claims to religious truth? It should be clear that Vattimo intends to surpass Lessing. For while Lessing may have adopted the view that we have no accessible warrant to determine the true religion, Vattimo insists that any notion of enduring truth is not only beyond us epistemologically, but is, in fact ontologically inappropriate.

Of course, if Vattimo's notion of revelation is unique, this is equally the case with his notion of faith. Faith is equated neither with trusting engagement with the person of Jesus of Nazareth nor with acceptance of Christ's claims as these have been mediated through Scripture and the fundamental creeds and doctrinal decisions of the early church. Vattimo himself says to profess faith in Christianity is to believe in the "inevitability of a certain textual tradition that has been passed down to me" (*ADG*, 36). As with his claims about Christ's kenosis and as with his belief in God, "faith" represents the fact that each person is heir to a sociocultural world in which he or she is embedded. We are unavoidably "saturated" with a tradition; we inescapably dwell within it. Consequently, faith is an acknowledgment that we live and think within a tight, thick web of socio-cultural-linguistic factors. If we go on to ask whether or not this thick web of acculturated belief is also true, i.e., is descriptive of states of affairs, is isomorphic with the world, Vattimo dismisses the question as philosophically naïve because it implies that there exists a "given" pre-existing *ontos on* waiting to be discovered.

Ultimately, for Vattimo, faith is the acknowledgment that, insofar as we dwell within varying traditions—and therefore have very different understandings of the "real,"—no one should press his or her interpretation as the "truth." This is what it means to have "faith" in kenotic Christianity: that *pensiero forte* is at an end, that belief can never be understood, even as one dimension of a multivalent reality, as assent to certain objective "truths." It must be repeated that Vattimo *does* insist that all interpretations must "strive to articulate, develop and advance arguments for itself" (*NE*, 94). But such action is intended simply to ensure that interpretations are themselves internally cohesive and that the genealogy of our own hermeneutics is plausible. It is certainly *not* for the sake of objectifying the *ontos on*; hermeneutical nihilism is a corrosive (but emancipatory) solvent on that kind of thinking. The essential Vattimian point is made when, still again, he cites Croce's essay, "We cannot not call ourselves Christians"; for faith is the acknowledgment that those living in the West are unavoidably swimming in a *Lebenswelt* thoroughly shaped by antecedent Christian meaning. Of course, Vattimo is entirely right when he says that doctrine cannot be an aggressive "hardening" of Christ's vital presence. As we have seen, theological language is well-aware that it has a strongly eschatological dimension, invoking promise rather than the fullness of unmediated presence. Nonetheless, such language necessarily possesses a descriptive dimension, at least analogically so. Indeed, the truth of Christian doctrine, in its most foundational affirmations, can never be reduced to the reversible, fallibilistic truth of time and history.

Vattimo wants us to understand that "revelation" and Christian doctrine is only acceptable if it can be healed and purified by kenotic *caritas*, by an acknowledgment of a hermeneutical nihilism that no longer looks to representational and objectifying thought. The symbolic self-emptying of God in the kenosis undermines natural religion including religion's reliance on "revelation" which itself, in its claim to abiding truth, constitutes part of the naturally sacred. This is why Vattimo says: "My basic opinion now is that people hate Christianity because of the priests" (*FR*, 68). Any minister of the Gospel who does not preach the hermeneutical plurality of kenotic Christianity remains mired in the discredited moral–metaphysical God of *pensiero forte*. As a logical implication of this position, *martyrdom*, the defining gold standard of Christian discipleship, would be impossible in Vattimo's thought. Why would anyone die for Christ if he is not, in fact, the way, the truth and the life? Why would anyone die for any principle that is not final, ultimate and "metaphysical"? Given that Vattimo says he renounces all claims, particularly claims to finality (*BE*, 44), how could Luther utter his "Here I stand?" Or the Confessing Church compose the *Barmen Declaration*? On these points, Vattimo's thought appears entirely inadequate. One is an *actual* disciple of Christ, on the Torinese's telling, to the extent that one renounces abiding and objective truth. Indeed, one gains one's life by losing it, but the price for *this* "emancipation" is steep indeed.

Theology, truth and "weakening"

There have always existed strategies for "weakening" theological truth-claims. Primary among these has been the very infinity of God, who in his sovereignty and transcendence, can only be "weakly" known by finite creatures. Closely following upon God's ineffable majesty has been the acknowledgment that men and women, even after receiving revelation, are under sin and deeply affected by it, further delimiting any attempt at "defining" knowledge of God. To such traditional claims have been rightly added those epistemological qualifiers indicating the historicity and socio-cultural embeddedness of the finite inquirer. Precisely because of such factors, theologians have, for a long time, recognized the "weakness" of theological claims, while insisting that the church, even with all of the conditioning factors attendant upon theological knowing, grasps the content of revelation, its mediation of states of affairs, never confusing such grasping with exhaustive apodicticity.

One can and should recognize that contemporary theology, too, has itself undergone a considerable "weakening." Is theological "weakening" the proper term here? Or is it a matter of greater sophistication, of deeper penetration into the mysteries of faith? The proper term for the phenomenon need not be decided here. My point, rather, is that the *effect* of theological nuance and deepening has, in fact, led to what Vattimo would describe, at least partially, as *pensiero debole*. Perhaps the reason Vattimo never averts to this weakening is because he would remain unconvinced by the effort. For the "softening" that occurs in theology is still far from the hermeneutical nihilism that he sanctions. Nonetheless, attempts aiming at greater theological humility have surely been undertaken and, just here, one sees the basis for certain links with Vattimian philosophy. I will concentrate below on theological hallmarks that are largely Roman Catholic in provenance even if they find profound resonances in all Christian churches (and, indeed, in other religions as well).[168] Catholicism serves here as the prime analogue not least because Vattimo always takes the Roman Catholic Church as the paradigmatic example of impenitent strong thought. But at Vatican II and afterwards, one discerns clear elements of just the weakening that Vattimo sanctions, contradicting some of his bald assertions that Christianity simply insists on the "absolute truth" of its own claims. It is to some of these conciliar affirmations that we now turn.

For example, Vatican II speaks of other religions with great respect, taking note of the grace and truth found in them. When speaking of Hinduism and Buddhism, the council avers,

"The Catholic Church rejects nothing of what is true and holy in these religions. She has a high regard for the manner of life and conduct, the precepts and doctrines which, although differing in many ways from her own teaching, nevertheless often reflect a ray of that truth which enlightens all men." The council continues, "Let Christians, while witnessing to their own faith and way of life, acknowledge, preserve and encourage the spiritual and moral truths found among non-Christians, also their social life and culture."[169]

This statement, with its recognition of the legitimacy of different spiritual and moral experiences, hardly sounds, contra Vattimo, as if Christianity fails to account for the truth found in other religions.[170] The declaration goes on to speak of the "high regard" that the church has for Muslims who worship the Creator of heaven and earth, insistently urging both Christians and Muslims to forget past enmity in the interest of achieving mutual understanding for the benefit of humanity (no. 3). Of course, because of the profound relationship between Christianity and Judaism, the Roman Catholic Church initiated at Vatican II a long series of reflections on the affinity between the two faiths. The council clearly acknowledges that the church received revelation by way of that people with whom God established his ancient covenant. Christians cannot forget, therefore, that they draw nourishment from the good tree onto which the branches of the Gentiles have been grafted, as Paul says in his letter to the Romans 11.17-24. Likewise, the church keeps before her eyes the clarion Pauline dictum: To the Israelites belong the sonship, the glory, the covenants, the law, the worship, the promises, the patriarchs and, according to the flesh, Jesus Christ (Rom. 9.4-5).[171]

Needless to say, from Vatican II onwards, the Catholic Church has considerably "weakened" its assertions regarding Judaism. At one time, the council of Florence taught that those who do not submit themselves to the Roman Pontiff (whether Jews or pagans) will be condemned to hell.[172] One can surely claim, then, that a "weakening" occurred at Vatican II although it is theologically more precise to speak of the "analogy of truth" that is here invoked. Christians are understood to possess truth in its fullness, to be sure, but it is undeniable that those of other religions participate analogically in this truth, often profoundly so, limited only by extent to which they diverge from the fundamental claims of Christian faith.[173] So when Vattimo counsels Christians to "abandon their missionary attitude, that is their claim to bring the sole truth to the pagan world" (*AC*, 48), he badly misses contemporary Christian attempts to balance carefully creative dialogue and missionary witness. Indeed, he even fails to understand a basic teaching of Catholicism: good fruits have been established by humanity in and through the very "autonomy" of human nature, apart from explicit religious faith of any kind. This is why Vatican II can affirm that the "Church looks with great respect on all that is true, good, and just in the institutions that the human race has established" (*Gaudium et Spes,* no. 42), that a bountiful God has distributed treasures among all nations (*Ad Gentes*, no. 11) and that one may find significant good in the various practices and cultures of diverse peoples, even if these must ultimately be healed and perfected in Christ (*Lumen Gentium*, no. 17).

The very same analogical notion of truth at work in Roman Catholicism's teaching about world religions may be found, in an obviously more concentrated manner, in its teaching about other Christian churches. In a famous passage, surely designed to "weaken" overweening Catholic claims, the council did not simply equate the Church of Christ with the Catholic Church (and, in fact, clearly rejected the simple correspondence indicated by the word "*est*"). In a sentence that still causes theological blood to boil, Vatican II "softened" prior ecclesial teaching by stating that the Church of Christ *subsists in* the Catholic Church.[174] The point of using *subsistit in* rather than *est* was precisely in order to affirm that the Church of Christ continues to be found, incompletely (from the Roman Catholic point of view) but nonetheless, really and actually, formally and substantially, in other Christian churches. The council affirms then, without hesitation, that "many elements of sanctification and truth are found outside of its [the Roman Catholic Church's] visible confines" (*Lumen Gentium*, no. 8). And the *Decree on Ecumenism* confirms ". . . all who have been justified by faith in baptism are incorporated into Christ; they therefore have a right to be called Christians and with good reason are accepted as brothers by the children of the Catholic Church" (*Unitatis redintegratio*, no. 3). Therefore, "the separated Churches and communities as such . . . have by no means been deprived of significance and importance in the mystery of salvation" (*Unitatis*

121

redintegratio, no. 3). Even though these statements are surely inadequate from the standpoint of Protestant Christianity (and, in fact, have been further developed by Catholic theologians), nonetheless, the essential point stands: in the authoritative teaching of the Roman Catholic Church there has been a significant "weakening" of the more traditional position which had regarded all non-Roman Catholic Christians as contumacious schismatics and heretics rather than brothers and sisters in Christ.[175] Yet this "weakening"—or, better, analogy of truth—goes unrecognized by Vattimo, who speaks as if Catholicism had not, indeed, undergone a significant shift in its self-understanding.

The same "weakening" is in evidence in the conciliar position on religious freedom. Vatican II, of course, did not abandon the strong biblical claim that Jesus of Nazareth is the way, the truth and the life.[176] But after many nineteenth-century documents of the "ordinary magisterium" condemning religious freedom, such as *Mirari vos* (1832) and *Quanta Cura* (1864), Vatican II taught clearly that freedom of religion is an objective right of every human being: "The council further declares that the right of religious freedom is based on the very dignity of the human person as known through the revealed word of God and by reason itself." This same declaration, *Dignitatis humanae*, insists that the truth can never be imposed or coerced: "Truth only imposes itself by virtue of its own truth, as it enters the mind at once gently and powerfully" (no. 1). Further, "the search for truth . . . must be carried out in a manner that is appropriate to the dignity of the human person and his social nature, namely by free enquiry with the help of teaching . . ." (no. 3). Debates continue to this day as to what extent this conciliar declaration is a complete reversal of prior ecclesial teaching or a legitimate, organic development of it. The salient point to be noted here is the considerable "weakening" which undoubtedly has taken place when one compares this document with earlier Roman Catholic teaching.[177]

Closely related to the issue of religious freedom is the very notion of salvation itself.

The Gospel of Matthew announces:

> Go into the whole world, preaching the Gospel to every
> creature. He who believes and is baptized will be saved;

but he who does not believe, shall be condemned.
(Mt. 16.15-16)

Over the centuries, in many Christian churches, there has been a "weakening" of the requirement of *explicit* faith in the Lordship of Jesus as essential for salvation. Summing up earlier teaching, Vatican II states that "those also can attain to salvation who through no fault of their own do not know the Gospel of Christ or His Church, yet sincerely seek God and moved by grace strive by their deeds to do His will as it is known to them through the dictates of conscience" (*Lumen gentium*, no. 16).

And again:

... God in ways known to Himself can lead those inculpably ignorant of the Gospel to find that faith without which it is impossible to please Him (Heb. 11:6) ... (*Ad gentes*, no. 7)

A host of theologians have developed this issue of "*fides impli-cita*" over the centuries, so that the third-century statement of Cyprian of Carthage, encapsulated as *extra ecclesiam nulla salus* (outside the church there is no salvation) has been interpreted as allowing for an implicit faith in Christ and an implicit belonging to the Church. Something of this is captured in John Henry Newman's Victorian prose.

The prerogative of Christians consists in the possession, not of exclusive knowledge and spiritual aid, but of gifts high and peculiar; and though the manifestation of the Divine character in the Incarnation is a singular and inestimable benefit, yet its absence is supplied in a degree, not only in the inspired record of Moses, but even, with more or less strength, in those various traditions concerning Divine Providences and Dispositions which are scattered through the heathen mythologies.[178]

Closer to our own times, Karl Rahner has spoken of "ano-nymous Christians." Rahner's argument is that all those who fol-low their consciences, thereby responding to the graced call of God, may indeed be saved (and saved by Christ, even though unknowingly) and can, therefore, at least analogously, be referred to as "Christians." Although contested on many fronts (both by those who insist that Rahner cheapens the noble title of "Christian" as well as by those who claim he engages in eleventh hour "imperialism"), Rahner's argument has offered a way of speaking about "salvation through Christ" which nonetheless respects human freedom and a host of issues related to humanity's profound socio-cultural embeddedness.

Utilizing Vattimo's terminology, then, we may indeed aver that a gradual "weakening" has occurred with regard to the kind of faith necessary for salvation. Once again, however, we do better to acknowledge that an analogical notion of faith and truth is at work in these various theological arguments. While explicit faith in Jesus of Nazareth as the Incarnate Son of God represents the fullness of truth, the prime analogue of belief, nonetheless, there is a participatory structure to believing that allows varying degrees of adherence to Christian faith. Many churches, then, acknowledge that explicit and formal belief in Christ may not be necessary in order to attain eternal life with God.

These several examples from Vatican II, duplicated in the formal statements and theological positions embraced by other churches, do indeed point to a certain "weakening" of strong assertions. But the weakness, we should acknowledge—and in distinction from Vattimo—is in service to the claim that the Lord of creation has spoken uniquely through the history of Israel and in the person of Jesus of Nazareth who bestows his Spirit on all of humanity. The "weakening," then, is an attempt to understand more consistently and precisely how the "strong" claims of Christian faith are to be understood in history.

Other theological examples of "weakening" can be briefly recounted: In an important passage, Vatican II's Decree on Ecumenism (*Unitatis Redintegratio*, no. 11) states: "When comparing doctrines, they [Catholic theologians] should remember that there exists an order or 'hierarchy' of truths, since [these truths] vary in their relationship to the foundation of the Christian faith." Although the specific phrase "hierarchy of truths" is a relatively new theological term, it resonates well with much of the prior Christian tradition.[179] The expression challenges theologians to display the profound unity that exists among all Christians on the primary and fundamental truths of faith. It hopes as well to make clear that there exists a significant distinction between the *certainty* that the (Roman Catholic) Church may claim about a matter and the *centrality* of any particular teaching.[180] As such, theologians should accent the deep concord that exists on the most foundational Christian tenets (the Incarnation and the Trinity) rather than concentrating on certain other doctrines which may be (from the Catholic point of view) certain even if not central to the Gospel message (such as certain Marian doctrines). Yves Congar has further developed this "participatory" insight, claiming that there exists a hierarchy not only of doctrinal truths, but also, clearly, of sacraments and of ecumenical councils of the church. And precisely this accent on "hierarchy" and participation allows for a theological "weakening" which tends toward Christian unity. This weakness occurs, however, not for the sake of diluting truth in service to a nihilistic *caritas*, but for the sake of showing that an inclusive *caritas* is to be sought precisely *on the basis of strong evangelical truth.*

One sees the same tendency toward "weakening," nonetheless based on firm evangelical principles, in several other contemporary developments. For example, John Paul II's *Ut unum sint,* an encyclical written in 1995, seeks to break the stalemate with other Christians by overcoming the age-old claim that Protestantism looks to Scripture as the source of revelation while Catholicism relies on Scripture and tradition. The pope offers the following language as a possible way forward: Scripture is "the highest authority in matters of faith" while tradition is "indispensable to the interpretation of the Word of God." Is this attempt to break a traditional impasse simply a "weakening" in the sense of a dilution of truth that is required because of our inability to know the *ontos on?* Or is it, rather, a salutary reformulation in service to the forceful claims of Christian belief?

The same questions may be asked when evaluating the demise of apologetics in much of mainstream Christianity, at least in any polemical sense. Hasn't a palpable weakening occurred in this discipline? Avery Dulles has pointed out that Vatican II, with its irenic and serene tone, undermined the polemical, aggressive attitude often connected with apologetics. At the same time, the council insists that the disciple of Christ is bound "faithfully to proclaim" and "vigorously to defend" the Christian faith.[181] By and large, however, the council engaged not in theological apologetics but instead adopted the rhetorical genre known as epideictic, holding up the beauty and radiance of the Christian faith and allowing others to be drawn by its innate attractiveness.[182] And while this has been the general approach of most Christian churches, presenting the Christian life itself, its accent on love of God and neighbor, its service to all people, its marked emphasis on the dignity of humanity, as the best source of "apologetics," this renunciation of aggressive and defensive polemics hardly amounts to the dilution and dissolution of Christianity's truth-claims. On the contrary, there remains popular what might be called "soft" apologetics—the appeal to the spiritual dimensions of humanity, to the elements of human life that inexorably open out onto the question of transcendence. This, in fact, is often simply a contemporary restatement of the "restless heart" or *cor inquietum* tradition bestowed by Augustine.[183]

Far from a defensive and apologetical attitude, as well, is the "purification of memory" countenanced by John Paul II at the turn of the third Christian millennium, a reality to which Vattimo virtually never refers despite his insistence that Catholicism is the prime paradigm of *pensiero forte*. Yet surely this undertaking, subject to much criticism even within Roman Catholicism, is a penitential "weakening" motivated by charity. So rare is this kind of institutional contrition that the document "Memory and Reconciliation," issued by the International Theological Commission of the Catholic Church, observed that very few instances of this kind of action can be recorded in the entire history of the church. Nonetheless, John Paul II boldly asked pardon for a variety of sins committed by Roman Catholics throughout the centuries, insisting that such purification was essential as the church moved toward the new millennium.

After briefly reviewing these (far from exhaustive) instances, the point remains a simple one: There has been a clear "weakening" of Roman Catholic teaching and theology at Vatican II and afterwards (a weakening to which Vattimo barely refers). But the crucial question is this: What is the *motive* for this "weakening" of strong thought? Is it hermeneutical nihilism, as Vattimo asserts, the recognition that we have no access to the *ontos on*, that we simply have endless interpretations which, finally, offer us emancipation from the tight strictures of *pensiero forte* and lead, inexorably, to the embrace of *caritas* over *veritas?* Is it the Vattimian-Heideggerian claim that manifestations of Being are transitory and evanescent, thereby disallowing any *final* naming of the Event that reveals itself historically? Such, of course, is hardly the case. At Vatican II there is a "weakening" of certain prior assertions on the basis of strong theological convictions, the oft-stated conciliar assertion that the church is duty-bound "to proclaim without fail Christ who is the way, the truth and the life" (*Nostra aetate,* no. 2). It is precisely because of the church's intention to adhere to Scripture and the early tradition in a stricter fashion, to become Christ's disciples more thoroughly, to implement his message more comprehensively (and, *in this sense,* to take the message of kenotic Christianity seriously, absent the renunciation of dogmatic claims) that a "weakening" occurs. It is precisely a restatement of *strong* thought about adherence to the message of the historical Christ, the *actually* Incarnate Son of God, that leads to a *weakening* of certain other positions. And this message is adhered to because of a firm conviction about its historical, final, indeed, irreversible truth.

Despite the concessions that theology has made about its own "weakening" over time, it remains that Vattimo cannot countenance any understanding of Christian teaching that relies on enduring truth (even if that notion is eschatologically and analogically tempered, renouncing claims to exhaustiveness or totality). For the Torinese, it is not the certainty that springs from faith that leads to a "weakening" of some theological positions; rather, it is the recognition of the "twilight of Being," of the ambiguous nature of "truth," and of the consequent "lightening" of reality, that lead, ineluctably, to *pensiero debole.* Insofar as truth is a productive interpretation that makes no representational claims, that renounces any isomorphism with the *ontos on,* then the Vattimian understanding of weakening is, despite some noted convergences, quite distinct from any theological developments that have occurred.

Vattimo, hermeneutics and theology

Hermeneutics (even if not hermeneutical nihilism) has become increasingly important for theology precisely because the robust truth-claims of Christianity have been forced to come to grips with the historical, socio-cultural and linguistic conditioning that necessarily attend such assertions. Abiding and enduring truth-claims have been met head-on by the acids of temporality. The result: metaphysics has transmogrified into continuing interpretation; stable truth-claims have acquired a new sensitivity to historicity; and hermeneutics has become the *koinē* of contemporary philosophy. This development accounts for the continuing and substantial influence of Heidegger and Hans-Georg Gadamer in present-day theology. Heidegger insisted that the primordial basis of existence is temporality. Humanity is always already constituted by historical embeddedness, by temporal immersion, by human finitude and thrownness. This explains Heidegger's attempt to return philosophical thinking to the pre-Socratics, to the locus where Being was thought more primordially and disclosively before it "hardened" and "objectified" into the Platonic-Aristotelian idea-essence-*ousia*.

Gadamer, for his part, intensifies Heidegger's thought (particularly his deconstruction of the prior metaphysical tradition), bringing it to hermeneutical fruition by showing how historical embeddedness has profound and irrefragable effects upon all textual readings. It is precisely the deeply conditioned nature of human existence that accounts for Gadamer's pointed remarks against Wilhelm Dilthey, who asserted that understanding (*Verstehen*) presupposes an ultimate substratum of a common human nature that serves as the matrix for reconstructive readings. Husserl, too, posited the transcendental ego of subjectivity as the ground from which to establish a rigorous science.[184] But, Gadamer argues, it is precisely this Platonic-Kantian-Husserlian "metaphysical" axis that must be rejected as ontologically and a fortiori hermeneutically inappropriate. And his logic has a sterling clarity: the "metaphysical" positions outlined here hold for some consistent notion of "human nature" which serves as an anthropological substratum for interpretation. In turn, this Archimedean point warrants the notion of reconstructive hermeneutics whereby one can "escape" the profound effects of temporality and human finitude by reconstructing the stable meaning embedded in texts centuries or even millennia later. The recovered, determinate meaning can then be re-expressed in new ways, in fresh linguistic formulations, even while preserving the essential "recovered" content. But it is precisely *this* notion of hermeneutics that Heidegger and Gadamer have rejected.

Vattimo's hermeneutical theory, for its part, is deeply influenced by Heidegger and Nietzsche (and by Gadamer as well, despite his disappointment that Gadamer reads Nietzsche out of the tradition and illegitimately sanctions a Hegelian "unity of history").[185] Nietzsche's insight that facts always devolve into embedded interpretations, that interpretation goes "all the way down," and that the "world has become a fable" together with Heidegger's recognition that Being manifests itself only irruptively, leads us to understand that there is no ultimate, overarching historical unity. We are left, rather, with a vast array of differing positions. The world is constantly "rewritten"; contingent and provisional interpretations are unceasing. Vattimo has little interest, then, in "reconstructive" hermeneutics, i.e., in the recovery of a stable textual meaning that endures over the course of time. Such "literal," objectivist interpretation is ontologically inappropriate for the simple reason that we have no philosophical warrant—such as a common human nature—to sanction it. With regard to Scripture, therefore, the locus of meaning is not to be found in the text itself (since there exists no theoretical basis for reconstructive understanding), but only in the *continuing reinterpretation of the Bible by the community*. We see here the roots of Vattimo's logic: (1) reconstructive interpretation, based as it is on some naïve and outdated metaphysical notion of enduring *physis*, is untenable (as Gadamer has already forcefully argued); (2) the locus of textual meaning, then, (in this case biblical meaning) is found in the community which is continually engaged in reinterpreting the Scriptures. To support his position, Vattimo argues that Christ himself says that he will impart the "spirit of truth" who will lead us into the fullness of truth (which, Vattimo says, occurs by continually reinterpreting the content of Jesus' own teachings) (*BE*, 49). And, he adds, with on eye on restraining any violent readings: "Charity is the only limit to the spiritualization of the biblical message" (*AC*, 48).

Very important to the Torinese on this point, and improbably adduced as a witness in several of his books, is the perennially fascinating Joachim da Fiore, whose work provides support for this "continual reinterpretation of the biblical message" (*BE*, 61). Who is Joachim? A brief word will indicate the essence of his thought as well as his continuing relevance for Vattimo. Joachim was a 12th century monk and abbot living in Calabria, Italy. He had a dramatic view of history, clearly discernable in his understanding of how the Holy Trinity is revealed over time. The Trinity is experienced in three stages: the Old Testament (with its accent on law) reveals the age of the Father; the New Testament (with its accent on humanity's adoption in Christ) reveals the age of the Son; finally, a new (and still coming) age will be representative of the Spirit, who will encourage a more "spiritual" understanding of both biblical testaments.[186] In the traditional typology, then, Joachim endorses three ages, with the final step being the crowning glory of *spiritual rather than literal* understanding. In one sense, history has been completed—revelation has, indeed, been given in Israel and in Christ Jesus. But in another sense it still awaits the Age of the Spirit, which will offer the fullness of eschatological and mystical understanding.

Vattimo's attraction to Joachim is not hard to discern. Joachim's "Age of the Spirit," of illuminative spiritual understanding, becomes the prototype that the Torinese uses to buttress his own claims about continual biblical reinterpretation, about the end of Christian doctrine, about a newly bestowed liberative and emancipatory hermeneutics far from constraining institutional and fundamentalist strictures (the very locus of the moral-metaphysical God). The Age of the Spirit, for Vattimo, is nothing other than the continued unfurling of *pensiero debole*, the progressive unrolling of the kenotic Christianity which dissolves all strong metaphysical claims, including religious ones. He declares, in tones reminiscent of Hegel, that "the history of salvation announced by the Bible realizes itself in world historical events . . ." (*AC*, 41). This is simply to say that in the continuing march of history, metaphysics is slowly resolving itself in interpretative nihilism and in societal secularization, a process which is itself, in Christian terms, the effect of *caritas* now temporally unfurled. All of civilization is directed toward this weakening of Being. History here has a clear meaning and direction: the dissolution of strong structures. And this interpretation is fully congruent with Joachim's "spiritual" understanding of the Bible, which "lightens" and surpasses the merely literal, doctrinal sense of the text.

Joachim's "method" allows Vattimo to interpret the Bible—indeed, to reconstruct the entire meaning of salvation history—in light of *pensiero debole*, that "weakening" which recognizes Being's destiny not as perduring, stable structure but as transitory disclosure. The ages of the Father and the Son now acquiesce before Joachim's age of the Spirit which, making no strong moral or doctrinal claims, supports the tolerance characteristic of vast hermeneutical plurality (*BYI*, 49–50). Joachim's hermeneutics allows Vattimo to overcome any "literal" interpretation of the Scriptures (especially those interpretations sanctioning "exclusionary" doctrinal or moral positions) in favor of a continuing reinterpretation limited only by the preclusion of violence. The Calabrian abbot has pointed us in the right direction by showing that the comprehensive meaning of Christianity still lies in the future, in the active reinterpretation that goes beyond the kind of simple ready-at-hand thinking that Heidegger condemned and that lurks in all moral-doctrinal teaching.[187]

Ultimately, Joachim serves as a legitimating prototype for Vattimo, signaling that his postmodern, postmetaphysical reinterpretation of Christianity is viable (and, indeed, deeply traditional), wherein "dogmatic" Christian faith is necessarily resolved into hermeneutical nihilism.[188] Vattimo argues that the literal interpretation of the Bible not only leads to the violence of the "natural sacred," but to countless aporeias, such as the defense of geocentrism against Galileo, the opposition to democratic constitutions for secular states and the insistence on the "absolute truth" of Christianity. These kinds of literal readings result in purely dominative, authoritarian approaches. What is needed is an *emancipatory*, spiritual reading of Scripture, something provided when *caritas* is taken as the foundational interpretative key. Joachim proleptically warns that the treacherous and permanent temptation of the church is to try to foreshorten the process of interpretation, to close down the meaning of texts, to "capture" the Event in a formulation and, even worse, to arrest historicity by appeal to some immutable natural law. But this results in a badly deformed hermeneutics both philosophically (since the Event continues to manifest and disclose itself in history) as well as theologically (inasmuch as the Spirit continues to illuminate the meaning of the text beyond the merely literal and "natural").

It is unsurprising, then, when Vattimo asserts: "It is not scandalous to conceive biblical revelation as an ongoing history in which we are implicated . . . which is not . . . the rediscovery of a core doctrine given once and for all as always the same . . ." (*BE*, 48). The Torinese's point is that revelation cannot be understood as materially identical Christian teaching enduring throughout history. Revelation is, rather, the working out of the parable of the kenosis, the resolution of all claims into weakness—obviously sanctioning, in the process, the continual and unending reinterpretation of both the Bible and Christian doctrine. That there can be a rewriting of even the most significant Christian teachings is defended by Vattimo on the basis of Joachimite spiritual teaching: the spirit of truth is sent by Jesus to allow the 'reinterpreting' of the content of Jesus' own doctrine (*BE*, 49). This is precisely what it means for the Christian church to be led by the Spirit—that there exists a continuing reinterpretation by the community of believers. And, for Vattimo, this "continuing reinterpretation" will be constituted by the dissolution of all strong doctrinal and moral claims in favor of the healing powers of the Bible's central message, inclusive, pluralistic, non-violent *caritas*.

For the Torinese, the most appealing aspect of Joachim's thought is the notion that salvation history is still in progress. This statement, of course, intends a profound truth: God's action is alive and vibrant today; revelation is, in one sense, always an ongoing event. But for Vattimo, we recall, "salvation" has a unique meaning: the dissolution of strong structures, the sanctioning of a capacious plurality which underwrites our emancipation. And this is precisely why Joachim is attractive. The Calabrian abbot provides proleptic support for the position that one cannot be "locked into" the literal meaning of texts; the text itself is now entirely *pliant and malleable*, patient of continuing reinterpretation.[189] Ultimately, for Vattimo, Joachim mystically underwrites Heidegger: there is no end to historicity, to the Event character of Being, to the dialectic of presence and absence. Joachim is an unwitting supporter of *pensiero debole* because continual reinterpretation in the age of the Spirit will, inevitably, break down strong structures with their imperious claims to final truth. For Joachim as for Vattimo, who knows what awaits us anew in the "age of the Spirit"? What new interpretation of human life will emerge next? Is it possibly the *caritas* of kenotic Christianity—the age of hermeneutical nihilism?

Reflections on Vattimo and theological hermeneutics

One may, of course, discern significant points of convergence between Vattimo's thought and contemporary theological reflection. For the Torinese clearly wishes to establish some strict correlation between the biblical message and the experience of the Christian community in the current historical moment. And this desire to call attention to the role of contemporary Christianity in its reception and "actualization" of the Gospel is entirely correct. For if the theological tradition is not to be lifelessly repeated, if it is to be vigorous and robust, it must be newly appropriated and, indeed, "performed" in every epoch. The Gospel message must be received and realized anew by each generation, in its own categories, according to its unique *Denkstil*. Absent some kind of correlation between the tradition and the present, there would result merely hidebound and monotonous reiteration. Correlation, then, rightly underscores unique appropriations that are simultaneously creative and complementary. This is what the 19th century Catholic theologian, Johann Evangelist Kuhn meant (in opposition to the neo-Scholasticism of his age) when he said that theology must be *zeitgemäss* and *geistlich*, timely and robust, capable of ever-new appropriations.[100] More recently, one sees just this kind of creative reformulation of the Gospel in feminist theology, in liberation and emancipatory thought, in Radical Orthodoxy, as well as in many other contemporary undertakings. Each intends to appropriate the tradition in a "performative" and vital way. In this sense, Vattimo rightly calls attention to the continuing hermeneutical role of the community, to the contemporary *actualization* of the Christian message.

We receive a deeper sense of Vattimo's point (and indeed, that of much contemporary theology) if we examine his discussion of the *érudit* in Nietzsche. In the essay, "On the Uses and

Disadvantages of History," Nietzsche heaps scorn on the mere *érudit* who knows the "facts of the matter" and is philologically competent. Of course, Nietzsche concedes, learned handymen are necessary for the cause of scholarship—but they can hardly be called thinkers (*DN*, 47). Their chief aim is to reproduce past historical events. And of this practice Nietzsche says with Christ: "Let the dead bury the dead!" He insists that historical knowing is not simply re-productive, a so-called, "faithful mirroring of the facts"; it must always be performative and vital, engaging in interpretations that are living and robust.[191] This is why Nietzsche found despicable the pedantic idea that the proper person to describe the past, the allegedly "objective" historian, was the one who had no actual interest in past events (94). This was a prizing of disinterested "objectivity" in the worst possible sense. For what gives life to history, truly enters into its dynamic and continuing meaning, is precisely intuitive force. Critical rigor is never suffi-cient since interpretation is always an act of engaged, vital life. As Nietzsche insists: "If you are to venture to interpret the past, you can do so only out of the fullest exertion of the present" (94).

With Nietzsche's (and Vattimo's) accent on interpretative perfor-mance, on living appropriation, theologians are in full agreement precisely because historical embeddedness does, indeed, dictate that the message of the Gospel be made *zeitgemäss* and *geistlich*, timely and vigorous, actualized for new epochs, cultures and peoples. Neither the biblical message nor Christian doctrine may be mum-mified and wizened; they need continual reformulation in order to be made intelligible and available for new cultures, ages and societies. Of course, Vattimo's dismissal of the mere "*érudit*" is ulti-mately in service to his accent on the role of the community in the continuing reinterpretation of the Gospel. When he states, for example, that not every interpretation is valid because "it must be valid for a community of interpreters" (*AC*, 67), he is both stress-ing the significance of contemporary experience as well as grop-ing for some criterion of interpretative adequacy beyond the random and the idiosyncratic. Although virtually all theologians would agree with this emphasis on the living community and, therefore, on the necessity of some kind of correlation between the biblical text, the creedal tradition and contemporary experi-ence, the truly contentious issue remains: how is this correlation precisely envisioned? How does the "present situation" of the engaged, graced community compare as a theological locus with Scripture and the early creeds of the Church? If the tradition, even its most solemn biblical and creedal pronouncements, does not sufficiently illuminate the culture, or seems no longer meaningful according to the standards of the contemporary historical moment or does not sufficiently implement (by Vattimo's standards) inclusive kenotic *caritas*, does this not mean that such statements are to be jettisoned, adulterated or radically reinterpreted?

As we have already observed, Vattimo is uninterested in the material continuity of biblical or doctrinal teachings. The standard of interpretation employed by the community of interpreters is never anchored, therefore, to any Scriptural or creedal *fundamentum in re*. And precisely here a major difficulty emerges. On the basis of his reading of Joachim, as well as his own understanding of *pensiero debole*, Vattimo would allow a re-reading of Scripture and the early tradition that is, in fact, a complete reinterpretation (indeed, often a total reversal) of their previous meaning. And this hermeneutical move is legitimate on several Vattimian grounds. In the first place, there exists no ontological warrant which would sanction reconstructive interpretation. That is to say, there exists no stable "ground" which would allow for the kind of hermeneutical strategy which supports—precisely by means of reconstructive readings—the material continuity of Christian doctrine in history. Without some kind of metaphysical anthropology, reconstructive reading (which Vattimo always brands as mere "literalism") is itself impossible. Secondly, Heidegger has shown us that the Being as disclosive is always deeply linked to temporality, a profound evanescence that itself militates against any notion of material continuity and identity over time. Thirdly, Joachim has shown that we are moving toward the "Age of the Spirit," allowing for a Spirit-guided interpretation which has kenotic *caritas* as its leitmotiv, thereby dissolving the merely literal which has reigned heretofore. Fourthly, Vattimo insists that his entire interpretative strategy simply replicates that of Christ who totally "hermeneuticizes" the Mosaic Law, effectively reducing it to the Great Commandment.

Of course, if one places such a pronounced accent on the experience of the community in reinterpreting the biblical and doctrinal tradition, this necessarily raises the question as to the extent that revelation, in its linguistic articulation in the Scriptures and creedal statements of the early Church, can be taken as ostensive and representational. Can Scripture and the creeds simply be "re-written" on the basis of the contemporary experience which is (finally) seeing the full implications of kenotic *caritas*? Vattimo would surely answer positively given that the *ontos on* is unavailable to us, the world is always subject to differing interpretations and objective, representational readings have no philosophical warrant. The "rewriting" of the world is, indeed, the only viable hermeneutical option as both Nietzsche and Heidegger (somewhat less ostentatiously) saw. Re-readings are only adequate, it should be added, to the extent that they have the support of a community of interpreters, but the community is never beholden to some apriori scriptural or creedal standard (which "standard" is itself, deeply historicized).

In clear distinction from the position held by Vattimo, Christian teachings, especially as stated in the creeds of the undivided church, can never be understood as simply provisional and contingent affirmations, open to reversal in their fundamental meanings—as if such claims were merely pragmatic and prudential judgments, having the status of Aristotle's *endechomena*, matters that could be otherwise. For the Christian faith holds that certain fundamental and authoritative beliefs, linguistically articulated as creedal statements, are universally, normatively and continuously true in and through varying cultures and generations. Christianity argues, then, that these beliefs are stable and selfsame, with a fundamentally perduring dimension throughout history.[192] Christian theology, consequently, needs a hermeneutical theory that is able to sustain and support two conjunctive elements: on the one hand perduring and stable identity over the course of ages and cultures; on the other, the possibility of change and development (thereby always allowing "actualization" by the community of believers). At stake is a hermeneutical theory that can take account of the horizons of historical embeddedness and socio-cultural determination (and in this sense Heidegger, Gadamer and Vattimo are entirely correct), while also clearly displaying the material continuity and identity of the Christian faith throughout history. What is required is a hermeneutical theory congruent with Pascal's aphorism: "A pluralism that cannot be integrated into unity is chaos; unity unrelated to plurality is tyranny."[193]

Context/Content

One way of seeking to preserve the material continuity of Christian doctrine—even while recognizing the indefeasible effects of historicity, including the socio-cultural determination of thought and language—has been to make a distinction between the materially continuous "content" of doctrine and varying and culture-specific contexts. In the Roman Catholic Church, for example, this hermeneutical approach helped to overcome the theological strictures of neo-scholasticism. John XXIII utilized the distinction in his opening speech of Vatican II and it has been endlessly cited by Catholic theologians as well as by official ecclesial documents.[194]

Other Christian churches have sanctioned this approach as well, either explicitly or—as is usually the case—implicitly, by means of their ecumenical statements. A couple of examples may be noted: Different churches have been willing to come to agreement on the nature of Christ's presence in the Eucharist even while invoking incommensurable models or paradigms describing such presence. No church sees itself as thereby abandoning the fundamentals of its faith, but as casting its substantial doctrinal affirmations in new lexicons that are less bound to one particular language or *Denkstil*. On the question of the Eucharist, for example, the Lutheran church has strongly affirmed Christ's "Real Presence" in the sacrament while demurring from the term "transubstantiation" lest a particular philosophy be seen as essential to the description of Christ's presence in the consecrated elements. Roman Catholicism sees the nub of the matter as Christ's subsisting presence in the consecrated bread and wine, regarding the term "transubstantiation" as one possible way of speaking, but as inessential to expressing its faith. For both Lutheranism and Catholicism, a variety of ways of expressing Christ's actual presence in the Sacrament is possible, thereby protecting the essential "content" of belief while allowing for a wide berth in theological expression or formulation.[195]

More recently, one sees the same approach in the *Joint Declaration on Justification* agreed upon by both the Lutheran World Federation and the Roman Catholic Church. Both communities see their faith represented in the document even if they use concepts and terminology that have not been traditional for them. In the *Declaration*, for example, the language of causality which had been dominant in Roman Catholicism since the time of Aquinas and authoritative since the council of Trent is nowhere to be found. And yet the Catholic Church is insistent that the more existential and biblical "form" which characterizes the agreement fully represents the faith expounded at Trent. For the Lutherans, the "forensic" paradigm which had dominated certain interpretations of Luther's thought on justification was read as not occluding the notion of graced, interior renewal that one finds in the *Declaration*.[196]

For all Christian churches, this distinction between content and context, although not without difficulties, has proven to be a fruitful strategy. It acknowledges that concepts and theological lexicons are deeply affected by a congeries of historical and socio-cultural elements while simultaneously recognizing the possibility of fundamental meaning-invariance over time. But this notion that there *can* be meaning-invariance in and through reconceptualization—that concepts may be reformulated while preserving an essentially stable and determinate meaning—itself demands certain philosophical commitments. I have recounted the basics of this position elsewhere, arguing that once one abandons an eidetically discernable *humanum* it becomes impossible to establish intelligibly (as opposed to fideistically asserting) the material identity and perduring truth of central Christian affirmations *in and through* profound differences in societies and cultures.[197] Here it is enough to say that Vattimo would, without a moment's doubt, reject this position as positing an ontological ground, a common *physis* among human beings, which would undergird both reconstructive understanding (and so stability of meaning) as well as the possibility of continuing reformulation, thereby theoretically underwriting the context-content approach. Vattimo (like Gadamer) would no doubt argue that the radically historical nature of human existence does not allow for the possibility of any such hermeneutical approach.

In addition, any accent on the material continuity of Christian doctrine, its stable and determinate meaning, cannot be countenanced by Vattimo for it violates several of his core principles: Joachim's opening to the new age with its "spiritual interpretation"; the transitory character of the disclosive Event of Being; and the "lightening" of structures called for by *pensiero debole*. Consequently, the church must always resist the continuing "metaphysical temptation" to come to a stable formulation such as a dogmatic definition, a perduring creedal statement or, worse, an authoritative decision in the bioethical realm under the rubric of human nature. What Vattimo rebels against here is the attempt to contain the Event within a particular formulation, to harden Being "within the authoritarian boundaries of dogma" (*AC*, 82).

The Torinese, on the contrary, wants to sanction not the material continuity and identity of meaning over time but a *formal continuity* of interpreters who, reflecting on the same text (the Bible), constantly offer new and productive understandings guided entirely by the living experience of the community rather than by the biblical or creedal statements themselves. Of course, this dilution of material continuity is inextricably linked with Vattimo's dissolution of "metaphysics": there can be no objectifying representations of "revelation"; new and possibly conflicting re-readings will surely emerge over time. It goes without saying that interpretative conflict is not only possible but entirely likely since the "march" of interpretation inexorably follows the Nietzschean notion that the world has become a fable, that there exists no discoverable *ontos on*. This allows for a continual rewriting of the world without much concern for synthesizing such wide-ranging plurality. And the Joachimite "Age of the Spirit" is adduced in support of this position because it goes beyond literal interpretation to a spiritual understanding of Scripture in which tolerant, non-exclusionary *caritas* will predominate.

Once again, virtually all theologians would agree with Vattimo that the fundamentals of Christian faith and doctrine, the affirmations of Nicea and Chalcedon for example, need to be productively reappropriated and "performed" in every new epoch and culture. But the ongoing interpretation of the contemporary Christian community must itself be guided and normed by the fundamental meanings found in Scripture and in the creeds themselves.

Vattimo speaks of the church as the community of believers who *hear and interpret freely* the meaning of the Christian message (*AC*, 9). But are there no constraints on interpretation, besides Vattimian non-exclusionary *caritas*? Further, it must be clearly stated that Christian doctrine never "closes down" historical consciousness inasmuch as all doctrine is subject to continuing development, balancing, refinement and precision. It is no surprise that Aquinas, as earlier noted, defined the article of faith as *perceptio divinae veritatis tendens in ipsam* (*ST*, II–II, q. 1, a. 6). It is precisely this *tendens* that recognizes the limited epistemological yield and ultimately eschatological nature of doctrinal statements And as Karl Rahner's seminal essay on Chalcedon has it, ecumenical councils offer a *beginning* for thinking about the mystery of Christ: "The clearest formulations, the most sanctified formulas, the classic condensations of centuries-long work of the church in prayer, reflection and struggle concerning God's mysteries: all these derive their life from the fact that they are not end but beginning."[198] And what Rahner says of Christology is true, of course, of all Christian teaching, whether concerning the Incarnation, the Trinity, Justification, the Eucharist and so the list continues. This is the thesis widely accepted by all theologians that no doctrine is ever exhaustive; the final intelligibility of Christian teaching will only be revealed in the heavenly Jerusalem. As Pannenberg rightly says: "Christians should not need to be taught this by modern reflection on the finitude of knowledge that goes with the historicity of experience."[199]

Vattimo, unfortunately, misses all of this careful theological reflection. He would reject it in any case since there remains a Christian insistence on some modest "objectifying" thinking. And, of course, the context-content approach to hermeneutics, even with its strong accent on the actuality of the socio-cultural conditioning of formulations, and with its emphases on the speculative incompleteness of every Christian doctrine, would be found wanting by Vattimo precisely because this hermeneutical path continues to argue for stable and determinate meaning through time, thereby limiting the possibility of endless rewriting and reinterpretation.

If one accepts Vattimo's principles in an unqualified way, with its hermeneutical nihilism, with Being as epiphanically disclosive, with the world now a fable, then the yield of interpretation is, needless to say, very different from epoch to epoch, from culture to culture, from generation to generation. The Torinese rejects any notion of a eidetically discernable human nature, which provides the ontological foundation for reconstructive interpretation. In this sense, both Gadamer and Vattimo are clearly Heideggerians, thinking that historicity has deconstructed the very notion of an enduring *physis*. Gadamer tries to stem the tide of interpretative relativism by arguing that all interpretations take place within an already established tradition so that there is a "fusion of horizons" between the past and the present; he invokes, as well, his notion of the perduring "claim" as one way of arguing for interpretative adequacy. But Vattimo, we remember, finds Gadamer entirely too wedded to his own Hegelian-inspired hermeneutics with its over-arching historical unity. The Torinese argues, to the contrary, that Gadamer himself needs a strong dose of nihilism precisely in order to temper his claim that he has finally found the "winning name" of Being. Vattimo, then, will hardly sanction Gadamer's moderating influences. He has told us, it is true, that interpretation is not a matter of "everything goes" (*AC*, 82). He implies, rather, that the community's recognition of the fruitfulness of an interpretation, its benefits as outlined in dialogue and consensus, now become the standard for interpretative adequacy even while renouncing any isomorphism with the *ontos on*.

Again, with Vattimo's accent on the hermeneutical importance of the living community of believers one can readily agree. But, he insists, this community can never be normed by apriori meanings stemming from the Scriptures or from early creedal statements. As such, interpretation is entirely unhinged from the founding, Spirit-guided decisions made in the church's own life. The interpretative process becomes for Vattimo a entirely malleable, open-ended, productive generation of Being, resulting, at least theoretically, in a Christianity without definitive content, or, perhaps more accurately, a content that is subject to consistent and continuing mutability.

Conclusion

What can finally be said about Vattimo and Christian theology? Are the two "ideas" so deeply disjunctive that one can hardly utter them in the same breath?

Desire for God

I think, in the first place, one should call attention to the desire for God that animates all of Vattimo's recent writings. Like a moth drawn to a flame, Vattimo comes back again and again to the God-question and to the person of Jesus of Nazareth. To be sure, Vattimo is no paradigm of Christian orthodoxy—as he willingly admits—usually offering thematic interpretations deeply incongruous with the God preached by historical Christian faith. Nonetheless, his work represents a desire for God, a desire making it difficult for him simply to "walk away" from religion entirely. Indeed, Vattimo attacks atheism on philosophical grounds, as a latter-day purveyor of *pensiero forte*—but one senses that this repugnance for militant atheism has personal as well as theoretical dimensions.

Vattimo's understanding of the divine resonates, at least in certain aspects, with Meister Eckhart's mystical God beyond God, with the Event who resists the surfeit of presence found in claims to final, concrete instantiations of the divine. Even though he rejects speaking of God as the "wholly other" and distinguishes himself from Derrida's bare expectation of *l'autre*—precisely because such language loses the New Testament accent on kenotic charity—one nonetheless sees convergences with the traditional "wholly other" approach. God is now conceived as entirely beyond concrete images, symbols and formulations; even the seemingly bare attribute of "existence" is threatening since it tries to "tie God down" to determinate historical events, to ontological bedrock, thereby violating the evanescent and irruptive nature of Being.

In one sense, Vattimo is saying that we fail to do God justice in our attempts to "enclose" him historically, representationally, objectively, "metaphysically." He seeks, rather, to develop the notion of a non-metaphysical God, a God "after metaphysics." Surely this is understandable for the God of Israel, the God of Jesus Christ, is hardly a "metaphysical" God in Vattimo's dyslogistic understanding of this ancient term.

There is also, in Vattimian thought, a championing of Christian charity, even if this *caritas* is uniquely understood as non-exclusionary tolerance, as the sanctioning of vast interpretative plurality, as the renunciation of any claims to final truth. Here, too, however, there are glimpses in Vattimo of a bolder, transcendent charity which supersedes mere tolerance and the abjuration of an aggressive and violent *pensiero forte*. There is an attraction to Christ and to the Christian message, to the vulnerable and loving God who is revealed in the story of the Incarnation, even if the Torinese does not allow himself to make any "strong" commitment to the actual existence of a Creator. But why then pray as Vattimo tells us he does (*BE*, 92)? Why bother with prayer if one sought only to construct the rationalist god of philosophy? Vattimo forthrightly calls himself a Christian (*FR*, 66), and a "good Catholic."[200] Indeed, at times, he appears only to protest against a suffocating ecclesial institutionalism which stifles proper Christian freedom, sounding more than a bit like the stereotypical village anti-clericalist.

Ultimately, however, one must ask Vattimo precisely what his firm affirmation of Christian identity means? As we have seen, he tends to attribute this identity to his socio-cultural embeddedness as a European and an Italian, endlessly citing Benedetto Croce's salute to cultural tradition, "We cannot but call ourselves Christians" (*ADG*, 36). He also tells us, invoking Voltaire as an example, that being a good Christian means standing for freedom (which we should read as the kind of emancipation wrought by hermeneutical nihilism). As he explains, ". . . by standing for freedom, this includes freedom from (the idea of) truth" (*ADG*, 37). And even though Vattimo prays the Lord's Prayer, he is compelled to add, "I pray these words more for the love of a tradition than I do for the love of some mythic reality" (*ADG,* 42).

As is clear, then, Vattimo backs away from committing himself to the kind of definitive claims that Christ and the Christian message indefeasibly make. These assertions seem to him, once again, to replicate a Platonic escape to a reified, ahistorical "being"—to a fable—far from the incessant and enveloping tides of contingency and provisionality. His religious identity, therefore, despite his continuing fascination with Christianity, is entirely reconceived according to his own philosophical faith, a faith that cannot see the "unconditioned" revealed in historical conditionality. Vattimo certainly wishes to give Christianity a hearing, even to reintroduce its lexicon into the public square, but it must now be deeply reconceived, indeed, even betrayed in its fundamental instincts. Because of his commitments to Heidegger and Nietzsche, one may legitimately suspect that a theological dialogue with Vattimo simply exemplifies the ancient axiom *bibere venenum in auro*, drinking poison from a golden cup—which is simply to say that while his work sounds beguilingly Christian, hidden poison lurks beneath the seductive and coquettishly "charitable" message. Even with this said, however, Vattimo's personal attraction to Christianity cannot be denied. And does he not stand where many men and women of our day stand—but perhaps even closer to Christianity, precisely because he is willing to give Christ some hearing?

Fides quaerens intellectum *or* intellectus quaerens fidem?

A central issue in Vattimo's thought, perhaps *the* central issue, is the relationship between reason and faith, between philosophy and theology. He tells us that he was able to establish a serendipitous link between rationality and Christianity with both resolved into *pensiero debole* (*BE*, 36). Vattimo's phrasing of this issue (with its claim of a new insight into the relationship between faith and philosophy) immediately calls to mind Heidegger's decisive letter of 1919, wherein he states: "Epistemological insights, extending as far as the theory of historical knowledge, have made the *system* of Catholicism problematic and unacceptable to me—but not Christianity and metaphysics (the latter to be sure, in a new sense)."[201] Something of this same sentiment, although in a different key, is at work in Vattimo. He seeks to be, in some sense, a

Christian, but one who, Heidegger-like, thinks about Christianity within the parameters of truth and Being as transitorily irruptive and historically evanescent rather than as consistently enduring. Consequently, Christianity itself needs to be rethought along very different lines than has heretofore been the case.

Heidegger, at least briefly, found a guide in Bultmann and the existentialist interpretation of Christian faith that clustered around Marburg. As Gadamer says: "It was clear to Heidegger that it would be intolerable to speak of God like science speaks about its objects; but what that might mean, to speak of God—this was the question that motivated him and pointed out his way of thinking."[202] And this intention surely motivates Vattimo as well and rightly so. For the Torinese is trying to think God anew, beyond the pitfalls of *Vorhandenheit* reasoning, beyond simple and unremitting presence and comprehensiveness. This explains his marked accent on Joachim's Age of the Spirit with its strongly eschatological and futurist dimensions (now coming to fruition in *pensiero debole*). It also explains the "happy convergence" he finds uniting the thought of Nietzsche, Heidegger and Christ. But it is just at this point that the questions become pointed: Having discovered some congruence among the three, which figure takes precedence? Are "spoils" taken from Nietzsche and Heidegger in order to elucidate the truth of the Christian faith? Or is it Christianity that yields "spoils" to a pre-existing Heideggerian notion of Being and a Nietzschean notion of a "constructed" world?

It should certainly be acknowledged that Vattimo does not blindly follow Heidegger and Nietzsche. The Torinese, in fact, chides the two philosophers for failing to see the possibilities of Christianity, the very "weakening" inherent in its accent on kenosis, an emphasis ultimately conjunctive with their own theoretical tendencies toward *pensiero debole*. Further, Vattimo takes his continual invocation of Christian *caritas* as a significantly limiting factor on the potential violence always lurking within nihilism. He is well aware that there are aspects of Nietzsche's thought that could result in self-assertive savagery if not tempered and domesticated by Christianity's insistence on charity and its parable of kenotic self-emptying (both of which bespeak inclusive tolerance). The creative "will to power," unconstrained by a *logos* order of reality, untethered to any objective, metaphysical laws, easily becomes the arena where the most ruthless triumph—and thus the essential adduction of Christianity's unique contribution. Vattimo does try to rescue Nietzsche from the most damaging consequences of nihilism by frequently citing his comments in the *Writings from the Late Notebooks* where he concludes, ". . . Who will prove to be the *strongest?* The most moderate, those who have no *need* of extreme articles of faith, who not only concede but even love a good deal of contingency and nonsense, who can think of man with a considerable moderation of his value and not therefore become small and weak. . . ."[203] But Vattimo realizes he is on much firmer ground when he drags Nietzschean nihilism through the ringer of kenotic Christianity. For Christianity restrains and dilutes the tendency of nihilism to result simply in a Hobbesian *bellum omnium contra omnes.* In this sense, then, Vattimo's Christianity serves to inhibit and constrain any tendencies to violence that could result from the sanctioning of an entirely unrestricted plurality.

Even with this limiting factor, however, it must be clearly stated that Vattimo remains deeply in thrall to Nietzsche and Heidegger, the twin thinkers who ultimately—surely more than the biblical Christ—guide his thought. The very trope of "spoils from Egypt" about which we have spoken, presumes a certain acceptance of Christianity as the story of the world, a story which, nonetheless, may learn from and, ultimately assimilate, elements from other narratives, even opposing ones. In Vattimo's telling, however, Christianity expresses theologically ("transcribes" is his usual description) what is true philosophically.[204] By this he means that Christianity sustains, gives impulse to, theologically underwrites, what ultimately is the philosophical *sublation* of Christianity. Even if kenotic Christianity gives birth to "weak thought" (by unleashing certain tendencies in the West), it is the philosophical *pensiero debole* into which the story of Christ and the church is integrated and, in its primary affirmations, diluted and dissolved. This, of course, is nothing less than the classical Hegelian *Aufhebung* of religion by philosophy—the annulment, accommodation and erasure of the Christian singular through the sublation of the finite. In Vattimian thought, the sensible form of Christianity is finally absorbed by a sophisticated, spiritually aware, philosophical consciousness. The *concretissimum* of Christianity is resolved in a secularizing *caritas* which is, ultimately, simply the tolerance extended to vast and inclusive pluralism. And this tolerance itself, in the last analysis, is the result of a purely philosophical idea: the move away from "objectivity," from representational thought, from Hellenism, from "metaphysics," toward the triumph of limitless plurality and *pensiero debole*. "Spoils from Jerusalem" rather than "spoils from Egypt" here becomes the guiding trope. And Jerusalem is adduced simply to confirm the perspicuous insights of a Nietzschean "Athens." One can understand, then, why Hans Urs von Balthasar reserved some of his most poisonous invective for Hegel and for speculative Idealism. And why Barth lamented that Hegel, despite his kaleidoscopic brilliance, could never serve as Protestantism's philosophical lodestar. Unlike Pascal and Kierkegaard who, despite all their limitations, came face to face with the crucified Christ, Hegel subsumes the historical form into the dialectic of Absolute Spirit. The finite is marginalized so that God's unique and specific act of love is no longer recognizable. In Vattimo's thought, one discerns an entirely parallel Hegelian move.

Of course, Vattimo wants us to think about religious disclosure *in history*, rather than regarding it as an essentialist, reified block of unchanging truth. And this view has significant purchase in that it legitimately concentrates on the actualization of truth in time rather than understanding temporality as "accidental" to theological thinking. Historicity surely cannot be understood dyslogistically, as an obstacle to the realization of revelation. Such a pejorative view would be entirely inappropriate given Christianity's own deep roots in God's salvific action in the history of Israel and in the life of Jesus of Nazareth. Ironically, however, while Vattimo wants to live an authentically religious life in a world profoundly marked by temporality, his philosophy tends to sublate the specific and determinately historical dimensions of Christianity in service to the philosophical *idea* of an overarching "weak thought," with religion now emptied of its historical specificity for the sake of the secularized philosophy of hermeneutical nihilism. Christianity here is a parable which only finds its fulfillment and reaches its zenith (now stripped of mythology) in the insights of Heidegger and Nietzsche. But this dissolution of Christian specificity into an alleged philosophical "universality" is the quintessential move of the modernity that Vattimo so vigorously opposes, leading one to wonder to what extent his *Verwindung* of the "modern" attitude toward religion has been accomplished. The fundamental narrative of modernity remains the same; only the philosophers invoked (Nietzsche and Heidegger rather than Hegel) have exchanged places. Vattimo often protests that he wishes to offer no full-blown schema of world-history. Nonetheless, his reflections on the meaning of *caritas*, the gradual working out of kenotic Christianity (which comes to fruition in secularization) certainly has the ring of a world-scale narrative in which transcendence is ultimately emptied out into immanence, the church into the world, revelation into secularization.[205]

For Vattimo, the Christian story is ultimately a parable, a cipher, which gives rise to certain ideas (such as kenosis and *caritas*) but which can never itself be regarded as ontological bedrock; indeed, Christianity comes to fulfillment in the very opposite of such bedrock, *pensiero debole*. As such, his interpretation of Scripture, as well as of doctrinal and creedal teaching, is normed by nothing other than philosophical reasoning itself. Of course, for any traditional notion of Christianity, faith purifies reason, teaching it, opening it up to new dimensions of human anthropology and the drive for self-transcendence. On the other hand, reason itself is not simply *discens* and not also *docens*. The first Vatican council of the Roman Catholic Church spoke of faith and reason as "mutually supporting each other." John Paul II adds that each offers to the other a "purifying critique" as well as a stimulus to pursue deeper understanding.[206] There exists, then, a kind of coinherence between faith and reason, with each allowing the other, by way of criticism and argument, to come to fruition. Vattimo, however, empties Christianity of its uniqueness, offering religion not a "purifying critique" but an imperialistic colonization whereby the central claims of the faith must be diluted and dissolved before the Nietzschean assertion that the world has become a fable and the Heideggerian unmasking of Being as epiphanic.

Given this strong accent on the sweeping reach of philosophy, it is unsurprising that, for Vattimo, the human drive for self-transcendence is resolved neither in God nor in faith, but in emancipatory freedom, in humanity's liberation from constraining moral or doctrinal strictures. The thrust for self-transcendence comes to fruition only in a creative freedom limited solely by the non-violent, non-exclusionary imperative. Absent any notion of human nature or of a *logos*-structure to reality, the possibilities for autonomous personal creativity are virtually limitless. And this accounts for Vattimo's profound voluntarism. For "nature" is here the irremediable and transparent enemy of human autonomy. Only if *kosmos* and *physis* are stripped of their pretensions to provide a rule and measure for human being and acting is existence entirely pliant and protean—and, therefore, free. Any attempt to establish an ontological norm or canon, to insist on a constraining *ontos on*, is to invoke "metaphysics" thereby illegitimately limiting personal independence.[207] It is no surprise that Vattimo says that those rediscovering Christianity look to the teachings of the church and find only a rigid understanding of human nature, not the words of eternal life (*BE*, 62). In this comment, Vattimo echoes the traditional Nietzschean theme that Christianity constitutes nothing less than *ressentiment* against personal freedom and even against the vitality of life itself.

Just at this point, however, one wishes that Vattimo had taken account of religion's marked accent on the vigorous and dynamic freedom of humanity, a liberty that, properly ordered, mirrors the creative inner life of God. Human beings are here understood as embodied spirits, entering freely into relationships of love and friendship, respecting the transcendence of others in their own God-given autonomy, an autonomy and independence reflective of their constitution as *imago Dei*. This reflection of God's image in all men and women comes to fruition in the manifold creations of human intelligence, in philosophy and science, in art and music, in literature and theology—all indications of humanity's freedom and wisdom, its dependence on, yet profound similitude to the Creator.[208] For Vattimo, however, religion (if taken in any objectively true sense) necessarily militates against humanity's personal independence. While he acknowledges that we live within the ineradicable cultural horizon of "God," his ultimate desire, it seems, is to live the life of the Nietzschean Overman: the man who happily exists without foundations, who lives a life of nihilistic moderation, who is not afraid of the "dictatorship of relativism" which, precisely in its toleration of a vast plurality of ways of (non-violent) being, endorses the life of *pensiero debole*. And embracing the life of the Overman means, in Vattimian terminology, to have achieved the essential *Verwindung*—the healing-alteration-deformation—of Christianity itself.

Vattimo insists that Heidegger and Nietzsche have "opened our eyes" to new realities. It would be foolish, therefore, to grasp clutchingly at a premodern Christianity no longer tenable according to the canons of contemporary philosophical reason. And with this general Vattimian *principle*, one must be in full agreement. For Christian faith can never violate the postulates of reason, nor can reason and faith ever be at ultimate odds. Aquinas peerlessly expresses this point in his *Summa contra gentiles*, I, 7, arguing that, since both faith and reason are gifts of God, they must always ultimately concur. Indeed, just here one may turn the tables on Vattimo, wondering about the Nietzschean and Heideggerian positions that he advances as axiomatic. Without pretending to offer a fully rounded discussion of their philosophical claims, surely some pertinent questions may be addressed to those assertions that Vattimo regards as indispensably constitutive of contemporary thought. Is it, in fact, a *sacrificium intellectus* to believe in historic Christianity? Do its affirmations really violate established philosophical principles that have been shown to be entirely apposite?

Vattimo's thought rests on certain positions compressed in the following points: (1) there are no facts, only interpretations; (2) the world has become a fable; (3) Being is epiphanically disclosed, subject always to the contingent tides of historicity.

But are these positions philosophically irrefutable?

Even if it is entirely true—and I think it is undeniably the case—that there is a deep intertwining of facts and interpretations, has the stability of "facts" been thereby overthrown? Surely it is one thing to say that all observations are, to borrow Kuhn's term, theory-laden. But even if our knowledge of the world is mediated by varying conceptualizations and paradigms, even if we reject Baconian presuppositionless observation and disembodied thinking, must facts be entirely collapsed into interpretations so that there exists only radical incommensurability among differing construals of reality? Do not facts serve as objective norms, even if they are used differently in competing construals of reality?[209] Aristotle and Galileo, for example, both observed the "fact" of a heavy body swinging at the end of a chain which comes to rest only gradually. Galileo used this datum to argue for the movement of a pendulum, while Aristotle spoke of bodies' "constrained falls." Is there not a common level of observation that indicates the existence of perceptible facts, even if these are variously employed?[210] The salient point is that standards of appraisal cannot be entirely internal to particular paradigms or lexical structures without the very standards for knowledge themselves collapsing.

Then, too, there is this related question: do we really possess only the "constructed world" of the fable which, in Nietzsche's telling in *The Twilight of the Idols*, far outstrips Kant's phenomenal-noumenal distinction (which is explicitly mocked)? Is the world shaped only by the Babel of interpretative plurality and the restless will to power? Is there a legitimate warrant for this massive rejection of realism? Vattimo's (and Nietzsche's) position is that, because of our embeddedness, it is useless to speak of the isomorphism between our theories and the world since there exists no neutral Archimedean platform outside of the historical flux by which we could make such a judgment about congruency. Much more radically, they challenge the claim that there even exists a subsisting *ontos on* apart from the interpreter precisely because every interpreter is deeply involved in the *creation* of the world. But are such positions justified? Can there be knowledge of truth even without some theory-less, perspective-less, access to reality? Can experiment and inference yield knowledge of the "world" even for those who are, indeed, embedded interpreters? And can we not speak of a "world" that is always known in and through the paradigms of the interpreting subject, a world with its own subsistence?

Is *ousia*, taken as essence or substance, simply a hardened notion of presence that necessarily excludes historicity? Or is it perhaps an eidetically (*eidos*) discernable structure *within* the complex of temporality? Why must a legitimate accent on finitude preclude the possibility of a perduring *physis*? Has it, in fact, been decisively shown that inasmuch as the subject is inextricably intertwined with historicity, society, culture and language there can be, therefore, no perduring "nature"? Is the human person infinitely malleable, without a fundamental structure that governs human being and acting?

Does metaphysics, with its attempt at a universal grasp of the being of things, necessarily entail an erasure of and flight from historicity? Or, on the contrary, is it not possible that there exists a participatory structure to reality itself, that the theater of the world, the knowledge of the *esse* of beings, opens up toward the Infinite ground of existence—that just here there is intermingling of the metaphysical and the mystical as Plotinus argued and as several Christian writers did as well?[211]

Of course, the foregoing questions are hardly intended as conclusive arguments. They are meant, however, to challenge certain positions that Vattimo seems to accept as axiomatic. Nietzsche himself, of course, rarely made arguments for his positions, preferring the clever maxim to rigorous analysis. And although Vattimo is a gifted interpreter of Nietzsche, he too often follows him in this practice, failing to mount a vigorous defense of his adopted positions. The Torinese tells us endlessly that Nietzsche and Heidegger have brought a close to an objectifying, "metaphysical" notion of reality. But to what extent, in fact, is this actually the case?

Vattimo's Gnostic tendencies: The Vattimian glossary

Even with all of his insights, and with his noteworthy attempt to reintroduce Christian discourse into the public square from which it has been banished, one is finally forced to conclude that Vattimo's *Verwindung* of Christianity has Gnostic proclivities. For virtually every key term in the Christian mystery is profoundly reinterpreted, treated as an old wineskin to be filled with, and indeed ruptured by, a new and alien vintage. Of course, the Gnostic alarm can be too facilely sounded, condemning every interpretation that deviates from historic orthodoxy as mere Gnostic ideology. Nonetheless, Vattimo continually uses classical Christian locutions in a way that is audaciously different from the prior tradition, injecting a meaning entirely foreign to them. Inevitably, this calls to mind the well-known comment of the second-century writer, St. Irenaeus, who says in his *Against Heresies* that Gnostics, in their use of the Scriptures, are like those who take a handsome portrait of a king (skillfully crafted from jewels) and make of it a dog or a fox, rearranging the original pieces in an entirely new and less attractive order. Gnostics even have the temerity to declare that *this* is the original, beautiful picture of the king, thereby "deceiving the ignorant who had no understanding of the king's form."[212]

Of course, Vattimo himself candidly admits that he is seeking a *Verwindung* of Christianity, a healing which is also a convalescence and a deformation—so one should hardly expect a reiteration of historic Christian orthodoxy. It is precisely that outdated story, with its tight constraints on human freedom, with its doctrinal and moral literalism, that is in dire need of supersession. But if one examines the terminology Vattimo uses, observes his consistent and forceful reformulation of classical Christian meanings, one cannot fail to see the extent to which the *concretissima* of biblical belief are so completely reinterpreted that Christianity itself becomes virtually unrecognizable. In a few passages, it is true, Vattimo refers to the Incarnation, death and resurrection of Jesus but these in a brief and adventitious manner. The resurrection, in particular, appears to be absent from his thought and this for good reason. For if the Incarnation/kenosis represents God's "self-abasement," the abandonment of power and transcendence, then the resurrection represents Christ's reassertion of his transcendent divinity. If Vattimo at times refers to the first part of Philippians 2.6-11—the vulnerable kenosis of God—he inevitably fails to complete the passage which insists that every tongue should confess Christ as Lord. The Torinese, who has already accused Christianity of drifting into cultural senescence given its continued assertion of *pensiero forte*, forthrightly and revealingly states: ". . . if I have a vocation to recover Christianity, it will consist in the task of rethinking revelation in secularized terms in order to 'live in accord with one's age', therefore in ways that do not offend my culture as, to a greater or lesser extent, a man who belongs to his age" (*BE*, 75).

But this wish not to offend one's culture, to "live in accord with one's age," leads Vattimo ineluctably to overthrow the *scandalum particularitatis* of historical Christian faith—which can now only be believably retrieved through a profound reinterpretation of its content, a rethinking which is, finally, a reinterpretation leaning heavily on Nietzsche's and Heidegger's protest against stable, enduring presence. Consequently, "revelation," for Vattimo, is nothing other than the working out of the (symbolic) kenotic event in history, which is itself equivalent to the gradual dissolution of strong structures of any kind, of *pensiero forte*. Revelation can *never* be understood as the "core doctrine given once for all as always the same . . ." (*BE*, 48). It is rather, the dissolution of every objectifying, "metaphysical" teaching. As such, one "receives" revelation to the extent that one recognizes that all truth-claims must be procedurally and, of course, always provisionally, resolved. The "weakening" and "lightening" of Being, along with the continual unfurling of the kenotic parable of charity, necessarily leads to the warm embrace of hermeneutical nihilism, to the acceptance of a capacious and continual Babel-like plurality. In the last analysis, revelation is equivalent with *pensiero debole* itself. The story of the kenosis is, in fact, the "sacred symbolization" of philosophical weak thought.

If this is the meaning of revelation, then how is revelation's traditional correlate, faith or belief, to be properly understood? For Vattimo, as noted, faith is hardly trusting engagement with Jesus Christ. Even less so is it the acceptance of Christ's claims as articulated by Scripture and the early Christological creeds. Faith, rather, is the recognition that we are profoundly embedded interpreters who "cannot not be Christians." To profess Christian belief, then, is simply to profess faith in the "inevitability of a certain textual tradition that has been passed down to me" (*ADG*, 36). Having passed through the fires of Heidegger and Nietzsche, we now recognize that we are unavoidably "saturated" with a tradition. Faith simply acknowledges that we ineluctably live within these tight socio-cultural-religious bonds, this thick and determinate framework of meaning. To ask if this "tradition" is also true—if it mediates the world and describes states of affairs—is to invite Vattimo's response that such a question is philosophically naïve, implying that there exists a pre-existing *ontos on* waiting to be discovered. "Faith" which regards the Christian story as the *actual* story of God and the world is precisely the root of exclusionary violence, of intolerant assertion, of *pensiero forte*. Ultimately, Vattimian "faith" is the recognition that, insofar as all men and women live within different traditions, within differing interpretations of reality, then no one should press his or her position as "true," as isomorphic with the "world." This is exactly what it means to have "faith" in the postmetaphysical era, in the epoch of the lightening and twilight of Being.

If faith is not directly related to Jesus Christ (other than in the sense that the kenosis symbolically confirms philosophical "weakening"), then neither is salvation. This pregnant Christian term traditionally indicates that in Jesus of Nazareth one finds forgiveness of sins and the path to union with God and eternal life. Vattimian salvation, on the other hand, consists in the dilution of *pensiero forte* with its attendant exclusionary violence, inexorably resulting in personal emancipation. As he says, "the meaning of Christianity as a message of salvation consists above all in dissolving the peremptory claims of 'reality'" (*FR*, 49). That is to say, personal emancipation/salvation only occurs when hermeneutical nihilism is embraced, when every strong thought is diluted—including the notion that Jesus of Nazareth offers salvation to all of humanity. Again and again, Vattimo insists that salvation consists in a freedom that is not determined by any apriori notion of human nature, by any preconceived "metaphysical" understanding of reality or by any "strong" biblical teaching. Human beings are free to "create" the world, a world which, in any case, is always a constructed rather than a "given" reality. We are called, Nietzsche-like, to the life of the moderate Overman who can live with contradictions, with relativism, with varying construals of reality, without insisting on any particular form of truth. *This* is the fundamental meaning of postmetaphysical, postmodern salvation.

Of course, the term *caritas* also plays a significant part in Vattimo's thought. But charity should not be understood in the usual sense, as a theological virtue indicating the supernatural love that is poured into our hearts by grace thereby uniting human beings to God and neighbor. Vattimian *caritas* refers to one's openness toward the infinite interpretability of the world, toward the acknowledgment of the world as an interpretative bazaar, toward the embrace of vast hermeneutical pluralism. The truly "charitable" person is the one accepting of and imbued with *pensiero debole*, who offers no strong assertions, who claims to have no "representational" answers, who renounces the *ontos on*, who is tolerant toward all positions. *This* is the only viable meaning of charitable love of neighbor in a postmodern world of interpretative nihilism.

Sin, too, is entirely reinterpreted in the Vattimian lexicon. It is not, of course, a violation of charity traditionally construed, with the latter's insistence on constraining moral norms and literalist biblical commands. Sin is, instead, a violation of *caritas* now understood as the willing acknowledgment of vast interpretative plurality, of hermeneutical nihilism. Sin is, in fact, the reversion to *any strong moral-metaphysical position* (which is necessarily exclusionary and therefore violent by nature). Christianity is actually execrable when it reverts to strong positions because this is to violate the very *caritas* which recognizes an endless plurality of interpretations; it is to pretend to an inexistent metaphysical certitude. Any regression to *pensiero forte* is, in fact, a violation of Christianity itself which finds its *radix et origo* in the story of the vulnerable God become man, the one who himself renounced authority and strength in favor of weakness.

This Vattimian reinterpretation of religion is, indeed, radical. And it prompts one to ask again if Vattimo really surpasses the Enlightenment notion of religion? Does he offer a transgressive, postmodern *Verwindung*? Or is this just more of the same, a repackaging of "religion within the limits of reason alone" with the Master Narrative of rationality (itself, of course, weakened) now subsuming and sublating concrete faith into the philosophical pretensions of *pensiero debole*? It is entirely true, of course, that Vattimian rationality is no longer conceived along the bold contours of modernity. The Kantian insistence on critique is no longer supposed as the bright line separating rational "faith" from superstitious *Priesterkraft*. At the same time, doctrine, morality, sacraments, preaching, liturgy—none of this has a place in the Vattimian rethinking of Christianity. But isn't such an approach simply modernity revisited—with every foolish "superstition," including the Bible "freighted with myths," now subordinated to weak thought—to a reason which, even in its weakened state, must still master and domesticate faith? One might think, perhaps, of Niebuhr's familiar broadside against a vapid, content-less Christianity: "A God without wrath brought men without sin into a kingdom without judgment through the ministration of a Christ without a cross."[213] But Vattimo makes Niebuhr's "cultural" churchman look like a scholastic divine by comparison.

In the Vattimian understanding of Christianity, transcendence is reduced to immanence; the church identified with the emancipated world; revelation equated with continued secularization. And this reduction, Vattimo argues, constitutes Christianity's triumph and glory. But is this not ultimately the Gnostic dilution of Christianity into a philosophical idea, the Hegelian diremption of Spirit into world? The Enlightenment recognized the prophetic and apocalyptic power of religion, and, for that very reason, sought to keep it far from the public square. At first glance, Vattimo appears to be an ally to religious thought since he dismisses as a remnant of Enlightenment *pensiero forte* the claim that religion has no role in public discourse. But, in fact, Vattimo, too, thinks religion must be defanged, only permitted into the drawing room with the proviso that it renounce its essential identity and transmogrify into an entity void of specific content (an act, ironically, that is itself saturated with exclusionary violence). Vattimo's *Verwindung* is, effectively, a simple recrudescence of the public square shorn of religious belief and discourse, an aping of Enlightenment mythology.

Vattimo's insights make him a provocative thinker, a man eager to engage philosophically with traditional Christian and religious beliefs. In the final analysis, however, his thought seeks a sublimation of religion within a wider philosophical narrative, a subsumption that, ultimately, eviscerates Christian faith of its very meaning in favor of Nietzschean nihilism and Heideggerian temporality.

Even with this said, one wonders, nonetheless, if Vattimian thought, struggling as it does with the presence and absence of God, with the meaning of kenosis, with the Christian sense of *caritas,* with ineradicable human dignity, reveals, amidst all of its glaring defects and unacceptable reinterpretations, nothing so much as the Augustianian *cor inquietum*, the unceasingly restless heart that cannot ultimately live without transcendence.

Notes

14. Vattimo is dissatisfied with what he takes to be the position of dialectical theology on the issue of secularization. In the dialectical construal, secularization is understood positively insofar as it forces us to acknowledge God as "wholly other." But Vattimo finds this line of thinking (and the entire "wholly other" designation) too closely allied to Old Testament rather than Christian patterns of thought (*AC*, 36–37). For this reason, he wishes to distinguish his position from both the older "death of God" theologies as well from the more recent approach of Jacques Derrida for whom religion represents openness to radical alterity, where one says "*Viens*" to an unknown. Vattimo insists, to the contrary, on relating secularization to the explicitly Christian notions of kenosis and *caritas*, an emphasis that has led John Caputo to criticize him for enclosing and hardening the "Event" of Being within a specifically Christian setting, with Judaism necessarily *aufgehoben* by a wider narrative (*ADG*, 78).

15. Vattimo cites Girard's *Violence and the Sacred* as important to his thought (*AC*, 38). For a crisp account of Girard's fundamental insights, see Michael Kirwan's excellent volume, *Discovering Girard* (Cowley Publications, 2005).

16. Vattimo himself has become a prominent public spokesman for homosexual rights in Italy and in Europe generally. He wonders if he can belong to a church which regards him as a sick person in need of healing, or a "monstrous brother who must be loved but kept hidden." The Torinese further observes that, for him, homosexuality has become the hermeneutical key for interpreting all forms of social exclusion both within and outside of the church (*BE*, 73).

17. As Vattimo says to René Girard in one of their dialogues: "If the orthodox Catholic declares that one is unable to abort, or to divorce or to experiment with embryos and so on, does there not persist here a certain violence of natural religion . . . ?" (*VFD*, 9).

18. Martin Heidegger, *Identity and Difference*, tr. Joan Stambaugh (New York: Harper and Row, 1969), 72.

19. Etymologically taken, of course, "ontotheology" simply means the conjoining of *ontos* (Being) and *theos* (God). When used pejoratively, as is normally the case, it means the subordination of God to an apriori philosophical idea. Such a position is rightly derided as a misshaping of theology in the worst possible sense. On the other hand, properly understood, ontotheology simply means that thinking about God is also concerned with the *ontos on*, the actually existing real. In this sense, a marriage between *ontos* and *theos* is exigent. For the meaning of ontotheology in several thinkers, see *Foundations of Systematic Theology*, 9–20.

20. Friedrich Nietzsche, *Twilight of the Idols*, tr. R. J. Hollingdale (London: Penguin, 1990), 50–51.

21. Vattimo is citing Nietzsche's *Will to Power*, no. 585.

22. *Will to Power*, no. 1 of *European Nihilism*.

23. Vattimo's comments here call to mind Nietzsche's distinction between a weary nihilism and an active nihilism that can "posit for oneself, productively, a goal, a why, a faith." *Will to Power*, nos. 21 23.

Notes

24. (*BYI*, 22). Vattimo clearly wants to distance himself from the thought of Hans-Georg Gadamer who has allegedly domesticated hermeneutical theory. Of course, Vattimo acknowledges that Gadamer has done more than anyone else to make hermeneutics the *koinē* of contemporary thought (*BYI*, 38) and it is clear that Gadamer is a significant influence on the Torinese. But, he states in a revelatory sentence, "it is on the theses of Gadamer that the nihilistic radicalization we wish to propose must be performed." Vattimo is convinced that Gadamer mistakenly fails to mention Nietzsche as one of his hermeneutical precursors (*DN*, 74–75) and he bemoans the fact that Nietzsche is often illegitimately "written out" of the history of hermeneutics. He also observes that Heidegger's overcoming of metaphysics plays "no more than a small part in Gadamer" (*DN*, 183). Consequently, despite his continuing influence on Vattimo, Gadamer is regarded by the Torinese as a domesticator of the more radical hermeneutical insights of both Nietzsche and Heidegger.

25. Vattimo is insistent that hermeneutics cannot seek to replace Plato, Descartes or Kant, presenting itself as a "comfortable meta-theory of the universality of interpretation" (*BYI*, 8). Hermeneutics must be convinced of its own historicity; otherwise, one is left with a "tamed" and "urbanized" theory which seeks to avoid the consequences of nihilism.

26. This is why Vattimo says that, for Nietzsche, even the tale recounted in *The Twilight of the Idols*—that the world has become a fable—cannot be taken as a true proposition or a stable foundation on which one may rest secure. On the contrary, it just here that Nietzsche proclaims *Incipit Zarathustra!* (*DN*, 152).

27. Vattimo insists, therefore, that Heidegger did not offer *Being and Time* as a "truer" representation than the inherited metaphysical tradition (*BYI*, 29). Heidegger's *magnum opus* should itself be seen as one disclosure, not the final disclosive manifestation of Being in history. The same is true of Nietzsche's Eternal Return. It is not intended as an ultimate structure of Being but precisely as a way of deconstructing such structures (*DN*, 146–147).

28. In general, Vattimo's comments on the hermeneutical character of science are weak and could easily be deepened by adducing the sophisticated debates in the philosophy of science on the relationship between "construction" and "constraint."

29. *Human, All Too Human*, tr. R. J. Hollingdale (Cambridge: Cambridge University Press, 1986), no. 18.

30. Vattimo frames one of his differences with René Girard precisely over the question of "human nature." He says that Girard seems to endorse such a concept while he "is convinced instead that . . . one is able to deconstruct also the concept of human nature as placing limits" (*VFD*, 13).

31. *The Gay Science*, tr. Thomas Common (Mineola, NY: Dover Publications, 2006), no. 125.

32. This is the ultimate meaning of Nietzsche's stirring comment, "It is still a *metaphysical faith* upon which our faith in science rests—and even we truth-seekers of today, we godless anti-metaphysicians, still take *our* fire from the

161

flame kindled by a belief thousands of years old, the Christian faith, which was also the faith of Plato, that God is truth and truth is divine." But, Nietzsche immediately adds, "What if God himself turns out to be our most persistent lie?" (*The Gay Science*, no. 344).

33. This is one significant thesis of Bernstein's well-known book, *Beyond Objectivism and Relativism* (Philadelphia: University of Pennsylvania, 1983).

34. Of course, the charge has long been made (for example, by Bernstein in *Beyond Objectivism and Relativism*) that Hans-George Gadamer, too, offers a weak account of interpretative adequacy and truth (causing Bernstein to seek further warrants from Habermas). Inasmuch as Vattimo thinks Gadamer's thought needs a salutary dose of Nietzschean nihilism, it is no surprise that criteria for interpretative adequacy do not constitute an essential concern of his work.

35. So Vattimo says that "The philosophical nihilism that I profess—which does not necessarily have a desperate, negative, pessimistic meaning, but wishes to be something like the active nihilism of Nietzsche (yes, that of the Overman). . . ." *La Stampa*, February 22, 2007.

36. Friedrich Nietzsche, *Writings from the Late Notebooks*, ed. Rüdiger Bittner, tr. Kate Sturge (Cambridge: Cambridge University Press, 2003), 121, no. 15.

37. Vattimo explains that the Overman is not the figure disastrously created by the Third Reich, but the one who seeks an alternative human project, an alternative moral content to life (*DN*, 95, 138). Nietzsche, of course, is the one who consistently offers a prescient understanding of *pensiero debole*.

38. Martin Heidegger, *Being and Time*, tr. John Macquarrie and Edward Robinson (New York: Harper and Row, 1962), 19 citing *The Sophist*, 244a.

39. Martin Heidegger, "Overcoming Metaphysics" in Richard Wolin, *The Heidegger Controversy*, 67.

40. For Heidegger's comments on the nature of Verwindung, see no. 3 above. As Vattimo says, *Verwindung* has none of the sense of an "overcoming" in which the past has nothing more to say (*EM*, 164; *OA*, 207). For Gadamer's insights into Heidegger's *Verwindung* of metaphysics, see his letter to Jean Grondin in Lewis Edwin Hahn, ed., *The Philosophy of Hans-Georg Gadamer* (Chicago: Open Court Press, 1997), 171–172.

41. Heidegger, *Being and Time*, 19. As Gadamer says, "What being is was to be determined from within the horizon of time. Thus the structure of temporality appeared as ontologically definitive of subjectivity." *Truth and Method*, 2nd revised edition, tr. Joel Weinsheimer and Donald G. Marshall (New York: Continuum, 2003) 257.

42. Richard Rorty, "The Challenge of Relativism," in Józef Niznik and John T. Sanders, *Debating the State of Philosophy* (Westport: Praeger, 1996), 31. In the introduction to one of Vattimo's books, Rorty says that both he and the Torinese are convinced that philosophy should not seek ultimate dimensions of human existence, whether Platonic, Kantian or Marxist; we are, indeed, at the mercy of contingencies (*NE*, xii–xiii). Similarly, in *Weakening Philosophy*, Rorty concurs with Vattimo's claims that neither the world nor humanity *has* a nature (150).

Notes

43. *The End of Philosophy*, 11, with translation slightly altered.
44. Heidegger argues that, for the Greeks, *phainesthai* means not "objectness" but appearance as "radiance," as rising into disclosure and unconcealment. See *On The Way to Language*, tr. Peter D. Hertz (New York: Harper and Row, 1971), 38.
45. Martin Heidegger, *Introduction to Metaphysics*, tr. Gregory Fried and Richard Polt (New Haven: Yale University Press, 2000), 90.
46. Apropos here is Gadamer's comment: "Heidegger's thesis was that being itself is time. This burst asunder the whole subjectivism of modern philosophy—and, in fact, as was soon to appear, the whole horizon of questions asked by metaphysics, which tended to define being as what is present." See *Truth and Method*, 257.
47. John Caputo, *Heidegger and Aquinas* (New York: Fordham University Press, 1982), 3.
48. Although I use the word "inaccessible" here, it should be remembered that the world has no "noumenal" existence that simply escapes the inquirer. As Vattimo says, "The images of the world we receive ... are not simply different interpretations of a 'reality' that is 'given' regardless, but rather constitute the very objectivity of the world" (*TS*, 24–25).
49. Friedrich Nietzsche, *Daybreak*, ed. Maudemarie Clark, tr. R. J. Hollingdale (Cambridge: Cambridge University Press, 1997), no. 547.
50. Friedrich Nietzsche, *Thus Spoke Zarathustra*, tr. Walter Kaufmann (New York: The Viking Press, 1966), 86–87.
51. Martin Heidegger, *Nietzsche*, v. I, tr. David Farrell Krell (San Francisco: Harper and Row, 1979), 58–66. Heidegger's brief is that Nietzsche once again, in his accent on *Wille zur Macht*, replicates the subjectivism of modernity (*DN*, 193).
52. *The Will to Power*, no. 493.
53. I have treated the fallibilistic understandings of truth developed by each of these thinkers in *Foundations of Systematic Theology*, 82–105.
54. Richard Bernstein, "Philosophers Respond to *Fides et ratio*," *Books and Culture* 5 (July/August, 1999), 30–32.
55. John D. Caputo describes a fallibilistic notion of truth in this matter-of-fact manner: truth is the "best interpretation that anybody has come up with yet while conceding that no one knows what is coming next." John D. Caputo, *On Religion* (London: Routledge, 2001), 21. But Caputo, it should be noted, is more clearly a classical fallibilist than Vattimo, with somewhat less attraction to the kind of nihilism that the Torinese sanctions.
56. Vattimo is convinced that Gadamer is much friendlier to the metaphysical tradition than is Heidegger, again indicting Gadamer's strategies for "presence" such as the "fusion of horizons" (*VM*, xxxii–xxxiii). As for Habermas, the Torinese is wary that his attraction to "transcendental conditions" for rational inquiry and to "universal validity claims" skates entirely too close to Kantian metaphysics (*BYI*, 21; *NE*, 84–85, 156–157).
57. Nietzsche, *Thus Spoke Zarathustra*, 91, with translation slightly altered.
58. See *Nichomachean Ethics* VI, 1140a.26–32 and VI, 1141b.11. For a fuller discussion of *phronēsis*, see *Foundations of Systematic Theology*, 87–91.

Notes

59. Stanley Rosen, *Hermeneutics as Politics* (New York: Oxford University, 1987), 138.

60. Martin Heidegger, "The Origin of the Work of Art" in *Poetry, Language, Thought*, tr. Albert Hofstadter (New York: Harper and Row, 1971), 17–87 at 32–35.

61. Hans-Georg Gadamer, *Heidegger's Ways*, tr. John W. Stanley (Albany: State University of New York, 1994), 103.

62. *Heidegger's Ways*, 105.

63. It is unsurprising, Vattimo states, that Gadamer was first discovered in North America by literary critics rather than professional philosophers given the marked accent on questions of logic and epistemology that dominate Anglo-American thought (*VM*, xxxvii).

64. As Vattimo says, "As we all know, *Being and Time* opposes, to the idea of truth as conformity of the proposition to the thing, that of an original disclo-sure—the disclosure, aletheia—that renders possible any access to beings and therefore also any eventual conformity or deformity" (*HNAP*, xiv).

65. For an extended historical treatment of the "spoils" question, see my *Founda-tions of Systematic Theology*, 269–310. I also rely here on material published in "Spoils from Egypt: Yesterday and Today," *Pro Ecclesia*, 15 (2006), 403–417.

66. Tertullian, "*The Prescription against Heretics*," *The Ante-Nicene Fathers*, v. 3, ed. Alexander Roberts and James Donaldson (Grand Rapids: Eerdmans, 1957), chapter seven, 246.

67. Origen, "*Letter to Gregory*" in *The Ante-Nicene Fathers*, v. 4 (Grand Rapids: Eerdmans, 1956), 393–394.

68. Origen argues that the truth of Christianity is not subject to alien warrants since, as Robert Wilken observes, the "gospel has a proof which is particular in itself and is more divine than a Greek proof based on dialectical arguments." See Robert Wilken, "Serving the One True God" in *Either/Or*, ed. Carl Braaten and Robert Jenson (Grand Rapids: Eerdmans, 1995), 49–63 at 54.

69. Helpful in this regard are the Gifford Lectures of Jaroslav Pelikan, published as *Christianity and Classical Culture* (New Haven: Yale University Press, 1993).

70. Basil, *Ad adolescentes de legendis libris gentilium*. The translation used here is "Address to Young People on Reading Greek Literature," in *The Letters*, v. 4, tr. Roy Deferrari and Martin McGuire (Cambridge, MA: Harvard Univer-sity Press, 1934), 365ff.

71. Ibid., IV, 7–8.

72. Ibid., VIII, 1–2.

73. Equally worthy of treatment (and duplicating the image of "spoils from Egypt") is the trope of the "comely captive" taken from Deuteronomy 21.10-14 and developed by both Origen and Jerome. For their use of this image, see Henri de Lubac, *Medieval Exegesis* v. I, tr. Mark Sebanc (Grand Rapids: Eerdmans, 1998), 211–224.

74. John Rist, *Augustine: Ancient Thought Baptized* (Cambridge: Cambridge Uni-versity Press, 1994), 13.

75. Joseph Ratzinger, *Eschatology*, tr. Michael Waldstein (Washington: The Catholic University of America Press, 1988), 143–145. Ratzinger, of course,

is arguing against the position that early Christianity uncritically adopted antecedent philosophical forms which subsequently (mis)shaped the Gospel.

76. Adolf von Harnack, *History of Dogma* I, tr. N. Buchanan (Boston: Roberts Bros., 1895), 17. Harnack adds, ". . . every dogmatic formula is suspicious because it is fitted to wound the spirit of religion . . ." Ibid., 71. On the contrary, the redoubtable historian of Aristotelianism, Joseph Owens, asks, "But where was there hellenization in any historical sense? . . . Where in Greek philosophy do you find the *notions* of person, essence or subsistence? Even when Greek concepts such as substance, accident, word and nature were used, were they not painfully hammered into a new shape to convey Christian content? . . . Do you need anything more to apply here than the observation of Galen that the doctrine of Moses differs from that of Plato and all right thinking Greeks?" See "Dewert's View of Christian Philosophy and Contemporary Man" in *The Future of Belief Debate*, ed. Gregory Baum (New York: Herder and Herder, 1967), 97–98.

77. Jacopone da Todi's poems can be found in a translation rendered by Anne MacDonell, *Sons of Francis* (London: J. M. Dent and Co., 1902), 369.

78. For Aquinas's scriptural justification for borrowing from pagan authors, see his arguments in *Commentary on Boethius's "De Trinitate"* q. 2, a. 3, sed contra. One trope he employs is that of the aforementioned "comely captive," an example taken from Deuteronomy 21.10-14 and earlier used by Jerome.

79. *De Trinitate*, q. 2, a. 3, c. (emphasis added).

80. For the circumstances surrounding this prohibition, see John Wippel, *Mediaeval Reactions to the Encounter between Faith and Reason*, The Aquinas Lecture of 1995 (Milwaukee: Marquette University Press, 1995), 11–12.

81. Tempier's condemnation of theological Aristotelianism is thoroughly examined by John Wippel in "The Condemnations of 1270 and 1277," *The Journal of Medieval and Renaissance Studies* 7 (1977), 169–201. For a useful summary, see Wippel, *Mediaeval Reactions*, 14–28.

82. For reason as "dame witch" see *Luther's Works (LW)*, ed. J. Pelikan and H. Lehmann, v. 24, 91. All citations from Luther will be from this series. For Aristotle as a "heathen philosopher" see *LW*, v. 52, 165; for "heathen philosophy" see *LW*, v. 2, 302. Commenting at length on Luther's discriminating use of Aristotle is Theodor Dieter, *Der junge Luther und Aristoteles* (Berlin: Walter de Gruyter, 2001).

83. John Henry Newman, *Development of Christian Doctrine* (London: Longmans, Green and Co., 1894), 382.

84. Ibid., 382. It is worth noting that Karl Barth also utilized the image of "Aaron's rod" (Exod. 7.9-12) when commenting on the relationship between theology and philosophy. See "Fate and Idea in Theology" in *The Way of Theology in Karl Barth*, ed. Martin Rumscheidt, tr. George Hunsinger (Allison Park, PA: Pickwick Publications, 1986), 25–61.

85. Henri de Lubac, *Catholicism*, tr. L. Sheppard (New York: Longmans, Green and Co., 1950), 149–153.

86. Henri de Lubac, *The Drama of Atheist Humanism*, tr. E. Riley (London: Sheed and Ward, 1949), vi.

87. Henri de Lubac, *A Brief Catechesis on Nature and Grace*, tr. R. Arnandez (San Francisco: Ignatius Press, 1984), 69. For Augustine, see *Confessions*, VII, 10.

88. Hans Urs von Balthasar, "On the Tasks of Catholic Philosophy in Our Time," *Communio* 20 (1993), 155. This is a translation of an essay originally published in 1946.

89. Ibid., 158–159.

90. *The Glory of the Lord*, v. 4, tr. Brian McNeil et al. (San Francisco: Ignatius Press, 1989), 320.

91. Hans Urs von Balthasar, *Truth is Symphonic*, tr. G. Harrison (San Francisco: Ignatius Press, 1987), 54.

92. Karl Barth, *Church Dogmatics* III/2, ed. G. Bromiley and T. F. Torrance, tr. H. Knight et al. (Edinburgh: T & T Clark, 1960), 282–283.

93. Ibid., 283–284.

94. John Paul II, *"Fides et ratio," Acta apostolicae sedis*, 91 (1999) 5–88. An English translation may be found in *Origins*, 28 (October 22, 1998), 317–347. Although the official Latin text was published in 1999, the encyclical is dated September 14, 1998.

95. *"Omne verum a quocumque dicatur a Spiritu Sancto est."* See ST I–II, q. 109, a. 1, ad 1.

96. At times, a distinction has been made between a Catholic assimilative and analogical approach (seeking comprehensiveness) and a Protestant-inspired dialectical perspective (stressing evangelical purity). While I think there exists an accent that is proper to each communion, this should not be regarded as an either/or issue. Both Catholic and Protestant theologians accept insights from every quarter and both are equally concerned with the purity of the Gospel. Catholics may, indeed, seek to show that the Incarnation of the Son of God is the highest exemplar of divine action to be found everywhere in the world, while the Protestant imagination sees the uniqueness of God better protected by showing the *difference* between God's action in Christ and the rest of creation. But does such a distinction constitute an essential difference?

97. Robert Jenson, *Systematic Theology*, v. I (New York: Oxford University Press, 1997), 20 (emphasis added).

98. Martin Heidegger, *The Piety of Thinking*, tr. J. Hart and J. Maraldo (Bloomington: Indiana University Press, 1976), 6.

99. Walter Cardinal Kasper, speech of November 23, 2007.

100. John Milbank, *Theology and Social Theory*, 260. See also Milbank's statement that theology "no longer has to measure up to accepted secular standards of scientific truth or normative rationality" in "'Postmodern Critical Augustinianism': A Short *Summa* in Forty Two Responses to Unasked Questions," *Modern Theology*, 7 (April, 1991), 225–237 at 225.

101. As he says elsewhere: "… I have learned from Heidegger and from Nietzsche that any fixation on structure is always an act of authority" (*VFD*, 15).

102. Vattimo would no doubt agree, then, with a recent decision of France's highest administrative court denying citizenship to a French woman of

Moroccan descent because she wore the *niqab*, a facial veil covering all but the eyes. It was judged that her "radical practice" of Islam was incompatible with the *laïcité* characteristic of secular France. See *The New York Times* article "A Veil Closes France's Door to Citizenship" of July 19, 2008. France's minister for urban affairs, herself a Muslim, is quoted as saying, in Vattimian tones, that the *niqab* "is not a religious insignia but the insignia of a totalitarian political project. . . ."

103. One thinks, in just this regard, of the millions of people who regard abortion as not simply an ethical mistake but, indeed, as murder. Whether or not one agrees with them, this strongly held belief has very rarely led to violence of any kind (and even when it has, it has been universally deplored by those opposing abortion). Isn't it true that the case against abortion has been made primarily by philosophical argument and by democratic election rather than by violence or unrest? Of course, Vattimo would undoubtedly respond that those opposing abortion are taking an apriori metaphysical position, thereby insisting that they have access to objectifying ultimates. He argues, rather, that all issues must be discharged into the realm of the procedural, precisely because no apriori "metaphysical" options are available to us, either theoretically or practically. On the issue of abortion, the Torinese claims that gynecologists with objections to abortions, like policemen with aversions to firearms, should find another job (*NE*, 106). He continues, "Talk about the rights of the fetus is little more than hot air."

104. Martin Heidegger, *Identity and Difference*, tr. Joan Stambaugh (Chicago: University of Chicago Press, 2002), 71–72.

105. *Identity and Difference*, 72.

106. Of course, Barth famously declared, "I regard the *analogia entis* as the invention of the Antichrist. . . ." See *Church Dogmatics* I/1, tr. G. T. Thomson (Edinburgh: T&T Clark, 1949), x.

107. Ibid., 40.

108. I have outlined the strengths and weaknesses of Barth's argument on analogy in *Foundations of Systematic Theology*, 218–238.

109. Karl Barth, *Church Dogmatics*, I/1, 42, 305.

110. *Luther's Works*, 24, 99.

111. See Paul Rorem, "Martin Luther's Christocentric Critique of Pseudo-Dionysian Spirituality," *Lutheran Quarterly*, 11 (1997), 291–307.

112. Luther's polemic against Dionysius was recently reprised in Colin Gunton's *Act and Being* where Gunton argued, like Luther, that the names attributed to God by the Areopagite have a genealogy that is essentially neo-Platonic rather than biblical. See *Act and Being* (Grand Rapids: Eerdmans, 2002), especially 14–18.

113. *Luther's Works*, 2, 124–125. Of course, Luther's concerns about the danger of philosophical imperialism are profoundly traditional. As earlier noted, Étienne Tempier, bishop of Paris, condemned two-hundred Aristotelian-influenced propositions on the grounds that they jeopardized evangelical purity. For more on Tempier's condemnations, see John Wippel, *Mediaeval Reactions*, 11–12.

114. Hans Urs von Balthasar, *The Glory of the Lord*, v. 4, tr. Brain McNeil et al. (San Francisco: Ignatius, 1989), 320.
115. Thomas Aquinas, *Summa theologiae* II–II, q. 2, a. 4. A thorough examination of how Aquinas corrected natural reasoning (and, therefore, Aristotle) by revelation may be found in Fernand van Steenberghen, *Thomas Aquinas and Radical Aristotelianism* (Washington: The Catholic University of America Press, 1980).
116. *Act and Being*, 15–16.
117. John Paul II, "*Fides et ratio,*" *Acta apostolicae sedis* 91 (1999), 5–88.
118. *Act and Being*, 5.
119. Jean-Luc Marion, *God Without Being*, tr. Thomas A. Carlson (Chicago: University of Chicago, 1991).
120. Ibid., 36.
121. A later, chastened Marion has, in several places, described the proper use of metaphysics within the theological tradition. For example, "Being offers a path, a humbly indispensable path, to the overeminent good of a God who must be loved. Although the question of being also concerns God, God is never circumscribed within the 'question of being' as a horizon that would precede or predetermine Him." This sentence could have been written by Aquinas and perhaps the later Barth as well. See *Cartesian Questions: Method and Metaphysics* (Chicago: University of Chicago, 1999) 160.
122. Despite these similarities, it is important to acknowledge the pronounced differences between Marion and Vattimo. Marion insists on developing the notion of *Gegebenheit* or givenness in its purity, allowing the *tout autre* to appear apart from any delimiting horizons. Vattimo, on the contrary, takes "givenness" to be itself an entirely constructed reality and so regards much phenomenology as philosophically naïve. Husserl's triumphal cry, *zu den Dingen selbst*, is itself a vaporous metaphysical dream.
123. In a comment also applicable to Vattimo, John Caputo says, "The death of God entails the deconstruction not only of the *ousia* of classical metaphysics but also the *hyperousios* of Neoplatonic mysticism" (*ADG*, 117).
124. Hans Urs von Balthasar, *The Glory of the Lord*, v. 1, tr. E. Leiva-Merikakis (San Francisco: Ignatius, 1982), 41.
125. See "What is Natural Law? Human Purposes and Natural Ends," *The Thomist*, 68 (2004) 507–529 at 524 (emphases added).
126. "*Evangelium vitae,*" AAS 87 (1995) 401–522 at 434, para. 29. Emphasis in the original. English translation in *Origins*, 24 (April 6, 1995) 689–727 at 700. The translation, however, does not italicize the remarks found in the authentic Latin text.
127. In response to this kind of natural law claim, Vattimo would insist, "To delude oneself that there is a core of knowledge proper to the 'natural' man and accessible to anyone with a bit of sound common sense is an error that is by now almost impossible to commit in good faith" (*NE*, 45). "Natural norms" must be seen for what they are: a deeply historicized, culturally conditioned legacy. For this reason, Vattimo pillories Catholicism for disregarding the democratic decisions of parliamentary majorities in the name of so-called "natural law" (*EWT*, 402).

128. The relationship between the relative autonomy of nature (and philosophy) vis-à-vis Christian faith, is perhaps best understood, invoking the *nexus mysteriorum inter se*, as analogous to the human nature of Christ, with its own integrity, subsisting in the person of the Logos Incarnate. The human nature loses nothing of its integral freedom within the hypostasis of the Eternal Word, even if the human nature is deeply affected by this union.

129. It has been argued, however, by Stephen J. Grabill, *Rediscovering the Natural Law in Reformed Theological Ethics* (Grand Rapids: Eerdmans, 2006) that natural law reasoning has a long history within the Protestant (and particularly Reformed) tradition even if this was largely displaced by Barth. One may also discern a certain Protestant-Catholic convergence on this question in recent ecumenical documents such as "That They May Have Life," issued by Evangelicals and Catholics Together: "We . . . affirm together that human reason, despite the consequences of sin, has the capacity for discerning, deliberating, and deciding the questions pertinent to the civil order. Some Evangelicals attribute this capacity of reason to 'common grace,' as distinct from 'saving grace.' Catholics typically speak of the 'natural law,' meaning moral law that is knowable in principle by all human beings, even if it is denied by many (Romans 1 and 2)." See *First Things* (October, 2006).

130. This issue, treated by Vattimo in *After Christianity*, 106–112, examines Dilthey's thesis as expressed in *Introduction to the Human Sciences*, tr. Ramon J. Betanzos (Detroit: Wayne State University Press, 1988), 229. Of Dilthey, Vattimo says, that he is essential for understanding "how Christianity could be taken as the starting point of the modern dissolution of metaphysics" (*AC*, 109).

131. Louis Dupré also speaks of the movement to modernity as involving the loss of meaning mediated by the objectivity of *kosmos* and *nomos*. But he roots this dissolution not in the advent of Christianity, which preserved the objectivism of Greek wisdom even while transforming it, but in the corrosive power of nominalist modernity with its emptying of the meaning-giving power of the world in favor of the form-giving subject. In this sense, Kant (and, earlier Ockham and medieval nominalism) are the key moments. See *Passage to Modernity* (New Haven: Yale University Press, 1993).

132. I rely here on material from my article "The God of Philosophy and of the Bible: Theological Reflections on Regensburg," *Logos*, 10 (2007), 120–130.

133. Joseph Ratzinger, *Introduction to Christianity*, tr. J. R. Foster (London: Search Press, 1969), 79.

134. In other words, one cannot simply argue for the substantial continuity of Christian truth on the basis of the Gospel of grace, absent confirming philosophical warrants, without lapsing into an untenable fideism. The other option, intelligible on its own grounds but a significant departure from the prior tradition, is to claim that the teachings of the church are in fact, entirely limited in their socio-cultural scope and necessarily have wide meaning-variance over the course of times and cultures. This would be to accept Vattimo's (and Heidegger's) philosophy on its own terms, transforming Christian belief accordingly.

Notes

135. Adolf Harnack, *What is Christianity?*, tr. Thomas Bailey Saunders (Gloucester, MA: Peter Smith, 1978), 204–205; 236–237.

136. *Idem, History of Dogma*, v. 4, tr. Neil Buchanan (Boston: Little, Brown and Company, 1898), 106.

137. *Luther's Works*, v. 31, 12.

138. Examples of a metaphysics disciplined by faith are offered, for example, by Thomas Weinandy, *Does God Suffer?* (Notre Dame: University of Notre Dame, 2000); Gisbert Greshake, *Der Dreiene Gott* (Freiburg im Breisgau: Herder, 1997); Klaus Hemmerle, *Thesen zu einer trinitarischen Ontologie* (Einsiedeln: Johannes, 1976); W. Norris Clark, *Person and Being* (Milwaukee: Marquette University Press, 1993) and John Zizioulas, *Being as Communion* (London: Darton, Longman and Todd, 2004). All these works utilize a notion of metaphysics deeply influenced by the communicative, dynamic and relational notion of Being found in Christian revelation. As such, they instantiate a performative, theological *Verwindung* of the notion of Being which acknowledges that there exists no speculative completeness of philosophy apart from Christ.

139. Martin Heidegger, "*Séminaire de Zurich*," tr. F. Fedier, *Po&sie* 13 (1980), 52–63, at 60. The passage may also be found in *Heidegger et la question de Dieu*, ed. Richard Kearney and Joseph S. O'Leary (Paris: Bernard Grasset, 1980), 334.

140. "Our thesis, then, is that *theology is a positive science, and as such, therefore, is absolutely different from philosophy. . . .* It is immediately clear that from this thesis that theology, as a positive science, is in principle closer to chemistry and mathematics than to philosophy." Martin Heidegger, *The Piety of Thinking*, 6.

141. At the same time, Vattimo is entirely unaware of the extent to which the adoption of "Hellenism" has always been disciplined by faith. The Torinese dyslogistically speaks of God as the "immobile foundation of history" (*RDV*, 81) and as an "immutable metaphysical plenitude" (*RDV*, 88). Are these not caricatures of a God who is preeminently inter-relational in his very existence (as three Persons)? And is it not a commonplace in Aquinas's thought, for example, that God does not even fall under the subject matter of metaphysics? See Rudi te Velde, *Aquinas on God* (Aldershot: Ashgate, 2006), 53.

142. As Vattimo says: "The itinerary of contemporary philosophy—from the language-games of Wittgenstein, to the idea of Being as Event of Heidegger, to the particular version of pragmatism of Richard Rorty—I see it as a passage from *veritas to caritas*" (*VFD*, 19).

143. "*Perché non possiamo non dirci cristiani*" in *Discorsi di varia filosofia,* v. I (Bari: Laterza, 1945).

144. John Caputo, too, finds doctrinal claims entirely unwarranted, desperately trying to "bottle up," so to speak, the Event character of Being. See Caputo, *On Religion*, 136. As he says elsewhere, ". . . truth demands an honest concession that we cannot contain the event harbored by the name of God." See *The Weakness of God* (Bloomington: Indiana University, 2006), 287.

Notes

Because of the very concerns noted by Vattimo and Caputo, several theologians (e.g. David Tracy) think that "art" most adequately explains the kind of truth mediated by theology. One understands this attraction since art allows for creative and imaginative dimensions of truth, without attempting to "harden" and therefore severely limit, interpretative plurality. At the same time, Christian doctrine has a perduring, descriptive and ostensive element which is not necessarily native to artistic interpretation.

145. Martin Luther, *The Bondage of the Will*, chapter two.

146. Wolfhart Pannenberg, *Systematic Theology*, v. 1, tr. Geoffrey Bromiley (Grand Rapids: Eerdmans, 1988), 48–52.

147. Gerhard Sauter, *Gateways to Dogmatics*, tr. Geoffrey Bromiley (Grand Rapids: Eerdmans, 2002), 6, 36.

148. Jenson, *Systematic Theology*, v. I, 20.

149. I have examined various ways in which truth is legitimately defended as universal, continuous and perpetual in *Foundations of Systematic Theology*, 107–139.

150. Martin Heidegger, *Introduction to Metaphysics*, 151–152. While Haecker tries to develop a philosophical/anthropological account of human nature, Heidegger dismisses his attempt as a "zoological" description. The same issue is at stake earlier in Heidegger's work when he says, "anyone for whom the Bible is divine revelation and truth already has the answer to the question, 'Why are there beings at all instead of nothing?' before it is even asked" (*Introduction to Metaphysics*, 7).

151. Karl Barth was fond of this formulation precisely because of its accent on the eschatological nature of divine truth. See *Church Dogmatics*, I/1, tr. G. T. Thomson (Edinburgh: T & T Clark, 1949), 307.

152. Avery Dulles, *The Craft of Theology* (New York: Crossroad, 1992), 19.

153. The convergence of Heidegger's thought with certain existentialist theological currents is captured by Gadamer in "Heidegger and Marburg Theology" in *Philosophical Hermeneutics*, tr. David E. Linge (Berkeley: University of California, 1976), 198–212.

154. Vattimo discusses Heidegger's *Einleitung in die Phänomenologie der Religion*, in *Phänomenologie des religiösen Lebens, Gesamtausgabe II*, v. 60 (Frankfurt: Klostermann, 1995), in *After Christianity*, 123–137. An English translation has been released as *The Phenomenology of Religious Life*, tr. Matthias Fritsch and Jennifer Anna Gosetti-Ferencei (Bloomington: Indiana University Press, 2004), 75–82.

155. Those commentators are likely right who argue that Heidegger sees himself, at least partially, as a philosophical counterpart to Luther. So, Herman Philipse argues that Heidegger's choice of the word *Destruktion* in order to describe his relationship with the earlier philosophical tradition echoes Luther's use of *destruere* in his *Heidelberger Disputation*. See *Heidegger's Philosophy of Being* (Princeton: Princeton University Press, 1998), 20. Benjamin D. Crowe adds, "It is, I submit, the theology of *Luther* which provides Heidegger with the basis for his own conception of hermeneutics." See *Heidegger's Religious Origins* (Bloomington: Indiana University Press, 2006), 38.

Notes

156. We see in Vattimo's summation a strong affinity with Derrida's desire for a deconstruction which is developed "without reference to religion as institutional dogma, without getting involved in some 'article of faith'. . . . while proposing a non-dogmatic doublet of dogma . . . a thinking that 'repeats' the possibility of religion without religion." See Jacques Derrida, *The Gift of Death*, tr. David Wills (Chicago: University of Chicago Press, 1995), 49.
157. Wolfhart Pannenberg, *Systematic Theology*, v. I, 55.
158. I have treated Aquinas's notion of analogy at length in *Foundations of Systematic Theology* (New York: T & T Clark, 2005), 239–253.
159. I discuss Pannenberg's objections, as well as possible answers, in *Foundations of Systematic Theology*, 235, note 12. Karl Barth's objections to the *analogia entis* are discussed in 219–223.
160. "*Dei Filius*" cited in Denzinger-Hünermann, *Enchiridion symbolorum definitionem et declarationem* (Freiburg im Breisgau: Herder, 1991), no. 3016.
161. For a summary of the dialogue between Rahner and Küng, see Carl Peter, "A Rahner-Küng Debate and Ecumenical Possibilities" in *Teaching Authority and Infallibility in the Church*, ed. Paul Empie et al., Lutheran-Catholic Dialogue 6 (Minneapolis: Augsburg, 1978), 159–168.
162. *Fides et ratio*, no. 27.
163. Richard Bernstein, "Philosophers Respond to *Fides et ratio*," 30–32.
164. It is important to recognize that Vattimo's thought is not entirely malleable to the standard principles of fallibilism as explained by Bernstein, particularly the latter's assertion that "fallibilism does not challenge the claim that we can know the truth." For "knowing the truth" is precisely what Vattimo calls into question under the aegis of hermeneutical nihilism. Doesn't the claim of "knowing the truth" itself smack of metaphysical representationalism, of the idea that there is an *ontos on* waiting to be discovered by the intelligent inquirer? Vattimo's position is that we can offer some coherent interpretations of experience, but this should not be confused with any sense of "correspondence" with the world. Precisely because of his hesitancy on this question, and his attraction to a nihilism limited only by *caritas,* it is no surprise that Vattimo leaves the truth-question undeveloped in his thought and never speaks of himself as espousing fallibilism. Just as he seeks to nudge Gadamer and Habermas in a Nietzschean direction, this is also the case with any fallibilistic approach to truth.
165. This is not to claim, of course, that revelation is reducible to its cognitive dimensions. This dimension of Christian life always exists within a more profound personal engagement with the mystery of the revealing God.
166. John Caputo, similarly, states that religion is about hoping, dreaming, sighing, weeping and praying—but knowing is not mentioned (*ADG*, 58). Of course, knowing cannot be included in this list because it tries to "objectify" the Event that is itself always beyond objectification. But doesn't this significantly underestimate the tradition's safeguards against a simpleminded presence?
167. Martin Heidegger, *Introduction to Metaphysics*, 151–152.

Notes

168. See for example, the Islamic statement "*A Common Word between Us and You*" and the Jewish statement "*Dabru Emet*" both of which can be understood as "weakening" understood in a properly theological rather than a nihilistic sense. The former document places a very strong accent on the love of God and neighbor found in both Christian and Muslim traditions; the latter statement argues that a stronger relationship of respect between Jews and Christians does not thereby weaken Jewish identity.

169. *Nostra Aetate* (Declaration on non-Christian Religions), no. 2. All translations taken from *Documents of Vatican II*, ed. Austin Flannery (Grand Rapids: Eerdmans, 1984).

170. Even well before Vatican II, the historian Henri de Lubac, reflecting on the spiritual experiences that animate the world's religions, had said "must everything be jettisoned to give place to the Gospel?" De Lubac answers with a resounding "no" stating that there is real truth to be found in the beliefs and consciences of non-Christians even though the church must deepen them and give them fresh life. See *Catholicism* tr. L. Sheppard (New York: Longmans, Green and Co., 1950), 144, 152.

171. Other statements on Judaism have followed *Nostra Aetate*. For example, *We Remember: A Reflection on the Shoah* (1998) and *The Jewish People and their Sacred Scriptures in the Christian Bible* (2001).

172. Denzinger-Hünermann, *Enchiridion symbolorum*, no. 1351.

173. I am, as is clear, recounting the official teaching of Vatican II and of later authoritative documents. I am not here entering into speculative thinking on inter-religious dialogue, which, of course, seeks to advance and, in certain ways, surpass conciliar teaching. See for example, the fine work of Jacques Dupuis, *Toward a Christian Theology of Religious Pluralism* (Maryknoll, NY: Orbis Press, 2000).

174. *Lumen Gentium*, no. 8. Recent articles on this issue include that of Francis A. Sullivan, "A Response to Karl Becker on the Meaning of subsistit in," *Theological Studies* 67 (2006), 395–409.

175. George Lindbeck, a Lutheran observer at Vatican II, has spoken movingly of the difference between Vatican I (1869–70) and Vatican II (1962–65). At the former, Bishop Strossmeyer had said something positive about the Reformation (March 22, 1870, general council 31) and was hooted down from the podium. At the later council, Leon Elchinger, bishop of Strasbourg, spoke serenely of the contributions made to the entire church by the Reformation. See George Lindbeck, "How a Lutheran Saw It [Vatican II]," *Commonweal* (November 22, 2002).

176. The uniqueness of the salvific path of Jesus of Nazareth was also strongly reaffirmed in *Dominus Iesus*, a document issued in 2000 by the Roman Catholic Congregation for the Doctrine of the Faith, reminding non-Christians that, from a Catholic point of view, they lacked the fullness of the means of salvation (e.g. faith in Christ, the Scriptures and sacraments) and so, "objectively speaking" were in a "gravely deficient situation." Regrettably, the document overlooked the significant advances of

contemporary interreligious and ecumenical dialogue and so was virtually stillborn from the moment of its promulgation.

177. Indeed, it may legitimately be argued that the world of Islam needs something like a declaration on religious freedom, recognizing the objective right for men and women to embrace a belief that, from the standpoint of Islam, appears to be deeply erroneous. This would constitute just the kind of "development of doctrine" in Islam that occurred in various sectors of Christianity: the ability to maintain the truth of one's own faith, even while recognizing that faith is a reality that can never be imposed but must be embraced in freedom.

178. John Henry Newman, *Oxford University Sermons* (London: Longmans, Green and Co., 1909), 33.

179. Yves Congar, for example, says that the idea of a hierarchy of truths may be found in various authors, including Luther, who distinguishes between what is "apostolic" (that which directly preaches Christ) and the other elements of Scripture. See *Diversity and Communion* (Mystic, CT: Twenty-Third Publications, 1982), 126–133.

180. I have treated the "hierarchy of truths" as well as "theological notes" (another strategy for "weakening") at length in *Revelation and Truth* (Scranton: University of Scranton, 1993), 138–161.

181. See Avery Dulles, *A History of Apologetics* (San Franciso: Ignatius Press, 2006).

182. For this approach, see John O'Malley, "Vatican II: Did anything happen?" *Theological Studies* 67 (2006), 3–33.

183. One thinks in this regard of Maurice Blondel's great philosophical work, *L'Action* of 1893. See *Action*, tr. Oliva Blanchette (Notre Dame: University of Notre Dame Press, 2004). Karl Rahner's *Spirit in the World* (New York: Continuum, 1994) has the same goal as Blondel's *magnum opus*, although written in an intellective rather than conative key.

184. Gadamer unfavorably contrasts Husserl with Heidegger saying, "Unlike Marburg Neokantianism and Husserl's Neokantian reshaping of phenomenology, Heidegger himself refused to remain with a tradition of modifying and perpetuating the heritage of metaphysics." H.-G. Gadamer, "Destruktion and Deconstruction" in *Dialogue and Deconstruction: The Gadamer-Derrida Encounter*, ed. Diane P. Michelfelder and Richard E. Palmer (Albany: SUNY Press, 1989), 110.

185. Jean Grondin, while admitting that there are many "relativism-friendly pronouncements" in Gadamer's work, defends Gadamer's exclusion of Nietzschean nihilism from his hermeneutical theory on the grounds that Gadamer was searching for a via media between nihilism and traditional theories of interpretation (*WP*, 203–216).

186. There are several excellent commentaries and interpretations of Joachim da Fiore's work. See, for example, George H. Tavard, *The Contemplative Church: Joachim and his Adversaries* (Milwaukee: Marquette University Press, 2005); Bernard McGinn, *The Calabrian Abbot* (New York: Macmillan, 1985); Henri de Lubac, *La posterité spirituelle de Joachim de Flore* (Paris: Lethielleux,

Notes

1979–81) and Marjorie Reeves, *Joachim of Fiore and the Prophetic Future*, 2nd revised edition (Gloucestershire: Sutton 1999).

187. John Caputo observes that Joachim da Fiore, beginning a line of thought that extends through Hegel and Schelling, tells a supersessionist story that shifts from the Old Testament to the New, always privileging Christianity while Judaism plays the "bad guy" (*ADG*, 80). He takes Vattimo to task for moving in just this Hegelian direction. Vattimo himself would likely respond that virtually all of his hermeneutical emphasis is on the coming age of the "Spirit" rather than a simple, diametrical opposition between "distant Father" of the Old Testament and "loving Son" of the New, even if Vattimo would also surely insist that kenotic Christianity is the proper theological "form" of *pensiero debole*. In a similar vein, Caputo expresses reservations about the "strength" given to the names of "Christianity" and the "Incarnation" in Vattimo's thought wondering if these become, too clearly, determinate (even fixed) instantiations of Being. In reality, however, Vattimo so empties these names of any traditional content that the distinction Caputo wishes to maintain between the *Ereignis*/Event and the concrete, determinate, historical "names" for it, is fully preserved in Vattimian philosophy.

188. Needless to add, Joachim himself does not sanction this approach. Vattimo makes entirely clear that he is not seeking a literal appropriation of Joachim, but only an interpretation (indeed, a *Verwindung*) of his most stimulating ideas.

189. This accent on continuing interpretation is why Vattimo finds "*sola Scriptura*" to be an unappealing axiom, smacking as its does of the "dead letter" of literalism (*BE*, 86). Roman Catholicism, often reproached for *not* following Scripture closely, does not fare better in Vattimian hermeneutics for the Torinese insists that Catholicism has strictly limited the interpretative role of the Christian community and, a fortiori, of the Spirit (AC, 81). Tradition itself quickly falls into representational, objectivist thinking by taking ecumenical councils and creedal statements as normative, thereby illegitimately attempting to "finalize" the truth of historicity.

190. See Johann E. Kuhn, *Einleitung in die katholische Dogmatik*, 2 vols. (Tübingen, 1846–47) 1:105–110.

191. Friedrich Nietzsche, *Untimely Meditations*, ed. D. Breazeale, tr. R. J. Hollingdale (Cambridge: Cambridge University Press, 1997). Page numbers are from the essay "On the Uses and Disadvantages of History."

192. I again note that there certainly may be changes in conceptual construct, i.e., in the unique *Denkstil* or grammar in which a particular belief or judgment is conceptualized, as we shall see below.

193. Blaise Pascal, *Pensées* (Paris: Charpentier, 1861), 388–389.

194. I have dealt at length with this hermeneutical approach, including an examination of the principal philosophical and theological objections to it, in *Foundations of Systematic Theology*, 141–208.

195. See *Lutherans and Catholics in Dialogue I–III*, ed. Paul C. Empie and T. Austin Murphy (Minneapolis: Augsburg, 1965) 187 197.

Notes

196. See *Joint Declaration on the Doctrine of Justification,* Origins 28 (July 16, 1998) 120–127.
197. See *Foundations of Systematic Theology,* 178–179.
198. Karl Rahner's original essay, "*Chalkedon—Ende oder Anfang?*" was subsequently redacted as "Current Problems in Christology" in *Theological Investigations,* vol. I, tr. Cornelius Ernst (Baltimore: Helicon, 1969), 149–200 at 149.
199. Pannenberg, *Systematic Theology,* v. I, 55.
200. See his online interview with *Corriere Canadese* of February 1, 2007.
201. Cited by John Caputo in "Heidegger and Theology" in *The Cambridge Companion to Heidegger,* ed. C. Guignon (Cambridge: Cambridge University Press, 1993), 272.
202. *Heidegger's Ways,* 182–183.
203. *Writings from the Late Notebooks,* 121, no. 15.
204. Vattimo usually says that philosophy is a transcription of an original Christian impulse, thereby implying that faith is the primary narrative. In practice, however, Vattimo regards weak philosophical thought as theoretically sublating the parable of Christian faith.
205. It should be noted that Vattimo does aver that ". . . the incarnation of God at issue here is not simply a way of giving mythical expression to what philosophy will in the end reveal via rational enquiry" (*RDV,* 92). In this sense, Vattimo distinguishes himself from the worst excesses of Hegel. However, his demurrer should be understood as reflecting the frequently stated Vattimian position that kenotic Christianity *gives rise* to weak thought, thereby allowing the New Testament a certain autonomy vis-à-vis philosophy even while making the concrete affirmations of Christianity subordinate to a philosophical idea. Further, Vattimo *does* think that Christian *caritas* is usefully invoked for the sake of limiting the worst excesses of the nihilistic will to power.
206. John Paul II, *Fides et ratio,* no. 100.
207. Vattimo would likely find unproblematic the contemporary decoupling of nature/form from personal meaning found in a recent proposal floated (but ultimately withdrawn) by the New York City Board of Health, disengaging gender from anatomy. The person here, in sovereign and promethean freedom, decides even the gender recorded on one's birth certificate— a constraining fact which must itself yield before the constructive, autonomous will. This insistence on the absolute plasticity of nature is "interpretation all the way down," indeed. The proposal was reported in the *New York Times* on November 7, 2006, by Damien Cave.
208. One may usefully compare Vattimo's understanding of emancipation with the notion of human freedom discussed at Vatican II in *Gaudium et spes,* no. 17: "Only in freedom can man direct himself toward goodness. Our contemporaries make much of this freedom and pursue it eagerly; and rightly to be sure. Often however they foster it perversely as a license for doing whatever pleases them, even if it is evil. For its part, authentic freedom is an exceptional sign of the divine image within man. For God has

willed that man remain 'under the control of his own decisions,' so that he can seek his Creator spontaneously, and come freely to utter and blissful perfection through loyalty to Him."

209. Jean Gronin, in his defense of Gadamer's scant use of Nietzsche in *Truth and Method*, argues that Gadamer would have interpreted Nietzsche's maxim "there are no facts, only interpretations" as "There are only facts *through* interpretations" a phrase which prevents the *Sache* from slipping away (*WP*, 207–208). Grondin's statement too, however, can be interpreted in a variety of ways. I am not certain that as understood by Gadamer himself, this formulation offers us anything more than Kantian constructivism and so is not at a significant remove from Vattimo's own nihilism.

210. Recently making a forceful argument against a collapse of facts into theories is Alexander Bird, *Thomas Kuhn* (Princeton: Princeton University Press, 2000), 117–118. Bird observes that "if there is no general rule that observation is dependent, then it is possible that on some occasions at least observations will be able to decide between competing theories or be an appropriate measure of the quality of both an older and a newer paradigm."

211. On the participatory structure of reality, see W. Norris Clarke, *The Philosophical Approach to God*. Second revised edition (New York: Fordham University Press, 2007). Also, David B. Hart, *The Beauty of the Infinite* (Grand Rapids: Eerdmans, 2004).

212. Irenaeus, *Adversus Haereses*, I, 8, 1.

213. H. Richard Niebuhr, *The Kingdom of God in America* (Middletown, CT: Wesleyan University Press, 1988), 193.

Index

Index

Index

Index

Index